大學之道在明明德

在止於至善

在格物

在親民

 The *Idea* of
a *University* in *East*
and *West*

A NOTE ON THE ILLUSTRATIONS, CALLIGRAPHY AND SEALS.

The pictures of incidents in the life of Confucius are from the hundred stone tablets in the Confucian Temple at Shantung. There are over three hundred of these and similar drawings belonging to the pictorial life and tradition of the Scholar of China. Some traditional captions have been associated with these stone engravings and these have in part been followed in the use of the illustrations in this book. For the most part, however, there is a slight departure from the tradition for the sake of appropriateness to the titles of the chapters and their divisions. In some instances where I felt a matter of taste might be involved, I have consulted colleagues and Chinese ikonographers and have followed their advice, though I must admit that I found their opinions rather liberal.

A larger selection of these stone engravings is found in Carl Crow's Master Kung published by Harper and Brothers in 1938. Mr. Crow supplies on pp. 17-19 of his book a description of the drawings and a discussion of their place in the history of Chinese art.

The jacket design by Ko Wai Bong of the Physical Education Staff of Chung Chi College carries the A B C motif in simulated Chinese seals with English letters in the place of Chinese characters. They are the seals of Abelard, the father of the medieval university of Paris, Bacon, who wrote the first important plea for a reorganization of the curriculum to include physical science, and Confucius the Sage of China and the world-wide symbol of humane learning. In the Abelard seal the title of his famous book Sic et Non is imposed upon the Yang Yin cosmological symbol and stands for philosophical studies.

The seals occur again in the design on the inside of the cover together with appropriate phrases from the Great Learning. Connected with the phrase "What the great learning teaches is to manifest illustrious virtue" is the seal of the Incarnatus (John 1:14). The fish is an ancient Christian symbol based on the Greek word for fish in which each letter is the initial for the words Jesus Christ, son of God, Saviour. Abelard's seal is affixed to the characters which read "To abide in the highest excellence" which is also the motto on the Chung Chi crest. The seal of Confucius is appropriately related to the characters which read "To renew the people." Wu Tee of the Chung Chi Chinese Department supplied the calligraphy.

The Confucian figure which appears on the facing page is taken from a rubbing of a stone column in Shantung and is one of the more famous engravings of the Master's likeness.

Of historical interest and of special significance to Chung Chi College is a reproduction of a small part of a rubbing from the famous Nestorian Tablet in Sian which is China's oldest Christian monument. It describes the coming of Bishop Alopen to China in A.D. 635 — the same year that Aidan came to Lindisfarne in Northumberland. The Chung Chi College shield is taken from the crest at the top of the stone that raises the cross above cloud and lotus. Below this design on the college shield is the quotation from the Great Learning — to abide in the highest excellence. These characters were chosen "as a compact summary of St. Paul's two sayings: "Till we attain unto the full grown man, unto the measure of the stature of the fullness of Christ", and "I press on toward the goal unto the prize of the high calling of God in Christ Jesus." The two characters on either side of the cross are the words for 'reverence' and for 'Christ' — Ch'ung and Chi."

THE IDEA OF

Noah Edward Fehl

II

Και ο
λογος
Σαρξ
εγενετο

A UNIVERSITY

A river, like truth, will flow on for ever and have no end!

EAST and WEST

CHUNG CHI COLLEGE   HONG KONG 1962

Published by Chung Chi College
January 1962
Second Printing October 1962

Made in Hong Kong

by

YE OLDE PRINTERIE, LTD., 6 DUDDELL ST.

Library Congress catalogue number: 62-5812

To Three Men who are Wise

THE REV. NOAH G. FEHL
my Father

CHI-TUNG YUNG, PH.D.,LL.D.
President of Chung Chi College

LESLIE GIFFORD KILBORN, M.D., PH.D.
Vice President of Chung Chi College

and who live under the demand

在止於至善，知止，而后有定

and

αἰὲν ἀριστεύειν καὶ ὑπείροχον ἔμμεναι ἄλλων

With some hesitation Confucius approached a Queen.

PREFACE

Some hesitation is proper in approaching a discussion of the university. With the church and the state, the university provides the third supporting pier of a civilized society.

There is no title more appropriate to a discussion of the university than that devised by John Stuart Mill which Newman borrowed and made famous. *Idea* is a Platonic word, and the university as a community of masters and scholars engaged in the pursuit of theoretical knowledge and its proper application is a platonic idea that first was made flesh in the Christian civilization of the twelfth century. The other term for the university in use in the late middle ages was *Studium generale*—the ideal of an international school, a society of scholars as inclusive as civilization itself, a community in which none was a foreigner. In this century that ideal has its first chance of realization, and it is significant that the first truly universal *Studium generale* is emerging in Asia. Newman's famous lectures are now too narrow in concept for two reasons. They did not take account of one whole hemisphere of human culture and they were written by a man who stood just before the threshold of the new physical and social sciences.

Now we are beginning to see something both of the glory and the horror of the new age—the *kairos* of a world-wide technological civilization. The East as well as the West is involved in this new age. In some ways the suddenness with which that ' dawn has come up like thunder *over* China cross the bay ' has made the East more sensitive to its total significance than is the West. Certainly, one important frontier of higher education in this *kairos* is the Eastern university where not only the study of the arts and the physical and social sciences must be re-conceived, but also a new kind of relation between the two great hemispheres of culture is in process of development.

This book began as an attempt to provide a general reader for our incoming students in the history and philosophy of the university at this moment when the college is on the threshold of university status within the Association of Universities of the British Commonwealth. As a community of masters and scholars—Chinese, American and British—we have given much thought to the crossing of that threshold. Our discussions have plunged from the periphery of formal matters such as are appropriate to the calendar (catalogue) to the central issue: what is the essence and function of the Eastern university as a new creation, a real meeting in the first truly universal *Studium generale* of arts and sciences and of East and West.

Out of the exhileration and the frustration—the greatness of this venture, daily made manifest in the meeting with colleagues and students, this book has come. It was written with horrible haste in the time that a sixteen hour teaching schedule has allowed over the past several months. It is, I trust, an honest book, reflecting the excitement of these months of lecturing on Plato and the Hebrew prophets, the interpretation of history and the philosophy of science in the setting of these green hills so close to the border of China. I have not censored the peculiar humour and the wicked thrust that are a part of academic life. But, of course, for these and for the opinions—at times extreme—I am responsible. The three wise men to whom I have, with genuine admiration, dedicated this book are not to be thought guilty of association with any of the opinions any reader would repudiate. My father has, for as many years as either of us cares to remember, disagreed with me on the principle that it was the only sensible policy, and I am quite sure that there would be a large measure of mutual understanding and sympathetic agreement between my father and Dr. Yung and Dr. Kilborn. Yet these three are men whom I admire with a feeling that borders on affection, and so for this and no other reason, I have offered this oblation of my first fruits on this subject to them.

Educational theory is of course not quite a subject or a science, at least no one else's notion of education can, by any respectable person, be considered scientific. Every master is, of course, an educator, and each of us feels that the highest excellence in this art can be attained only by the physicist, historian or theologian who has not allowed any reading on the subject or any of his colleagues' opinions to prejudice his own clear thinking. And this is as it should be. Nowhere else is there a greater need for the courage of one's vices than in a university. Such courage has always been the badge of honour of distinguished professors.

There is, therefore, after the fact, a justification for this book. Every master has a right to one digression with impunity into the field of education. For none, ought there to be a second forgiveness on the indisputably orthodox principle that ' no man can be trusted who lets himself be bitten twice by the same mad dog . . . in the noon day sun.'

N. E. F.

Ma Liu Shui
December, 1961

Confucius was for a time the collector of the produce of the workers.

ACKNOWLEDGEMENTS

Chung Chi College is grateful for the generous contribution given by Harvard Yenching Institute through the good offices of Dr. William Fenn of the United Board for Christian Higher Education in Asia to this publication in our Philosophy of Life Series.

I should like to acknowledge a happy indebtedness to the many people who let themselves get involved in helping me with this book. First I must mention my wife, Ethel Janet, who suggested that I write it; and who, like all good women that give men ideas and then try to prevent them from being carried out, has rendered invaluable service in censorship, general criticism and proof reading. In transcribing my handwriting she has mis-read several passages to make better sense than I intended.

Tam Woon Ting by his patient research has done his best to keep me from disgrace in the matter of the etymology of Chinese characters. Wu Tee, a senior member of our Department of Chinese Studies, contributed the calligraphy that appears on the fly leaf.

Ko Wai Bong is the creator of the seals on the jacket and the fly leaf and is the artist responsible for the improvement of the Shantung drawing on the title page. Kwong Kong Kit read the section on " The Language Problem " and gave valuable insights into the problems of the Chinese student in the bi-lingual university.

The free translations of passages from the *She King* and the *Li Chi* in the " University Reader " were made in the happy company of colleagues and students ' who sucked out much amusement therefrom.' Ho Shuk Yee helped with the index and Chiu So Lan did everything possible to find texts and materials in the library. She also introduced me to the Chinese text of *The Great Learning.* Dr. Bertha Hensman suggested readings in Literature. Chau Yiu Kee, Li Seung Ping and Dr. Shu Ting Chang made the photographic reproductions of the Shantung stone engravings.

I am particularly grateful to Lee Tsu Wei for her many talents for helpfulness and to Lau Ho Wai Ching, Wong Chi Kit and Helen Chiu for typing, many times late into the night after busy days in the office or at their studies, and to Chan Ho Hua who would have considered tea for Samuel Johnson scarcely worthy of mention.

I am pleased to acknowledge the permission granted by the several publishers to reprint selected passages in the " University Reader."

" On Being the Right Size " from *Possible Worlds* by J. B. S. Haldane. Copyright c 1928 by Harper and Brothers. Reprinted by permission of Harper Brothers.

Selected paragraphs from " Science as a Vocation " in Gerth and Mills, *From Max Weber.* Reprinted by permission of Oxford University Press.

" Turtle Eggs For Agassiz " by Dallas Lore Sharp. Reprinted by the kind permission of *The Atlantic Monthly.*

" Why Philosophy " by Susan Langer.   Reprinted by
the kind permission of the *Saturday Evening Post.*

"A Reading of King Lear " Reprinted by permission
of the *Chung Chi Bulletin.*

Finally, I am pleased to mention the exceptionally
happy relationship with Ye Olde Printerie, and the many
excellent discussions with Lam Yung Fai, the manager,
on the making of books and the weariness of the flesh.

We are pleased that a second printing has been
necessary within the year.   I gratefully acknowledge the
aid in corrections given by Dr. Leslie Kilborn and Mr.
John Bar.

N. E. F.

Hong Kong
Feast of St. Francis of Assisi 1962

CONTENTS

PART THREE

UNIVERSITAS

PART FOUR

THE UNIVERSITY, THE TOWN AND THE INDIVIDUAL

PART FIVE

THE EASTERN UNIVERSITY

A UNIVERSITY READER

As a boy Confucius imitated the ancient rites.

CHAPTER I

CROSSING A THRESHOLD

ENTERING the University marks one of the great crises of life. University education is a crucial threshold for the individual and it stands at the watershed of a culture. All education involves crisis. From the simplest to the highest levels, education is a series of thresholds, a series of crises. What distinguishes man from other animals is not his instinctive behaviour but rather a positive and creative response to his environment. He has *learned* to live. His learning is essential to his survival. Apart from learning there is no meaning to his existence. Without learning he would be merely a pathetic freak in the animal kingdom.

The youngest Chinese student is called a *hsüeh-sheng* (學生 a learning-to-live person). At the age of seven he comes to the first great crisis of his life. His family pauses with him, taking the necessary precautions before sending him over the threshold (the Gateway of Confucius) to a new life. It is a serious moment for the young lad and it is a serious moment for the family; for by his going forth to learn there is set in motion the vital process that

1

links past and present, and is the substance of hope for the future not only of the child himself but also of his family and of his nation. " Watch him, on the great day, trudging off in his new clothes, the *San-tzü Ching (The Three Character Classic)* . . . in a neatly tied cloth cover in one hand and a small teapot in the other. His father or his mother accompanies him, carrying the bundle of incense sticks which he is to burn before the portrait of Confucius." [1]

Leaving home is a crisis. Something of his earliest and happiest years must be left behind when he first ventures forth. To some of his first playmates he will never be so close again. With all whom he knows and loves some change in his relationship will occur, at first, perhaps, unnoticed even by his parents. The old ties will not be broken but new qualities of awareness and meaning will emerge, modulating his relationships toward another key, even though their original theme is maintained. Only long afterwards will that lad, looking backwards, realize how decisive was the step that he took over the threshold of his home toward his first day at school.

But the great moment is not his going forth. It is his entering in—the inward crossing of another threshold, that of his first school. Nor is this new world to be entered into casually or carelessly. The learning-to-live person must burn incense. The torch of learning is a " hard gem-like flame " that burns in each age because someone has kept it alight and passed it on. The incense of reverence and of remembrance is always perceptible to those who bear that torch. There followed nine prostrations before the Confucian shrine and three to the

---

[1] Han Yü-shan, "Molding Forces" in H. F. MacNair, *China,* United Nations Series (Berkeley: University of California Press, 1951), p. 9.

2

teacher.[2] This was probably the most ancient ceremony of matriculation. It was a gesture of commitment—a binding of the student to the heritage of the past and a binding to the authority of the teacher, that is, to the discipline of scholarship. It was a dying to the old, carefree ways of childhood and a being born anew to a life of duty and dignity. The young scholar is known henceforth by a new name. His " milk name " is not forgotten but it is under his new—his book-name (書名) that he becomes a disciple of Confucius " the Teacher and Pattern for all Ages." [3] The first sentence of the primary school classic presses upon him the importance of learning.

> In men at birth, Nature is basically good:
> Nature is similar; through learning, a difference
> results.

He has become a learning-to-live person.

Entering the university means the crossing of an equally important threshold. The matriculant at Chung Chi will be, by the motto of the College, reminded of those first words his fathers learned from the San-tzü Ching. " To rest in the highest excellence " [4] (止於至善) this is the great " difference that results from learning." Never to be satisfied with less, never to falter nor to turn aside from the way of excellence no matter what weather he may meet nor for any accident of the road that may befall him. Whichever word of power, with the centuries' increment of richness of meaning, a Chinese university may choose as its motto from *The Great Learning*, that word will bring to mind for the entering student all the others: to make manifest the illustrious virtue (明明德),

---

[2] Victor Purcell, *Problems of Chinese Education,* (London: Kegan Paul, Trench, Trubner & Co., Ltd., 1936), pp. 18, 19.

[3] Han Yü-shan, *op. cit.,* p. 9.

[4] *The Great Learning,* i.

3

to renew the hearts of the people (親(新)民), to press with sincerity and faithfulness toward the furthermost reaches of knowledge (致知), to examine exhaustively the principle of things (格物). Of such is the higher, the great, learning that marks the deep divide in education, that sets the university apart from all other training and from every other kind of school.

To become a university student is to join an aristocracy. This word comes to us from the oldest and greatest of the Greek poets, from Homer, the first educator of Greece. The *aristos,* the aristocrat, is the one who strives for the highest honour. The words 'honour' *(areté)* and 'nobleman' *(aristos)* are of the same root.[5] In Homer's *Iliad* the healthy pride of the aristocrat in his family, his sense of duty to his fathers and to his calling to be a knight is expressed in a famous line which has been throughout Western history both the motto of knightly chivalry and the model of the scholar's courage: " Hippolochus begat me, and I claim to be his son. He sent me to Troy, and often gave me this command, *to strive always for the highest excellence (areté),* and to excel all others." [6]

To enter the university is to be brought face to face with excellence.[7] The lower schools must, by the nature of their task, be content with lesser aims. They have a mixed purpose: to train younger students for the intermediate positions and to prepare their best students for the university. The university claims only the best for her own, and of these not all are destined to fulfill their quest: to rest in the highest excellence. Thus to enter

---

[5] See Werner Jaeger, *Paideia* (Oxford: Blackwell, 1957, I. pp. 4 ff.

[6] *Iliad* vi. 208.

[7] See address, "God Is the Teacher" by the Rt. Rev. Stephen F. Bayne, Jr. in *the Christian Idea of Education,* ed. by Edmund Fuller (New Haven: Yale University Press, 1957), pp. 260 ff.

the university is to cross the most important threshold of the long process of learning to live. At this threshold the lines of life's crucial transitions come together—the transition from adolescence to adulthood, from the general society into a special association, *collegium, universitas,* from the ordinary responsibility of the common man to a special vocation, a higher calling. The first regulation for admission to Chung Chi College provides that an applicant, even though he holds the School Leaving Certificate and is a successful candidate in the post-secondary Joint Entry Examination, must be " not less than seventeen years of age at the time of admission to the College." The University of Paris in the middle ages granted its degree after the seven year course in the arts only to those who had attained the age of twenty.[8] From the Li Chi (禮記) it would appear that a young man of the Chou Dynasty spent the ten years between twenty " when he was capped " and thirty, when he had a wife, at the higher studies.[9] Chu Hsi's commentary on *The Great Learning* interprets the title to mean " the Learning of Adults " as opposed to that of children and regards the document as the syllabus of the ancient, advanced academies.[10] From middle school to the university measures the distance from adolescence to adulthood. Again entering the university is an entering into a special society. It is to become a member of a special community of masters and scholars, of teachers and students. This is the basic meaning of the word " matriculation." It comes from the Latin *matricula*—the list, the list of members.

---

[8] Hastings Rashdall, *The Universities of Europe in the Middle Ages,* 2nd ed. by Powicke and Emden (Oxford: Oxford University Press, 1936-reprinted 1958), III pp. 352 ff.

[9] Purcell, *op. cit.,* p. 5. See also the reconstruction by Dr. Kuo Ping-wen in the Columbia University Series on Education.

[10] Cf. James Legge, *The Four Books,* (Hong Kong University Jubilee Publication 1961), p. 307.

In a spiritual sense the matriculant has become a member of a new household, a new family, the aristocratic family of scholars. His name is entered upon the tablets of the ancestral hall, the register of the university. Finally, entering the university marks a transition that is more crucial than the frontiers of age or class. This is the initiation reserved in most cultures for those set apart not only by special endowment but also by a strong sense of vocation. In primitive societies the medicine man and the shaman would be the best known examples. The shaman is one who " knows and remembers," who penetrates the mystery of life. In modern society it would be one of the more exclusive religious orders or an institute of men of pure science. It is the dedication of the scholar who sees his learning as a mission to which he has been called.[11]   Confucius spoke of such a commission under the will of Heaven, and Socrates, of the God whose voice was an inward oracle. Both had the vision of scholarship as the improvement of the soul. This is the wisdom of the first characters of the *Great Learning;* to make manifest the virtuous nature which man derives from heaven. Plato uses a more radical symbol. The highest education is conversion, a turning around toward the *Idea of the Good.* Hsun Tzu comes quite close in the tradition of Chinese educational theory to Plato.[12]

In the three types of initiation there is a common pattern:

1. a ceremony of separation from the careless ways of the past. The common symbol is that of death, a dying to the old life;

2. a new birth or resurrection to a new life;

---

[11] Jaeger, *Paideia* II pp. 295 ff.

[12] See J. K. Shryock "Confucianism" in MacNair, *op. cit.,* p. 249.

6

3. a period of testing, a striving against "the enemies of promise."

In each instance the initiate becomes another man, a new person, he enters anew into life on a higher level of insight and a deeper sense of purpose.[13]

The new life is symbolized by a new name, a new vestment, and a new language. In no other culture has the appropriate name for the stations of academic achievement received such careful attention as in China. The successful candidates in the first important examination were called "flowers of talent" and the degree awarded them was that of hsiu-ts'ai (秀才 budding genius). At the second station they received the degree of chu-ren (舉人 promoted man), and at the third of chin-shih (進士 advanced scholar).[14]

In European tradition name-giving was not so imaginative or complimentary. The official terms were scholar (belonging to a school), bachelor, master, professor and doctor. The last three were, throughout the middle ages, used synonymously. The student jargon was more colorful. Freshman and Sophomore probably originated in England. The Freshman was the freshly (newly) arrived student, as yet "green" and untutored. He was not yet fully separated from his provincial or rustic ways and hence not yet fully a member of the new society. *Soph-Mor* first appears in annuals of Cambridge University as designating the "second year man" who now knows his way so well around his college, the university, and the town that he is the "wise" man, wise at least in some simple things, but thinking himself wiser than he is. In the medieval university the matriculant did not become a

---

[13] See Mircea Eliade, *Birth and Rebirth* (New York: Harper & Bros., 1958), pp. 1 ff. and 103 ff.

[14] Han Yü-shan, *op. cit.,* pp. 12-14.

scholar until he had been initiated. At first he was a
bejaunus or " yellow-bill " (from bec-jaune—yellow beak)
—a young bird who did not yet have all his feathers.[15]
After several years of study he became a bachelor, a poor,
young apprentice. It is probable that the word originally
referred to the tenant of a farm *(baccalaria),* and was
applied to the candidate for the lecturer's certificate in
the first instance as a slang expression. The bachelor
was an academic serf. Its use in the medieval university
described the status of a pupil-teachership, a senior student
granted the privilege to teach as an apprentice to a
master.[16] He would not yet be in the position to marry,
and, if he were to seek academic preferment, he would
be obliged to take clerical vows and hence the term has
its secondary meaning: one who is not married.

University life is also symbolized by a distinctive
vestment. The college blazer, bearing the school shield,
is the modern, secular equivalent of the scholar's gown.
A distinctive dress was probably in the earliest universities
of Europe the privilege of the masters. The dress of the
students would have been simply the outer cloak of the
secular clergy. Neither classrooms nor college hostels
were heated and so the overcoat became the typical student
dress. Bachelors were privileged to wear hoods of rabbit's
fur or lamb's wool. The silk hood now worn in academic
processions had its origin in the fourteenth century as a
concession to the comfort of the masters in the summer
term. The " mortar board," worn now as an academic
hat in addition to the hood, is a descendent of the clerical
cap that could be worn inside the class room or the church
except at the most sacred moments of the several sacraments and other solemn rituals. The soft round cap of

---

[15] Rashdall, *op. cit.,* III p. 377.
[16] *Ibid.* vol. I pp. 207 ff.

Oxford and Cambridge graduates was in the middle ages
the *pileum* worn by those in the faculties of law, medicine,
and music.[17]   When the universities were no longer largely
clerical so that students did not by rule wear the clothes
befitting an order of the Church, a wide variety of student
costumes appeared on the campus.   Even the medieval
universities were forced to adopt regulations prohibiting
" indecent and dishonest attire."   " Trunkhose," puffed
sleeves, pointed shoes, red and green stockings were
particularly forbidden.[18]   In part to avoid such offenses
to the cultivated taste of the masters, the undergraduate
gown was adopted by most European universities.

The new life of the university is also symbolized by
a new language.   For the European universities the new
language was Latin.   At Oxford students were fined if
caught speaking English.   Only on the occasion of a
" gaude " or major feast was the rule relaxed.[19]   The
university has over the centuries developed its own peculiar
language.   The entering student may find that he is
obliged to learn, during the course of his ' orientation
week,' a formidable table of new expressions, or at least
to learn to use these sacred words of the academic world
with greater care for their precise meaning.   Curriculum,
faculty, matriculation, major and minor, lecturer and tutor,

---

[17] *Ibid.* vol. I pp. 389, 90.   The modern academic gown
derives in part from the Roman dress.   It is the toga rather than
medieval gown which was the *cappa* or cope.   When the Roman
student had completed his study of grammar and reached the age
of 16-17 he was privileged to wear the *toga virilis* and proceed
to the study of rhetoric.   Grammar (Latin) was only rarely in the
medieval university considered a "University Subject."   It was a
"lower form" study.   When it was completed, the student went
up to the university and in some instances wore the grammarian's
gown (undergraduate gown) as a mark of his new status.   See
Quintilian, quoted by S. J. Curtis, *A Short History of Educational
Ideas* (London: Univ. Tutorial Press), p. 55.

[18] *Ibid.* vol. I p. 386.

[19] *Ibid.* vol. III p. 374.

are but a few of the words from the " new language " of the medieval university that continue to be common to higher education in Asia as well as Europe and America. The " language barrier " in university education is an old tradition. It plagued the student at Paris and in Oxford during the middle ages and even in modern times almost as much as it does the Chung Chi student today. In fact the medieval method of enforcing the new language to the exclusion of the native tongue was the opposite of our ideal of the bi-lingual university. At Heidelberg and other German universities the official statutes ordered the appointment of *lupi* or " wolves " who acted as spies for the masters and informed them of the *vulgarisantes,* students who persisted in the use of German when they were in their rooms or otherwise away from the watchful eye and sharp ear of their tutors.[20]

These brief glimpses into university life in the past are parts of one picture: university matriculation as an experience of initiation involving separation and re-formation or re-birth, in short, becoming a new person. A late fifteenth century university manual describes an initiation ceremony which still retains under its mock-seriousness and the burlesque of academic ordination, all the elements which we have described.[21] The initiation at the German university was the student side of matriculation. First the new student applies to the rector to have his name recorded on the university register and to make his pledge of obedience to the statutes of the school and to the authority of the rector. Soon after he has returned to

---

[20] Quoted by Rashdall, *op. cit.,* III p. 376 from Zarncke, *Statutenbücher* (A.D. 1499) p. 477.

[21] From the *Manuale Scholarium,* transl. by R. F. Seybolt (Cambridge: Harvard Univ. Press, 1921). The medieval text is found in Zarncke, *Die deutschen Universitäten im Mittelalter* (Leipzig: 1857).

his room, he is visited by two representatives of the
student body who have come, so they say, to complain
of an unbearable stench which they have traced to his
room. Upon careful investigation it is found that the
foul odour is the smell of the *beanus,* a wild, unclean,
and dangerous beast. It is of course the new student
who is thus identified. For some time the " beast " is
badgered and taunted. Then, after solemn consultation,
a *depositio,* surgical operation, is ordered. The horns
are to be removed, the tusks extracted, the fur sheared,
the ears clipped. Saws, knives, shears, and pliers are
produced and sharpened while the freshman is pinned
down on his table and smeared with grease in preparation
for the operation. It is likely that the old students'
enthusiastic concern for a realistic performance sometimes
led to an actual letting of blood or the pulling of a tooth.
At this point, even in the mock ceremony, the operation
is stopped. The surgeons agree that the patient is dying
and a priest is called to hear his confession and prepare
him for death. A mock priest appears and the freshman
is encouraged to whisper into his ear all the evils of which
he has been guilty. As the dying *beanus* is absolved
he is also ' revived.' The ' priest,' however, imposes a
penance. The initiated scholar is ordered to provide a
feast for his masters and fellow students.

This outline of a German university initiation is taken
by Rashdall to have been a private rehearsal in the
candidate's room for the public ceremony that followed.
In the actual initiation he probably wore a costume with
hood resembling the coarse features of a grotesque beast—
horns, tusks, huge ears and a tail.[22] From the sixteenth
century a curious little book has been preserved which
provides a pictorial account of such an initiation together

---

[22] *Op. cit.,* III p. 380.

with a speech, — delivered on the occasion of a *Depositio* performed at Erfurt, — by the Reverend Doctor Martin Luther! [23] The pictorial account is similar to a modern cartoon strip beginning with an academic procession led by a master in academic dress with his students following in mock costumes. Then the freshman is shown lying upon a table about to be de-horned. A saw lies on the ground beside the table. In another scene the initiate is held with his nose to a grind stone while another student turns the wheel. The text describes other incidents in the re-formation of the beast into a scholar. Scissors were used on his hair. His nails were cut by a knife and a surgical instrument, the *auriscalpium*, was used to trim his ears. Finally a purgative medicine of salt and wine was administered. Luther's commentary on the initiation at Erfurt is actually a kind of homily on the ' sacrament.' The various acts are explained as symbols of an intellectual, moral, and spiritual pruning and purgation to fit the entering student for the new life which he henceforth shall lead.

Behind the crude symbols of the ceremony lies the long history of initiation that is as old as human society itself. Before the important thresholds of his life in his passage from childhood to puberty, his crossing of the frontier of marriage, his entry upon a special vocation, man has always paused for a moment of serious reflection and of sober anticipation. "Initiation lies at the core of any genuine human life." [24] It takes account of the crises and the ordeals through which every life must pass.

---

[23] Cited by Rashdall, III p. 380 from Dinkel, *De origine, causis, typo et ceremoniis illius ritus, qui vulgo in Scholis Depositio appellatur.* (Erfurt: 1528). Rashdall assumes from the frequency of contemporary quotation from Luther's little address that his prestige accounted for the perpetuation of such initiations in German universities for over a century. n. 2. p. 380.

[24] Eliade, *op. cit.,* p. 135.

It recognizes in sober realism that every new venture into the future will ask its price of the past and that every truly significant advance is a new birth that comes only after a death and entombment in some sense of the spirit. Initiation is the solemn recognition of the recurring need of the conquest of the self, that one cannot stay the way he is. It is also the expression of the hope of beginning life over again.[25] Entering the university is the invitation to become another man, a new person. This is the claim that the great universities of the world have always made as the real reason for their existence. " When you have been a member of a university in a true sense for any length of time you will be thenceforward and for ever a different person." [26] Almost twenty-five hundred years ago Alcibiades said of his school-master, Socrates,—" He made me feel as though I could hardly endure the life which I am now living." And Apollodorus, in the opening lines of the *Symposium* shows how well that master had communicated the spiritual side of philosophy to his disciples. Since having known Socrates, he says " whenever either I am talking about my instruction or I hear others doing so, I receive the very greatest pleasure in addition to the sense of having good done to me." This also is the testament of the noble Roman, Seneca, addressed to Lucullus. " I understand," he writes, " that I am not only being improved but that I am being transformed." [27] We remember also the quiet words of Szema Ch'ien, quoting the *Book of Songs:* " High is the mountain I look up to, and bright is his example for our emulation. Although I cannot reach the top, my heart

---

[25] *Ibid.*

[26] Quoted by Sir Walter Moberly, *The Crisis in the University* (London S.C.M. Press, 1949), p. 24.

[27] *Epistle vi* 1.

leaps up to it." [28] And then he looks upon the few simple things that were the possessions of Confucius and he thinks of the man clad only in a cotton gown who had transformed the minds of so many. Such is the heritage of higher learning,[29] the greatness of the university whose sons are like those of Athens, whose

> . . . citizens, imperial spirits,
> Rule the present from the past.

---

[28] See Lin Yutang, *The Wisdom of Confucius,* (New York: Random House, 1938), pp. 99 f.

[29] See A. N. Whitehead, "Universities and Their Function" in *Aims of Education,* (New York: Macmillan, 1929), p. 106.

Duke Gay asked Confucius foolish questions about the dress of a scholar.

CHAPTER II

THE UNIVERSITY IN HISTORY

INHERITING A PAST

UPON his entry into a university a student inherits a tremendous past. He is adopted into an ancient family. The matriculant finds a new mother, his *alma mater*. The student who enters Chung Chi is not only the inheritor of a decade of devotion of founders, administrators, academic staff, students, and alumni. The College itself has an ancestry. It is, as Professor Kilborn has reminded us, in " direct descent from the thirteen Christian universities and colleges which were founded on the Mainland of China and survived until 1951. . . . And these in turn were descended from numerous complex unions of still earlier colleges. One of these, Tengchow, an ancestor of Cheeloo University, was ' recognized as a college ' in 1862. On the basis of this ancestry, Chung Chi will celebrate its tenth anniversary in 1961 and its centennial in 1962." [1] And so the lines of inheritance go backward from decade to

---

[1] "Universities, Jubilees and Arithmetic", *Chung Chi Bulletin,* April 1961. No. 26. p. 1.

century and then to millenium; for Tengchow too had its parents, both Chinese and Western. Its Western parent could boast a family tree whose roots drew nourishment from the soil of the middle ages—from the University of Paris. Its Chinese parent would have been in some way the inheritor of the first imperial academy founded in 124 B.C.[2] The text of a memorial, sent to the emperor by Tung Chung-shu, which led to the establishment of that school of higher learning is still preserved: "Among the things paramount for the upbringing of scholars none is more important than a state university. It is intimately related to the fostering of virtuous scholars, and it is the foundation of education. . . . Your servant desires Your Majesty to erect a university and appoint illustrious teachers for it, for the upbringing of the empire's scholars." [3]

The deepest root of a university is the concept of higher education and a concern for the kind of institution where excellence can be pursued and communicated. The university is thus the inheritor of the wisdom of many cultures. The universities of Europe in the middle ages which appear suddenly to have arisen, in response to new demands, out of the cathedral schools, had in part an Eastern parentage. The Moslem colleges at Alexandria and Cairo in Egypt, at Cordova, Granada, Toledo, and Seville in Spain, had not only preserved Greek science when it fell into decay in the Christian West, but had, indeed, made significant advances in mathematics, medicine, metaphysics, and jurisprudence beyond the Athenian academies.[4] Abelard, whose name is usually associated

---

[2] MacNair, *op. cit.*, p. 226. *Sources of Chinese Tradition* ed. by W. T. de Bary (New York: Columbia University Press, 1960) pp. 256 f.

[3] *Han Shu,* 56:126-13a.

[4] See T. J. Boer, *History of Philosophy in Islam,* also G. von Grunebaun, *Medieval Islam.*

with the beginnings of the University of Paris, was well aware of "Arabic science" as was also Roger Bacon at Oxford. The controlling ideas that gave life to the great universities of Europe arose when scholars, recognizing the achievements of the Moslem world, turned from Latin studies to the Greek science and philosophy of Aristotle. It is significant to observe that the West had in this instance gone to the East. The literal journeys were of mixed purpose—the Crusades and later the caravans of trade. They sought a material reward but they found a richer treasure—the philosophy and science of Islamic scholarship. They returned as missionaries from the East to their own homes. Missionaries bringing a gift from their own culture to another people are seldom as successful as those who bring a gift from abroad back to their own homes. One simple yet fundamental souvenir was a new numerical system. Roman numerals had made the study and use of mathematics almost as difficult for the medieval European as the Chinese numeration by characters.[5] St. Augustin confessed that he was able to do addition and subtraction with the Latin letters but had never progressed to the efficient solution of problems in multiplication. Europe adopted the more efficient system of the Moslems and still refers to it as Arabic. But the Moslems had in turn borrowed this numerical notation from the Hindus, and it was in part due to this borrowing and to a knowledge of a superior Hindu Algebra that they were able to excel the West in the foundation of the sciences. Behind the modern university are also the Brahmanic colleges of India, the Parishads— a tradition of scholarship in a special community of priests and pupils that began a thousand years before Christ.

---

[5] See F. P. Graves, *A History of Education* (New York: Macmillan, 1931), vol. I *Before the Middle Ages, p.* 86.

The elements of philology (the comparative study of language) taught in Oxford at the turn to the present century were based upon the work of Sanskrit scholars of ancient India.[6]

Thus the roots of the university represent the unlimited inheritance not only of one past but of many. The heritage of the university is the universe of knowledge. And each university, in so far as it is a good one, participates in the glories of all others. A university need not be old to be good. Chung Chi is as truly the heir of Roger Bacon as is Oxford. Nor is an illustrious past any guarantee of continuing excellence. There was a period in the history of Oxford when the masters took too seriously the warning of Francis Bacon that a little learning is a dangerous thing [7] and so decided to have none at all! In studies and in the community of masters and scholars the newest school can be the favoured heir of its richest ancestor, and it can be so without the encumbrance of either the trivial or the tedious in tradition —if its masters and scholars are of the stuff of which tradition is made.

ROOTS OF HIGHER EDUCATION

The elemental presupposition of a university is the concept of higher education. In both China and the West this concept has been in force from ancient times. It was probably Confucius who first drew for China the critical line between the usual and ordinary and the higher and ideal.[8] Pre-Confucian literature makes no reference to schools for the young aristocrats of ancient times other

---

[6] *Ibid.* p. 84.

[7] *Essays* "Of Atheism."

[8] H. G. Creel, *Confucius and the Chinese Way* (New York: Harper & Bros., 1949) p. 82.

than those of archery and charioteering. There is ample reference to these in the inscriptions on the bronze vessels of earlier times,[9] but from Confucius' day onward such schools are the lower as opposed to the higher education in the true art of being a gentleman and in understanding what kind of knowledge it is that comprises the great learning.

In Western tradition the great figure is Socrates who enquires of the sophistic teachers and all others what is the purpose of education and how this purpose is to be realized. Some have found in Plato's *Meno* the first critical essay on the distinction between ordinary and higher education. Professor Jaeger defines the problem of the dialogue with the question, " What kind of knowledge is it which Socrates considers the basis of *areté?* " [10] What is the nature of that knowledge that leads to the highest excellence and how shall it be gained? The conclusion is one to which Plato comes after many attempts to find an easy answer. In the earlier dialogues he had explored one by one the separate disciplines of the spirit, the virtue most appropriate to the intellect. Here he first proposes that wisdom is neither a simple science nor is it simply an accumulation of knowledge from individual sciences. The highest knowledge is unitive. It is a virtue which is the ground and structure of all other virtues. It is that virtue which provides the pattern according to which all other virtues are related. Socrates in the *Meno* calls it the *eidos*—the *form* of virtue.[11] Jaeger interprets this quite simply as " the view of the Good as a whole." [12] Higher education deals with principles, with understanding.

---

[9] *Ibid.* p. 75.

[10] Jaeger, *Paideia* II pp. 160 ff.

[11] *Meno* 22 c-d.

[12] *Op. cit.,* II p. 163.

The lower schools are concerned with skills and with specific knowledge in particular fields.

Generally speaking, formal, Western education developed according to a notion of three levels. The first, the elementary or primary, had the task of instruction in the basic skills of reading, writing, and simple arithmetic. It enabled the student to be a free and independent citizen in the sense that he could communicate without the services of another, that he could carry on the affairs of simple business by himself. The second stage was preparatory for the third. At the intermediate level, the student studied rhetoric, that is, literature and history. He became a knowledgeable person, participating in the culture of his nation, capable of appreciating the work of others. Finally, the highest level, philosophy, is critical, interpretive and creative.

During Socrates' lifetime a crisis had arisen in the concept of higher education. Previously philosophy had been synonymous with natural philosophy, that is, with physical science, and there had since the time of Thales (c.600 B.C.) developed in Greece a division of learning, separating poetry (Homer) and philosophy (natural science).[13] " More truth than poetry " is a saying of Greek origin, and it probably originated with the philosophers! Just before Socrates' time, however, philosophy had reached an impasse. Contradictory theories had been developed with respect to almost every important problem, and there seemed to be no way by which opposing points of view could be resolved. Sophistic education arose as a new alternative. If the great questions about the universe could not be answered, it would be better to concentrate upon the human side of things, upon anthropology and

---

[13] See J. Baillie, *The Study of Religion* (New York: Charles Scribner's Sons, 1928) pp. 3 ff.

sociology, the sciences of man and of society. Man then, not God or the universe, is taken to be the measure of all things, and the aim of higher education is to develop the *areté* of success in politics and professional undertakings. Socrates did not disagree with the Sophists' contention that the higher education should be devoted to the study of man rather than to that of nature. His stand against them was taken on the issue of what the proper study of man should be. Protagoras, one of the greatest of the Sophists, had defined higher education as a training in the social sciences that would lead to success in the management of private affairs and advancement in the career of politics.[14] Later Plato's rival, Isocrates, defined the substance of higher education as a learning to understand one another—a factual knowledge of human relationships and of social institutions. On the basis of such knowledge, he claimed, his students would be able to speak effectually upon the affairs of the polis (the city), that is, they would be successful politicians.[15]

Socrates, on the other hand, contends that the study of man should be the study of " the things of the soul," and that its aim should be the improvement of the soul.[16] Now the study of the soul involves an examination of the religious consciousness, and it is at this point that the crisis arose which led finally to Socrates' trial and martyrdom. The older education had combined religion and literature. Homer was the theologian as well as the poet of Greece. Grammar, literature, tradition, history— all these Socrates regarded as elementary, preparatory studies. Religious knowledge, on the other hand, he considered to be the highest of all studies and one which

---

[14] *Protagoras* 312 e.
[15] *Panegyricus* 48. f.
[16] *The Apology* 30.

must therefore be approached as a critical enquiry. Literature might add to the enjoyment of life as a pastime for the empty hours. He would not have denied to the lighter side of the human spirit the satisfactions to be found in the delicate turning of a phrase or the playful and imaginative telling of the story of men's follies or even the occasional, humorously naughty treatment of the serious issues of life. But these must be elementary or extra-curricular. They cannot be the subject matter of the higher studies.

Plato went even further in his exclusion of such poems from the curriculum of the academy. For the advanced education in the arts he substituted mathematics, and for the attainment of the highest excellence, the true *areté*, the student must take leave even of the sciences in order to proceed to the first principle—to the Idea of the Good.[17] He would not accept Homer even as the basis of a primary or preparatory education. It was the early Christian scholar who preserved the study of literature as a legitimate subject for secondary education.[18] But this was possible only on the basis that the subject matter of literature was to be considered neither useful nor serious. The study of literature was justified as the means by which the skill of precise and forceful expression could be learned. The content of poetry could be ignored, it was unimportant. Only the form should be valued. Indeed, in the West, it was the Christian scholar who first " taught men to appraise poetry by a purely aesthetic standard " and to find a place in Christian learning for the recreation of the aesthetically delightful.[19] There was a humanity in

---

[17] *Republic* 533.

[18] See E. H. Harbison, *The Christian Scholar* (New York: Charles Scribner's Sons, 1956), Ch. I "Scholarship as a Christian Calling: Jerome, Augustine, Abelard, Aquinas" pp. 1-30.

[19] *Paideia* II p. 35.

Clement of Alexandria and in St. Augustin which is not to be found in Plato. Christian education retained the study of literature both as a preparatory (encyclical) and an aesthetic curriculum. In this choice the Christian scholars followed the Stoics rather than Plato. But the Christian scholar gave little place to science; for he substituted philosophy—logic in its broadest sense—for the place Plato and Aristotle had given to mathematics and the physical sciences. The highest education was that of theology. Philosophy stood between literature and theology. It enabled the student to see the emptiness of literature as content, the follies of the poets, while he rejoiced in the beauty of their language and the refinement of their style. It was also the foundation (reason) upon which the higher truth (revelation) was fixed.

Primary education in ancient China also was devoted to the study of language. Three elementary classics led the student to a mastery of the most important characters to be met in the great classics. There was first the *Three Character Classic* (*San-tzu Ching* 三字經), then the *One Hundred Surnames* (*Pai Chia Hsing* 百家姓) and finally, the *Thousand Character Essay* (*Ch'ien-tzu wen* 千字文). The higher learning began with the *Four Books* (*Lun Yu* 論語 *Analects of Confucius, Ta Hsüeh* 大學 *the Great Learning, Chung Yung* 中庸 *the Doctrine of the Mean,* and *Meng Tzu* 孟子 *the Works of Mencius*) and proceeded to the *Five Classics* (*Shu Ching* 書經 *Book of Documents*— history, *Shih Ching* 詩經 *Book of Songs*—poetry, *Yi Ching* 易經 *Book of Changes, Li Chi* 禮記 *Book of Rites,* and *Ch'un Ch'iu* 春秋 *Spring and Autumn*). These remained throughout the scholar's career the programme of his studies but he progressed in his understanding of them through three levels of attainment. The first level prepared the student for the *hsien* 縣 or county examination which consisted of two essays and one original poem. The successful candidate was awarded the degree of *hsiu-ts'ai* (秀才 budding genius) and proceeded to his preparation for the provincial examination. By A.D. 622 (the year of the Hijra and the founding of Islam in the Near East and just after the papacy of Gregory the Great in the West) this examination was firmly established under imperial order. It was divided into three parts and covered, in a series of thirteen essays or papers, the whole of the classical literature and its relation to the art of government. The successful candidate received the degree of chu-ren (舉人 promoted man).[20]   He was given a scholar's gown and academic cap and proceeded to the final level. This was the palace examination, established in 1066 (the year of the Battle of Hastings), which tested the candidates' mastery of the classics on the level of ready application to the affairs of the state.[21]   One third of the candidates was selected to enter the Hanlin Academy (翰林 Forest of Scholars)—a Royal Society of Letters. It would appear that something of the same syllabus of studies obtained both in China and in the West. The county examination would correspond to the science of grammar which also in the West covered much more than was indicated by the word in its narrower sense. The provincial examination presupposed a syllabus on literature in the broader sense of the arts. Finally the palace examination was designed to select those of highest competence in the distilling of knowledge into wisdom for the management of public affairs.

The lower schools are concerned with acquiring the tools of knowledge and their mastery with a view to

[20] Han Yü-shan, *op. cit.,* pp. 12 ff.
[21] Teng Ssu-Yu, "China's Examination System and the West" in MacNair, *op. cit.,* pp. 441 ff.

immediate application to life either in terms of skill or of enjoyment. But it must be remembered that even on the lower level neither the Greeks nor the Chinese thought of skill in calligraphy or the composition of poems as a mechanical skill or a technical knowledge related to wage-earning occupations. Aristotle, who was far more practical than Plato, would not accept the training in crafts as a part of formal education on any level. Such knowledge, he wrote, will " absorb and degrade the mind." [22]

Professor Whitehead has suggested that the stages of learning are not points on a simple progression graph but rather phases of a cycle that recur at all levels though each phase is characteristic of a certain level. These are the stages of romance, precision, and generalization. Romance " is the stage of first apprehension. The subject matter has the vividness of novelty. . . . It holds within itself unexplored connections with possibilities half disclosed by glimpses and half concealed by the wealth of material. . . . Romantic emotion is essentially the excitement consequent on the transition from the bare facts to the first realizations of the import of their unexplored relationships." [23] Memorization at this level is almost unconscious. The young student takes facts in almost effortlessly as fast as they come to him. Newman described primary education as the seven years of plenty when the school boy gathers in by the handfulls, " like the Egyptians without counting—he acquires and little more." [24]

With the stage of precision comes the necessary discipline of exactness of formulation. This is the time of the science of language and the grammar of science.

---

[22] *Politics* 1339.

[23] *Aims of Education* pp. 29 ff.

[24] J. H. Newman, *University Subjects* (New York: Houghton Mifflin Co., 1913), p. 28.

Middle school years are the hardest. The romance of learning may easily be lost under the burdens of grammar, chronology and mathematics. As Whitehead remarked, " the hardest task in mathematics is the study of the elements of algebra, and yet this stage must precede the comparative simplicity of the differential calculus." [25] College maths are a threat only to the student who has not known the necessary discipline of middle school. In some schools of the middle ages the bachelor's degree was almost exclusively associated with the science of grammar, and the conferral of the master's privileges upon the grammarian differed from that of all other faculties. For the latter the graduate received a book as the symbol of his office but the grammarian's instruments of office were a " palmer " (the ' ruler ' for smacking the palms of careless students) and a birch rod to be applied to the dorsal surfaces in the case of more serious mistakes. As a new deacon is directed to read the Gospel at the Eucharist following his ordination, so the master in grammar proved his new powers by flogging a boy 'openlye in the Scholys ' as a part of the solemn ceremony of inception. We are relieved to note that the boy was paid a groat for his services and the bedel (the college warden) received the same for the use of his paddle.[26] Elsewhere Rashdall remarks that there has always been " some peculiar and mysterious connection between the rod and classical scholarship." [27]

The final stage of generalization, Whitehead describes as a ' return to romanticism with the added advantage of classified ideas and relevant technique.' Learning as

---

[25] *Ibid.*

[26] Rashdall, *op. cit.,* III p. 347. The source is *Stoky's Book* —Cambridge University 16th cent. A similar inception ceremony was in use at Oxford as indicated by the *Oxford Register* 1509.

[27] *Ibid.* 359.

romance and adventure is found anew as the adventure of research and the romance of wisdom.

THE CONCEPT OF HIGHER EDUCATION

Higher education deals with principles. Plato introduced his discussion of the highest science, philosophy, with the simple statement that it consists in the ability to give and take account of something.[28] One can conceive of an education rising from elementary to university level in which the student learned first his native language, next another language similar in structure, and finally a third quite different language. Such an education might possibly be a good one. There were some students so trained who became great minds, and who, looking backward, were convinced that the road they had travelled in the schools was the only one by which they could have come to an appreciation of the past, a breadth of understanding, and a vision of creative scholarship upon the frontier of human reason. John Colet would have said this of his own academic pilgrimage.[29] He had learned the peculiar patois of his own island, and through it grasped the particular qualities of the English mind and the British heart. He had learned Latin, and had by this study entered into a living relation with the past and with the common heritage of European civilization. Finally he learned Greek; and there opened before him an exciting new world of criticism and of the re-conception of spiritual values. But language itself was not the road that brought him to his journey's end. Grammar was at best the shoes without which he could not have trod the rough places of his journey. You could learn twenty

---

[28] *Republic* 531 e.
[29] See Harbison, *op. cit.*, pp. 55 ff.

27

languages and if you used them to read the equivalent of the multiplication table or the *San-tzü Ching* you would not be advanced beyond a primary education. One of the very great dangers in the modern world is the extension of middle school studies into the university both in the arts and in the sciences. Too much that passes under the name of advanced scholarship is simply middle school scholarship in a little known subject. Higher education deals with the theory of things. Theory of course cannot be divorced from things, but it is the emphasis, the side which matters most to teacher and to student, that distinguishes the university from the middle school. Higher education deals with principles that have universal rather than limited application. It should begin with general ideas for which a few significant concrete exemplifications are sufficient. Plato chose to treat both politics and education in his ideal republic without any reference to particular states or particular peoples. He tells us nothing of the physical conditions of his ideal city. " The training described in the *Republic* has nothing to do with the race that lives in the city." [30]

Higher education is critical and interpretive not catechetical or mechanical. It aims at the making of a mind, not the filling of a head with facts. "A merely well-informed man is the most useless bore on God's earth." [31] Whitehead speaks with a medical vividness of " the consequences of a plethora of half-digested theoretical knowledge," [32] and with a Platonic sarcasm about that kind of learning which is a " watching of the open pages of all the books which we have read, and then, when occasion arises, . . . select(ing) the right page to read

---

[30] *Paideia* II pp. 198-9.
[31] Whitehead, *op. cit.,* p. 13.
[32] *Ibid.* p. 16.

28

aloud to the universe!" [33] Similarly the reformer, Wang An-shih, complained of the narrow catechetical education of his day as consisting merely of " explanations of the texts of the Classics, analyzed into sections and sentences." [34] Such was not, he insisted, the ancient method. When Maynard Hutchins came to the University of Chicago as its Chancellor, he was determined that it should be in the tradition of Socrates, not of the Sophists. " It is not the university's business to teach practical, professional and vocational courses, for practice changes too rapidly. What the student learns in such practical courses, even if his professor is up to date, will be out of date when he gets round to using it. All that can be learned in a university is the general principles, the fundamental propositions, the theory of any discipline." [35]

Higher education is characterized by both a depth of competence and a breadth of perspective. American education has sometimes been caricatured as the attempt to know less and less about more and more until one can know absolutely nothing about everything. A well-known story about such a programme tells of the examination in one course : " Describe the universe and give three examples." But there is also the danger of knowing more and more about less and less until one knows everything about nothing. One doctoral dissertation, written at the height of the fashion of specialization in a German university, that has often been mentioned but seldom read is *The Use of the Comma in Medieval Icelandic Literature.* The sins of the universities have been many. We cannot label them, according to a popular custom with respect

---

[33] *Ibid.* pp. 38-39.

[34] Creel, *op. cit.,* p. 95. The date of the quotation is A.D. 1058.

[35] G. P. Schmidt, *The Liberal Arts College,* p. 80.

to disreputable diseases, as national types. All have sinned, and the prayer of all must ever be: " God be merciful to me a sinner! " The history of the greatest universities is the story of God's mercy to both masters and scholars. This problem of the tension between a special competence and a broad perspective belongs to a later chapter. Here it is sufficient to recall the wisdom of a contemporary American historian: " The calling to teach is the calling to know something well. The teacher need not know everything, even everything pertaining to his own speciality, but he must know something thoroughly. And to know something thoroughly means to see it in the longest perspective and with all its implications." [36]

Higher education is structured with a view toward an ultimate concern. This has been true of the greatest universities in the periods of their highest excellence. It has also been true of the few philosophies of education that have provided the organizing principles of a systematic approach to higher learning. In the history of Western education there has been only one such basic philosophy— the work of Plato. Aristotle did not deal systematically with the subject, largely because he believed Plato had already done so. His own academy represents amendments, important to be sure, to the Platonic schema. The great Christian contributors from Clement of Alexandria through Origen, St. Augustin, St. Jerome, to Abelard, Thomas Aquinas, Luther, Bacon, Commenius, Newman and others have all laboured within the framework of Plato's programme. For the most part other philosophies of education have followed the basic pattern of sophistic notions, pointing out from time to time as did Isocrates and Dewey some of the inert ideas and ineffectual methods

---

[36] S. Mead, "The Vocation of the Teacher", *Divinity School Bulletin,* University of Chicago, 1948.

of the Platonic academy.   What the university aspires to develop is a capacity of response to that kind of excellence of the intellect which accords with that perfection of the body which is called health and that perfection of the moral nature which is called virtue.[37]   Plato can use the Homeric word *areté* with its earlier meaning transformed from honour into that wisdom which is a directing of the " best part of the soul to see the best thing that exists." Then can the soul rest in its journeying.   For this is " to rest in the highest excellence," " to know one's abiding place " 至善知止 ;[38] for as Newman paraphrased Plato, " in the nature of things, greatness and unity go together, excellence implies a center." [39]   There is a set of general principles along which all knowledge is organized and these in turn are interrelated.   Francis Bacon spoke of the " chain of the sciences " and of the " circle of learning." [40]   Philo, the great Jewish scholar of Alexandria, used the phrase " the art of arts and the science of sciences." [41]   The highest task of the university is precisely this : to exhibit in its total working the science of sciences. All curricula explicitly or implicitly exhibit a *systema,* a circle of sciences, and for all systematic curricula there is an end in view.   Ultimately these ends imply one of the two basic categories of interpretation : *1.* man is the measure of all things or *2.* God is the measure of all things.   The first is neither more profound nor more liberal than the second.   Protagoras was neither more profound nor more humane than Plato.

---

[37] See Newman, *op. cit.,* pp. 24-5.

[38] *The Great Learning* i 2. See E. R. Hughes, *The Great Learning and The Mean-In-Action* (New York : E. P. Dutton & Co., 1943), p. 146.

[39] Newman, *op. cit.,* p. 11.

[40] De *augmentis scientiarum* iii.   See A. Dwight Culler's brilliant chapter "The Circle of the Sciences" in his *Imperial Intellect* (New Haven : Yale University Press, 1955) pp. 173 ff.

[41] Philo, *De congressu* xxv.

A statesman of Lu recognized the need of a new kind of school and appealed to Confucius to teach his son.

THE UNIVERSITY

Thus far we have dealt with the pedigree of those ideas of higher education that could be called the seed from which the university has sprung. The plant itself, as an historical institution, was germinated in a particular soil: the religious, political and cultural life of medieval Europe. When the word 'university' is used to describe a well-defined society of teachers and students, pursuing a programme of studies according to faculties under a special charter with the authority to grant various degrees, or, in other words, when 'university' is used with reference to such schools as Heidelburg, Harvard or Hong Kong, it describes a particular kind of educational institution that had its beginnings in Medieval Europe.[42] Previous schools of higher learning in Spain or France or Italy or Greece, in the Middle East or China were not universities in the sense in which the word itself came, during the middle ages, to be applied to a particular kind of higher school. The schools of Plato and Aristotle were academies, not universities.

In telling the story of the birth of the university, if

[42] Rashdall, *op. cit.,* III 458 f.

it is to be a true story, we must speak of quite common-place incidents in the commonplace development of trade and of commonplace political and ecclesiastical incidents leading to obvious solutions of quite practical problems. But what transpired in the ordinary course of dealing with these commonplace incidents was the creation, partly unconscious, certainly without definite intention, of a wholly new and unique institution of profound significance for the subsequent cultural history not only of Europe but of the world. The greatness of medieval Europe was a unique capacity in response to the past, to create institutions, and a unique sense of vocation for that task.[43] Living as we do in an age of analysis and discovery, we have, perhaps not of our own choosing, bought our brilliance and our comforts at a price. We have bartered for them that which all previous ages considered their greatest treasure: a sense of the past and an uninhibited love of ancient things. The middle ages, throughout the world, were a time of assimilation and incorporation in which the ideal achievement was the weaving of a classical heritage into the very fabric of life, i.e. into institutions. We live amidst the chaos of new inventions and new ideas, resigned to the frustration of being strangers and barbarians in our own culture. The medieval scholar in China and in Europe had the leisure and luxury of savouring one by one the riches of the past. He was thereby led to the vocation of securing for each part of his heritage its proper place and of organizing society in such a way that all that he cherished could find concrete expression in an ordered structure of institutions. Ours is an age of invention, his an age of construction. The medieval man was a builder.[44] Our energies are spent

---

[43] *Ibid.*

[44] See C. G. Coulton, *Medieval Faith and Symbolism,* Harper Torchbooks, (New York: Harper and Bros., 1958).

in making new bricks out of new materials. The medieval man had his bricks already to hand, weathered to the pleasant tone of the familiar. He had the joy of fitting old things into structures of usefulness and beauty. His appreciative awareness of the sublime led him to value structure above novelty, and synthesis above analysis. He built from the materials of ages past that which shall endure for years to come. His cathedrals rising from their firm foundations reach with the spires of hope toward heaven, the symbols in stone of his cherished harmony of the diverse elements of solidity and delicacy, of severity and sensuality, the sublime and the grotesque, the austere and the tender, of faith and fear, of all things human, and of things divine. We would, of course, quite miss the point were we to picture the medieval genius as the man of naive piety and purity, the savant or the courtly servitor of genteel tradition. He was, far more than we, the realist. What we would probably feel first, if suddenly we should be carried from our age back to his, would be the violence of the time whether the scene were Paris or Peking. And it is in the debt of his realism, as much as of his aspiration or his architectonic genius, that we continue to live in our day within the structure of his institutions so long after the beliefs that gave character to his cathedrals have lost their relevance.

The opening sentence of Dean Rashdall's huge history of European universities in the middle ages recalls the pride of a medieval author in the three great institutions of his age: *Sacerdotium, Imperium et Studium,* the Church, the Empire and the School.[45] But what is more significant in this quotation than the naming of these institutions is the implication that they are linked together

---

[45] Rashdall, *op. cit.,* I pp. 2 ff. Cf. Ulich, *The Education of Nations* (Cambridge: Harvard University Press, 1961), pp. 5 ff.

as a trinity of powers expressing a trinity of virtues, the spiritual, the temporal and the rational. It is indeed the last which binds together the spiritual and the temporal, the Church and the State; for it has as its task the study of things human and things divine, of law and of theology and above all of that reason which is the life of law and the mediator between experience and revelation. So there abideth faith, justice and wisdom, and many of those, even among the monks and priests, who as men of faith brought forth the European university, would have said: ' and the greatest of these is wisdom.' The university was the child of the church and its father was the state.[46] It was the issue of a notion of the state that rose above nationality. The gleam in its father's eye was Alexander's dream of the cosmopolitan empire. The Patristic synthesis of the kingdom of Caesar and the Kingdom of the Christ was in part a concept of a science, not so much of a knowledge as of a wisdom, which both exposed the temporality of the kingdoms of this world and pointed toward eternal verities.

As the daughter of the church and the empire the university inherited a basic structure. Both church and state were hierarchical which means that in ideal their several offices were linked by loyalty.[47] The chivalry of the state involving the loyalty of knight to lord and lord to king and king to emperor was paralleled by the orders of the church involving the loyalty of priest to bishop and of bishop to prelate and of prelate to pope. So also the university was a society of levels and responsibilities.

---

[46] Charles V spoke of the University of Paris as 'the eldest daughter of the King.' See Rashdall, *op. cit.,* I p. 542.

[47] See E. W. Watson, "Development of Ecclesiastical Organization and Its Financial Basis" in *Cambridge Medieval History* vol. VI. In the eleventh century the priest was commonly called the 'Bishop's man.'

The ideal of the middle ages is captured in the Latin word for university—*universitas*—which means ' a whole.' The Christian people as a whole are addressed by the popes as *universitas vestra,* ' the whole of you.'[48] It is the whole society, the whole body of a particular group. Its first use with respect to education was *universitas scholarium* and it then referred to the body of students who formed a corporation at the medical school at Salerno in Italy. It had previously been used in the eleventh century as the synonym for ' guild ' or ' fraternity ' and it is in fact to the phenomenon in that century of the guilds of clergy, merchants and craftsmen that we must look to find the genesis of the university as an institution.[49] Our first glimpse of these societies is in connection with trade and travel: an association of travelling merchants who have banded together to share the expense of their journey and to provide mutual protection against the hazards of travel and the risks of residence in a foreign state. The first guilds were probably caravans—a company of travellers who sought the safety in numbers that the individual merchant could enjoy only with a paid retinue. The members of the caravan were bound together by the pledge of mutual assistance and sworn brotherhood. When they returned home they continued their relationship, seeking in a society the benefits of corporate action with respect to matters of mutual interest.[50] The first association of students was probably also for the sake of the greater benefits of corporate action to secure fair treatment from their instructors and from the

---

[48] Rashdall, *op. cit.,* I pp. 5 ff. See also Graves, *op. cit.,* II pp. 86 ff; Rashdall, "The Medieval Universities" in *Cambridge Medieval History* VI pp. 559 ff; Culler, *op. cit.,* p. 179.

[49] See Charles Gross, "Guilds" in *Encyclopaedia Britannica*[11] and Coulton, *op. cit.,* pp. 198 ff.

[50] See Henri Pirenne, "Northern Towns and Their Commerce" in *CMH* VI pp. 511 ff.

landlords, tradesmen and authorities of the city in which they went to school. The first university was a *universitas* of students who had come from other cities and foreign countries to study medicine at Salerno. Similarly at Bologna in northern Italy students who had left their homes in southern Italy and France and Holland to study Law were obliged to seek in corporate action the rights which as individual foreigners they could not have obtained. The *universitas scholarium* which first appeared at Salerno and Bologna was a guild of scholars patterned after the guilds of merchants and craftsmen.[51] The guild of masters or teachers which was formed at Paris, the *universitas magistrorum* was also a society for mutual protection—a trade union which guarded its members against the abuses of non-union competitors and insured that no student without due qualifications could claim the title of master.[52] What we mean by the term ' university,' a programme of instruction in several fields, was in the middle ages called a *studium generale,* that is to say a school. But *generale* then referred to the breadth of its policy of admissions not to the variety of the courses which it offered. A *studium generale* was a school to which students from all parts of the empire could come. A *studium particulare,* on the other hand, was a school open only to those of the locality.[53] Three great schools *(studia)* emerged with the beginning of the thirteenth century as the foremost international centers of learning. All three had become universities in the previous century in the sense that a guild of scholars or of masters had been formed and recognized. Of these Salerno, the foremost center of medical studies which had for many years

---

[51] J. B. Mullinger, "Universities" in *EB* xxvii.

[52] Graves, *op. cit.,* II p. 88.

[53] Rashdall, *op. cit.,* I pp. 6 ff.

the fame of its mineral springs and its physicians, was the first. It was a university of scholars and a college of doctors.[54] The second and far more influential university was the *studium generale* of law at Bologna. Its scholars' guild became the model for most of the schools of Italy and hence the first of the two basic types of university organization. Paris was the third great *studium generale* and the model of the universities of masters such as Oxford and Cambridge. At Bologna the authority resided in the guild of students. At Paris it was in the guild of masters. By the fourteenth century the phrase *universitas magistrorum et scholarium* was in common use and by the fifteenth, beginning in Germany, the term *studium generale* fell into disuse.[55] The great centers of learning were known simply as universities, and by a gradual process, the term ceased to be applied to other kinds of institutions.

In the Parisian type of university, organized under the guild of masters, there was a division of teachers according to *faculties*.[56] This term originally designated the departments of special knowledge such as law or medicine. Since the masters were grouped according to the subjects they taught, the word came to mean the instructors in a particular field or science. The masters were the voting members of the faculties each of which elected a head to direct the internal matters of the department and to represent it in the administrative councils. The head of a faculty was a ' dean.' The Latin *decanus* indicates the first among ten—the captain of a small group. The French *doyen* indicates the eldest of a group. The medieval dean

---

[54] J. B. Mullinger, *op. cit.*, p. 750.

[55] *Ibid.* p. 749.

[56] Graves, *op. cit.*, p. 88; Rashdall, *op. cit.*, I 321 ff. and 433 ff.

was probably most often the eldest of the masters teaching within a department of special knowledge.[57]

Each of the first three universities appears to have grown around a particular faculty for which it had become famous. At Salerno it was medicine, at Bologna law, and at Paris, theology. These were higher studies and each demanded a special grounding in those disciplines which had heretofore been themselves the higher learning, that is, the famous *quadrivium* and *trivium* which the middle ages inherited from the academies of Greece and Rome.

Philo, the great Jewish philosopher of Alexandria, was possibly the originator of the phrase ' the seven liberal arts ' which he finds symbolized in the notion of the seven pillars of wisdom attributed to Solomon.[58] The division of these seven sciences into the *trivium* of grammar, rhetoric and logic and the *quadrivium* of music, arithmetic, geometry and astronomy was probably a medieval development.[59] Today we would speak of the seven as for the most part undergraduate studies. In this sense the medieval universities began as primarily graduate schools with faculties of law, medicine and theology but retained the liberal arts both because of their traditional prestige and because they were basic to the advanced studies. Philosophy was a major requirement for medicine.[60] In the course in rhetoric, introductory law was taught.[61] Theology demanded a particularly high competence in all the arts. There is always the ugly duckling, and, in the medieval university it was the grammarian who had his

---

[57] Rashdall, *op. cit.,* I p. 326.

[58] *De congressu* 31, 177.

[59] Rashdall, *op. cit.,* I p. 37 n. 2.

[60] Jaeger, *Paideia* III pp. 3 ff. Rashdall I p. 234.

[61] Rashdall I p. 93.

difficulties.[62] Perhaps the association of grammar and the rod was not easily forgotten even by the older masters in advanced studies. Four faculties thus comprised the programme of the oldest universities—theology, law, medicine and the arts.[63] The dean of each faculty became a member of a college of electors in which also the students were represented for the choosing of a rector, the administrative officer of the university. The term had previously been used in the early university of scholars for the head of guilds in general. In the early university of scholars the rector was usually a student, though in this type of school it must be remembered the students were not only of mature age but also were men of prominence in the church.[64] Many were deans of cathedrals, some were even bishops. In the university of masters the rector was often by rule selected from the masters in the faculty of arts.

The guild of masters was similar to the guilds of craftsmen with respect to the regulation of the training of the apprentice and his inception into the guild. The masters were qualified, licensed lecturers who protected their rights and also the honour of their calling with a trade union monopoly of the teaching profession. At the top of the guild stood the masters of the higher faculties. In some universities the highest rank, that of doctor, was reserved for the highest faculty, theology.[65] Most schools called only those professor or doctor who were of the superior faculties (theology, law, medicine). Some schools did confer the degree of *doctor notariae* to masters in the faculty of arts but it was seldom if ever bestowed upon the grammarian. Many schools had a special and

---

[62] *Ibid.* pp. 240 ff; Graves, *op. cit.,* II p. 88.

[63] *Ibid.* 433 ff; 471. See Graves II p. 88.

[64] *Ibid.* 176 ff. Some chairs were also held by students, p. 215.

[65] J. B. Mullinger, *op. cit.,* p. 564.

lower degree in grammar and rhetoric than that given in the other arts.[66] To be a master meant primarily to be a member of the guild of teachers.   There were two stages or degrees in the progress of the scholar toward the rank of master.   The first of these was the grade (*gradus*— degree) of bachelor.   As such the scholar had taken a step toward his goal, *gradus ad magisterium*.[67]   He had entered upon a period of probation in which certain minor tasks of instruction were entrusted to him.   He was permitted to lecture on certain specified portions of a required text and he was admitted to masters' disputations on certain subjects.   A curious function of bachelors at Bologna was the exercise of the office of Repetitor. Students were required to hear certain lectures at least twice.   Also it was not always possible or approved by the lecturer that lower form scholars should crowd his hall.   The Repetitor attended the lecture and then repeated it as best he could to the students.   He then proceeded to question them on their understanding of the material. Bologna required an appointment of *repetitor generalis* attached to the chair of logic.   The *repetitor speciales* tutored individual students.[68]   It is here at Bologna that we first meet the office of tutor in the history of the university.   The second stage in the progress from scholar to master was that of licentiate.   The recommended bachelor was licensed by the rector to lecture.   Finally, he had to obtain the consent of the members to be admitted into the guild of masters.   Only then was he free to teach as a fully qualified lecturer in the university.   The symbol of his privilege was the magisterial biretta—the academic cap.   Here again we see the close connection between

---

[66] Rashdall, II p. 243. Graves II 88.

[67] J. B. Mullinger, *op. cit.*, p. 564. Cf. Rashdall, I 282, 287.

[68] Rashdall, I pp. 246-9.

41

the guild and the university of masters. An apprentice was indentured to his master. Graduation was an emancipation and the old Roman ceremony of manumission— the placing of a new cap upon the head of the freed slave symbolized the release of the student from his servant status to the master under whom he had studied.[69] Upon his admission to the society of masters he was obliged to deliver an inaugural lecture to his colleagues as the final act of his inception. A master of the three great schools was henceforth qualified to teach without further examination in any university. Theoretically the license to teach derived from the authority of the church. At Paris long after the chancellor of the cathedral had ceased to be a power at the university he still retained the authority to issue in the name of the church the license to teach. No *studium generale* could be established without the consent either of the pope or the emperor and this indicates a further aspect of the conception of the university; for the general school was in no sense provincial or national.[70] Under either its imperial or papal charter it not only received scholars from all parts of the empire but its graduates as masters were empowered to pursue their careers in any school of the empire. In modern parlance we would say that their degrees were universally recognized.

The international character of all universities is seen also in the internal organization of the inferior faculty, the faculty of arts. Both masters and scholars in arts were organized into divisions known as the four nations.[71] At Paris these were 1. the French nation which included

---

[69] *Ibid.*, p. 285.

[70] Coulton, *Medieval Panorama*, p. 395. By A.D. 1300 it amounted to legal theory that either papal or imperial foundation was essential to a *studium generale*.

[71] Mullinger, *op. cit.*, pp. 752 f.

Spaniards, Italians and Greeks, 2. the Picard nation which included members from the northeast and the Netherlands, 3. the Norman nation, and 4. the English nation including continental provinces under English rule and masters and students from Ireland, Scotland and Germany. Each nation had its head who was called the proctor. It would appear that the proctors were largely influential in the election of the head of the arts faculty who then automatically became, in some schools, the rector of the university. The major administrative body of the university as a whole was called the congregation, comprising the deans of faculties and the proctors of the nations. Voting was by faculty and the vote of the arts faculty could be cast only after ascertaining the majority opinion of the nations.

In the United States of America the inferior faculty of the university is known as the college and the superior faculties as graduate departments and professional schools. *Collegium* and *universitas* were in the eleventh century practically synonymous. Both were in common use as designating the societies of the guilds and other special groups either within the larger whole of the empire or the church. At Bologna *universitas* was first used with reference only to the guild of students. *Collegium* was the term for the several guilds of the teachers. Thus the guild of doctors of medicine was a *collegium*, the guild of the doctors of canon law, the guild of the doctors of civil law were other *collegia*.[72] Each college appears to have been academically autonomous. It was the college that conferred the degree. Bologna was thus at this stage of its development a university of colleges.

The word was used at Bologna also in another sense— as houses founded for the benefit of poor scholars or of

---

[72] Rashdall, I 82, 145; II 315.

a group of students from the same province or under the patronage of a bishop. In 1256 such a college was founded by the Bishop of Avignon at Bologna for the benefit of eight scholars from his diocese.[73] In the same year the Sorbonne was founded at Paris for the benefit of sixteen scholars in theology, four from each nation. Prior to the rise of the colleges as places of residence poor students were sheltered in the humble *domus* which was little more than a *dormitorium*—a place to sleep. In England the colleges of Oxford and Cambridge, which in the beginning were exactly similar to those of Bologna and Paris, developed an amazing individual vitality, and in the course of three centuries became by the middle of the sixteenth more important than the university. These *collegia* were corporations in the legal sense composed of a ' master ' and fellows. The fellows were graduate students and the master was elected by them and from among their number. They would from the medieval period until the nineteenth century have been young clergy in their early twenties staying on in the college until a living in the church might come their way.[74] Living with them would have been a larger number of scholars, undergraduates in their middle and later teens. At first these colleges like those of Paris were simply hostels organized for a common life of study and worship. Each college had its chapel, usually far larger than its numbers warranted, at which daily services were said and masses sung on appointed days for the repose of the founder's soul. Sometime, however, during the latter days of the middle ages, the fellows began to guide the scholars in their studies. From houses of residence and coaching, the colleges then suddenly became the real centers of

---

[73] Mullinger, *op. cit.*, p. 751.
[74] See C. P. Snow's interesting "Appendix" to his *Masters*, Penguin ed., pp. 300 ff.

education in the university. With the large gifts that came to them, especially in the seventeenth century, they were able to attract into their corporations the more promising graduates until the university was largely dependent upon the colleges for its lecturers. It was in this century, quite apart from the university programme that the new physical sciences were noted and explored by the fellows of the colleges. The sciences still belonged to the arts as the new content of the old *quadrivium*. During the next century English learning as a whole enjoyed a sabbatical and the universities declined. Some of the colleges fell back to the number of scholars provided for in the original foundation five hundred years before. The fellows remained in force as gentlemen in waiting for clerical livings and sipped their port at leisure. In the nineteenth century the long shadow of seventeenth century discovery had fallen upon the detached scholarship of the arts and there came the reorganization of the university's programme of studies to meet the nation's demand for scientists. Again the university with its greater resources to foot the huge costs of laboratories rose to its old stature above the colleges. But colleges continued to secure the lecturers and provide the comfortable livings for their distinguished fellows who were thus enabled to serve the university. The rise of the sciences was not, however, at least in the nineteenth century, at the expense of the arts. Indeed the ancient ' Greats ' enjoyed during the century the championship of some of the ablest men in the history of the colleges. New research in classical studies and distinguished publications in history reflected the needed impetus that the competition of the physical sciences had supplied. And throughout the century science scholars were still privileged by their associations in their colleges to enjoy a civilizing of the intellect.

The University of Paris began with its guild of masters about A.D. 1170.[75] Salerno and Bologna had already their guilds of students. Within the twelfth century six universities had arisen in Europe, three in Italy, two in France, and Oxford in England. Seventeen more appeared in the next century including those of Spain and Portugal. By A.D. 1400 thirty-five universities dotted the map of Europe from Cracow in Poland, Fünfkirchen and Buda in Hungary to Lisbon on the western coast, and from Salerno in southern Italy to Cambridge in England; and by the end of the century thirty-four more, including the Scandinavian and the later German universities, had been founded. In little more than three hundred years, eighty universities had arisen. At the close of the middle ages Europe's great centers of learning had all been established.[76]

How shall we give an account of this mighty movement, how can we explain why it took place? In the instance of each of the first universities we could tell the simple story, colorful in detail yet commonplace as a whole, of the bald events: the incidents in the streets of Salerno and Bologna where German students suffered the harsh treatment accorded to the stranger for whom the laws of the city provided no rights yet imposed harsh restrictions.[77] So much of the surface history of the rise of the student guilds is the commonplace story of the gown torn in the town.[78] At a little lower level it is the story of the aspiration toward cosmopolitan citizenship. The guilds as corporations could wrest from the city what amounted to a special citizenship for their alien members.

---

[75] Rashdall, I p. 292. For the first statute of Paris (A.D. 1210) see p. 311.

[76] See the "Table of Universities" in Rashdall, I xxiv and the map of medieval university towns at the back of vol. III.

[77] Mullinger, *op. cit.*, p. 750.

[78] Coulton, *op. cit.*, pp. 401 ff. and Rashdall, III pp. 79 and 353 ff.

In part the rise of the universities is the story of men, of mature men like William of Champeaux in whom old experience had attained to something like prophetic flame, of younger men like Abelard, impetuous geniuses, driven by ambition to break through old walls and seek self-expression which the ancient institutions could not provide. In part it is the story of adventure in young hearts, of young men who left their homes in pursuit of knowledge and travelled as did the young knight on crusade. All these little stories are vignettes of the epic of the later middle ages. The larger story is one of a waning of lethargy and of an increased capacity to respond to the past and to the 'insistent present.' The 'dark ages' were years not so much of the dullness of mind and the depression of spirit as they were a time of struggle for sheer survival. Some time during the early part of the twelfth century the cities of Europe, which had in the seventh and eighth centuries declined in importance as trade dwindled, began once more to grow. The battle for survival had been won, not as by one great and final onslaught, but little by little, almost imperceptibly, the harsh conditions of life began to give way. There was more energy in the farmer, more initiative in the towns-man, more lively interest in the scholar for his tasks. By the middle of the twelfth century trade had quickened almost to the point it had attained in the last lively days of empire of the Caesars. Europe had not had so much excitement since the fall of Rome. The demands of life changed from the necessitous drudgery of the hand-to-hand conflict with the soil to the higher skills and abilities of international commerce. A new class of men was needed and the training that would fit them for their new tasks was not to be had either in the monasteries or in the cathedral schools. These had developed the virtues of obedience and asceticism and applied them to both the content and the method of instruction.[79] Their aim was to train men for the life of contemplative prayer in the monastery and for the ministry to the hard-pressed veteran of the battle for survival in the parish. Now there were needed schools where either the implications for contemporary situations of the ancient canon and civil law could be explored or adventures in new approaches to positive law undertaken. With the recovery of the cities, particularly those of northern Italy, a concern for the rights of the city over against the claims of empire and church gave impetus to the study of Roman law, especially those documents upon which their ancient claims to independence were founded.[80] Even before these needs became acute a subtle change had occurred in the cathedral schools. Quite gradually, and apparently without plan, these schools found among their teachers fewer monastics and more of the secular clergy. The monastics had emphasized grammar, the secular clergy tended to be more interested in logic and more sensitive to the winds of change blowing through the streets of the cities. Abelard was not yet in priest's orders when he came to Paris to study under William of Champeaux. William had his licence to teach from the Chancellor of the Cathedral of Notre Dame and he taught in the cathedral school on the Ile de la Cité. To this and other such schools the secular clergy could come as free-lance lecturers.[81] Like the Sophists in Greece their living would depend upon the number of students they could gather round them. The cathedral school did not assure its teachers of any students. Some lecturers might have only

---

[79] Graves, *op. cit.*, II pp. 4 ff., 63 ff. and 72 ff.
[80] *Ibid.*, p. 78.
[81] Rashdall, I p. 150.

a few or none at all. Others might attract large numbers. When Abelard became dissatisfied with the instruction offered by the best of the teachers on the island in the Seine he simply left the school and with youthful daring crossed over to the left bank and set himself up as a master extraordinary at the Collegiate Church of Ste. Genevieve. It is sometimes claimed that Abelard and his students at Ste. Genevieve mark the beginning of the University of Paris. More precisely this school of Abelard's was an ancestor of the University. Later William, who had left the isle himself after the defection of Abelard, returned to Paris and inaugurated a third school at the Church of the Canons Regular of St. Victor.

Attention focuses upon Abelard not only because he was himself a colourful character, brilliant and erratic, with a capacity for the enjoyment of logic but capable also of responding to the beauty and tenderness that he found in Heloise, but primarily because he is the classical type of the new man who was the precursor of the new school, the university.[82] His youthful arrogance is now unimportant, even to William, I suspect. What he said in those lectures that were the wonder of the academic world of his day, so that students higher than bishops crowded his hall, is also now for the most part unimportant. His insights into the great doctrines of the church, for which he was prepared to risk everything including Heloise except his intellectual pride and his academic reputation, are now points of view on which neither Roman nor Protestant would care to take an unequivocal stand. But it is just in this quality of Abelard that we find one of the few truly essential foundations of a

---

[82] See Helen Waddell's charming biographical novel *Peter Abelard* (London: Fontana Books, 1958) and her *Wandering Scholars* 4th ed. (Boston; 1929). For Rashdall's estimate of the place of Abelard in the history of the university see I pp. 25 ff.

university—the intellectual pride of its masters. At its best it is a sense of commitment to enquiry or to academic excellence. At its worst it is an unlovely sin. It is seldom if ever either all best or worst. Scholars are rarely saints, unless, as in the case of St. Jerome, everyone has forgotten everything else about them. Nowadays their wives are bound to tell you so in strictest confidence. Bishops and kings, too, have their failings and even popes have been known to have missed full marks at times. Yet perhaps stronger even than the lust for power, certainly than the love of fellow human beings, is the passion of the scholar. It is a very high calling and as such it betrays its votaries so easily into pride. But it is this very pride that gains for the university its excellence even at the loss of the scholar's own soul. For the scholar, too, is a Greek hero and a knightly adventurer. In his sometimes Fallstaffian figure there beats a stout heart with its proud boast 'to strive always for the highest excellence, and to excel all others.' And here is one difference between the Chinese and the Western ideal.[83] Each has its merits but it is by the latter that the university lives.

For another reason also Abelard is the man, the individual intellect, standing behind the university. He had made a brilliant contribution to the discussions of classical theology in his solution of the controversy over individuals and universals which had been the major problem of medieval philosophy for three hundred years. He wrote what may be called the opinion of the high court on this case of nominalism versus realism. But he sensed that this was not the basic issue in theology. The controversies of his day seemed to him to hover round

---

[83] See Chi'en Mu, 「中國歷史精神」(國民出版社印行 1952) p. 68.

the important issues without affording any clearer view either of the matters themselves or of the landscape around them. During his brilliant years when he lectured to the admiring crowds and during his season under the shadow of personal despair and official censure he appears to have been struggling with the problem of method, seeking a more effective instrument for the assessment of truth and the testing of falsehood. For over a century medieval thought had been at an impasse. The famous controversies between Lanfranc and Berenger and between Anselm and Roscellinus had demonstrated that something more than grammar and rhetoric or even a knowledge of authorities was needed. William of Champeaux revived the study of dialectic at the cathedral school of Notre Dame and the young Abelard learned there, in part through the inadequacy of William's approach, where the problem lay. We appear to be dealing here at the cathedral school of Pairs in general outline with a situation similar to what had occurred in fifth century Athens. There the impasse reached by the natural philosophers had encouraged the seeking of new methods. The Sophists had taken one tack and Socrates another. Behind the academy of Plato lay Socrates' controversies with the Sophists. In recounting these debates between Socrates and Protagoras, Plato evolves his own educational theory. Loosely parallel was the issue between William and Abelard that led the latter to set up for himself on the left bank of the Seine. Like Socrates and Plato, Abelard was an asker of questions. His famous *Sic et Non* (Yes and No) is simply a propounding of questions. He gives no answers but his questions initiate a new kind of learning—scholarship as a search, education as enquiry. " For by doubting," he wrote, " we come to enquiry, by enquiry we discover the truth." In the cathedral schools education

51

had been the transmission of a body of knowledge from teacher to student, the pouring from the big jug into the little mugs. Abelard envisioned another kind of education—a different kind of school, the *studium* as a center of enquiry. What he sought was a kind of science of sciences and it is with this rebirth of the Greek mind that the university emerged. The proper study from the standpoint both of the Sophists and the cathedral school teachers was grammar and rhetoric. Such studies are the foundation for education conceived as the transfer of knowledge from the past, from one generation to another. But grammar and rhetoric are not alone adequate tools for the school of enquiry. The medieval university could appear when this shift of emphasis had occurred within the three primary liberal arts from grammar to dialectic.

Both of the qualities of intellectual pride and of the emphasis upon enquiry which we have found in Abelard as the herald of the university are related to his writings. The first to his work in the *Trinity* which led to a trial for heresy and the second in his syllabus for students, the better known *Sic et Non*. We have yet a third quality to be mentioned and it also found expression in a book, the least known of Abelard's works, *The Three Leges* (Laws). It is a discussion undertaken by representatives of the three cultures of the medieval West—the Jewish, Mohammedan and Christian, perhaps in imitation of Cicero's *De Natura Deorum* wherein Stoic, Epicurean and Sceptic present their respective views under the pleasant conditions of a Roman house party. Cicero in his account gave the better speeches to the Sceptic and Abelard gives to the Jewish protagonist the role of the wise mediator between the Moslem and the Christian. The point to be made for our purposes is the breadth of Abelard's interest, his appreciative awareness of other cultures, his concern for a supranational and supra-cultural dialogue. To the end of his life he believed himself to be a Christian scholar.[84] He had no issues with either the Church or the Empire as the two fundamental and all-inclusive institutions of Western society. But he claimed also for the school a place of importance in its own right, not simply as an agency of the state or of the church. There is that in Abelard which anticipates the unique position essential to the university as intimately and responsibly related to both great powers yet enjoying an internal freedom and integrity upon which they do not encroach. Finally, in being the first to attract to his kind of lectures a substantial number of students from the many nations of Europe he was not only the precursor of the university professor but also illumined the nature of university studies as of that kind and quality that are of international interest.

We have spoken of two parent universities, of Bologna as the *universitas scholarium* and of Paris as the *universitas magistrorum*. They are types also in another sense. Bologna in the beginning was concerned almost exclusively with professional education, fitting men to meet the demands of an expanding trade and to deal with the new problems of civil and international law. Paris was primarily theoretical, concerned almost exclusively with the science of sciences, serving the nations, the empire and the church in terms of the first principles underlying all science, the principles of method and the integration of fundamental insights. The modern university bears in trust the heritage of both.[85]

---

[84] A careful estimate of Abelard as a Christian scholar is found in Harbison, *op. cit.*, pp. 19 ff.

[85] It is interesting to observe that the University of Hong Kong as the University of Salerno began as a medical college. Chung Chi as the University of Paris began in part as a faculty in theology. Salerno antedated Paris. The University of Hong Kong antedates Chung Chi.

One footnote should be added to this thumbnail sketch of the rise of the medieval university. We have said that the full story of the surface incidents, the journalistic account of the specific events, in the case of each early university would be commonplace indeed. The story of Paris, the parent of the English universities, is the romantic story of the new wine of genius bursting old wine skins. It is the story of a man in love not only with Heloise but with his first and great passion, the queen of the sciences. The stories of other universities are less romantic. For the most part they are either the story of the migrations, so common in the middle ages, of students or of teachers to another city that promised a freer life, less hampered by provincial laws unfavorable to the alien, and a larger exercise of the peculiar talents of scholarship. Oxford had its origin in such a migration—a migration of masters from Paris, partly because of new restrictions upon foreigners in that most cosmopolitan of European cities, partly due to the pressures exerted by their own King upon masters and scholars to return home.[86] Cambridge a little later had its origin in a migration of masters, a flight from Oxford to the rural Cambridge fens. We can not tell the story of the University of Paris without reference to Heloise, and of Cambridge as well the story begins with a woman. She was privileged to have been killed by an Oxford scholar. We know nothing of her life. The priest who records her death is certain that it was accidental, but the townsmen were furious, and led by the Mayor, they entered the hostel and carried off several students who were later executed. Masters and students then fled the town. Some of the three thousand Oxford refugees came to Cambridge and from this

---

[86] Rashdall, I pp. 12 ff.

time (A. D. 1209) Cambridge was a *studium generale*.[87]
Rashdall has found in the Oxford coroner's record of
' inquisitions ' evidence that Cambridge continued throughout the middle ages to receive transfers from Oxford.
" Over and over again," he writes, " occurs the dismal
record, ' Such and such jurors on their oaths present that
M or N, clerk (student) killed A or B citizen . . . with
sword or pole-axe or a knife or an arrow; that he has fled
and that there are no goods left which can be distrained
upon." [88] The Oxford authorities had handled the matter
themselves. They did not lightly regard such misdemeanors
and so compelled the offending student to go to Cambridge.

No better pencil portrait of the distinguishing features
of the university as the unique contribution of the middle
ages can be found than Rashdall's summary [89] of his
three volume study:

> If higher education is to exist there must obviously
> be teachers to impart it, and it is likely that particular
> places will become famous for particular studies. But
> it is not necessary that the teachers should be united
> into a corporate body enjoying more or less privilege
> and autonomy. It is not necessary that the teachers
> of different subjects should teach in the same place
> and be united in a single institution—still less that
> an attempt should be made to make the teaching body
> representative of the whole cycle of human knowledge.
> It is not necessary that studies should be grouped into
> particular faculties, and students required to confine
> themselves more or less exclusively to one. It is not
> necessary that a definite line of study should be marked
> out by authority, that a definite period of years

---

[87] *Ibid.*, III pp. 33, 34.

[88] *Ibid.* pp. 432 ff.

[89] *Ibid.* pp. 458 f.

should be assigned to a student's course, or that at the end of that period he should be subjected to examination and receive with more or less formality and ceremony a title of honour. All this we owe to the middle ages.

Confucius ordered the immediate execution of an unworthy person.

A Postscript Impertinent, Being a Gentle Word to the Wise Student on You and the University: Beware!

YOU have matriculated. Your name is written on the college registry. Already you have achieved a status not to be despised. You have a School Leaving Certificate. You have passed the Joint Entry Examination. You have been selected as one out of three who have all these qualifications who applied for admission to Chung Chi College. Under a British colonial educational system you have already learned that advance from primary to secondary and from secondary school to university is a selective process. All of the students in the University of Hong Kong and the three Post-Secondary Grant Colleges added together total only six hundredths of one percent of the population of the Colony. Only two of every ten students who began their primary education in Hong Kong have been privileged this year to go on to secondary school. You are one out of forty-four students who began middle school education who is privileged to go on to college. You are the one out of two hundred students who started with you in primary school who is now a college matriculant.

Education is a highly selective and a highly competitive venture and it will continue to be so throughout your college career. Less than one half of the students who began their courses in the science departments in 1957 graduated at the commencement of 1961. Two graduated in English out of a beginning class of forty. These are raw statistics but even after interpretation they speak for themselves. The student's life is not an easy one. You may be somewhat consoled to hear of the requirements in another British colonial college over three hundred years ago. The first president of Harvard set down the following entrance requirements for the entering class of 1642:

> When my Schollar is able to understand Tully, or such like classical Latine Author extempore, and make and speak true Latine in Verse and Prose, *suo ut aiunt Marte;* and decline perfectly the Paradigm's of Nounes and Verbes in the Greek tongue; Let him then and not before be capable of admission into the College.

We assume that you are a student of like quality and that you have the courage to hazard sometimes beyond your strength. You are now a scholar. We shall expect from you all that is implied in the honour and the excellence of this high status. The words with which Martin Luther concluded one of his university sermons at Erfurt over four hundred years ago apply to you: *Werde was du bist.* Become what you are.

You have not chosen your college. Your college has chosen you. Of over five hundred qualified students who applied for admission this year the college could accept only one hundred and sixty. A college education is not something that a student can choose. No student could pay for it on the open market. Your school is operated on an austerity basis. The University of Hong Kong is

58

definitely in the economy class in comparison with the average modern university yet its cost per student education in raw figures is about twenty thousand Hong Kong dollars per year. At Chung Chi it is less than five thousand. Of this amount the student pays less than eight hundred. Yet in addition to tuition and the fees charged for library and laboratory that are included in this figure, the College provides scholarships for more than one half of the student body. No student pays his way. All are supported by the Government, the Church, foundations and individuals. In most universities students are supported also by their teachers whose salaries are not comparable to their training and ability even according to government standards let alone according to the scale of the business market. Your privilege to have a college education is by the sacrifice of many people you will never meet. It is, in the case of Chung Chi, by the pennies and dollars put into the missionary box by people in foreign countries, many of whom have not themselves been privileged to attend a university. It is also by the taxes and fees paid by the hawker who sells shrimp or fruit in the street, by the whole populace of Hong Kong who pay a levy on all income over seven thousand dollars a year. All this sacrifice goes into your subsidized tuition and into the buildings and facilities necessary to the enterprise. The economy of the Colony is your benefactor: the farm woman standing thigh-deep in the night soil of the paddies, the merchants smiling and coaxing in their never-closing shops, the tailors with their needles, the fishermen with their lines and nets. You, who are the privileged few, have been chosen from so many to receive the sacrifice of the multitude. Even your college, on its austerity budget, represents a prodigal investment of wealth and talent. The investment is made to produce something truly unique—a product that is not for sale.

You have been singled out for this venture because we believe that you are adventurous. Only a few in the population of any city have either the power or the discipline to serve as bridges between the generations, to receive from the past and transmit to the future. You are such pontiffs. It is a high calling but it bears great responsibility.

Each student must in some way, beyond purely personal ambitions, justify his right to be in a university and to study in his chosen faculty. He is in the debt of too many just to please himself. What the student receives in knowledge by dint of hard labour in library and laboratory, what he achieves in wisdom from the experience of others —all this he holds in trust for those whose right it is to receive it from him. It is highly improbable that he who thinks otherwise will ever really get a university education. The student who goes to college to secure an exit visa from Hong Kong or to get a ' union card ' that is simply a pass to a few hundred dollars more per month, the university usually finds, is uneducable. You may choose this or that faculty because it is the surest way of getting such a pass and you may study this or that book because it is required for such a course. That is a dreary business and a wretched life. Necessity of this kind is the mother of only futile dodges. College life is not easy but it should be joyous and exciting. The science and the wisdom to which you will be introduced in lecture hall and library is itself the outgrowth of pleasurable intellectual curiosity. The nightly study is a knightly adventure.

I should like to place side by side for you two famous quotations, one from the *Great Learning,* the other from John Henry Newman. In the first university, matriculation was not only a matter of fixing the student's name on the list. It was not completed until the student had pledged his loyalty to the *studium* and to its rector and to the motto of the school. You will not choose unwisely whichever you affirm as your college creed.

"The Way of the Great Learning consists in manifesting illustrious virtue, in creating a new people, in abiding in the highest excellence. To know the abode of excellence leads to fixity of purpose, fixity of purpose to calmness of mind, calmness of mind to serenity of life, serenity of life to careful consideration of means, and this to the achievement of the end."

"A university training is the great, ordinary means to a great but ordinary end; it aims at raising the intellectual tone of society, at cultivating the public mind, purifying the national taste, at supplying true principles to popular enthusiasms and fixed aims to popular aspiration, at giving enlargement and sobriety to the ideas of the age, at facilitating the exercise of political power, and refining the intercourse of private life."

Confucius enquired of Lao-tsze concerning the ancient arts.

CHAPTER III

A PROGRAMME OF STUDIES: HISTORY OF CURRICULUM

' The time has come,' the Walrus said,
To talk of many things;
Of shoes and ships and sealing wax
Of cabbages and kings
And why the sea is boiling hot
And whether pigs have wings.

' But wait a bit,' the Oysters cried,
Before we have our chat;
For some of us are out of breath,
And all of us are fat! '
' No hurry ' said the Carpenter.
They thanked him much for that.

Lewis Carroll.

OBVIOUSLY the walrus has raised the central issue of university education, the question of curriculum. He proposes to discuss trade, navigation, chemistry, agriculture, politics, geology and physics, and finally biology. Obviously the oysters are not quite prepared for so much so soon.

The entering student who examines the syllabus of studies thrust into his hand on registration day is likely to have the same reaction to the vast array of lectures offered in any one term. Many of the courses are on subjects of which he has never heard. In some instances he will suffer the same fate as did the oysters for a failure with such fair warning to draw back into their shells and leave the walrus and the carpenter (the lecturers) to carry on their dialogue in splendid isolation.

Only the glutton can contemplate the menus of the several departments without a slight feeling of indigestion even before his own plate is served. When he has read the fine print of the requirements for graduation he will be further dismayed to learn that whatever entree he has chosen, he is required by the etiquette of this academic restaurant to mark, learn and inwardly digest a whole array of side dishes which, eaten together, are bound to produce gastronomic convulsions of astronomic proportions. He is the captive guest at a thirty-dish feast and his hosts (the lecturers) are apparently employed to heap his bowl with combinations of the ineffable and the inedible from every dish.

In some ways an ignorance of all that is to come, as in the case of an adventure on the operating table or a visit to the dentist, may provide the better part of valour. Some curricula are so elaborately designed to conceal any intelligible order that the student may fairly conclude that such was the merciful intention of its architects. However, education, whether it be the drawing out of something the student already possesses or the filling of cavities, does not call for the passive resignation that the dentist encourages in his patients.

A servant may be instructed step by step to fulfill what would otherwise be far too complicated an undertaking but the student on the university level may be a far more competent and intelligent workman if he has in his hands a blueprint of the structure he is to build brick by brick and some notion of the landscape and adjacent structures.

A closer look at the syllabus should reveal to the alert, entering student that the programme of studies, despite the diversity of the offerings, is not wholly arbitrary. He is already aware that the university as a *studium generale* has the major divisions of its faculties—arts and sciences—and that these are each subdivided into departments. He has already learned that he must first be admitted to a department before he is accepted as a matriculant by the university. He has already made the fairly crucial decision as to his first and second choices with respect to departments. In some instances the choice will have been a difficult one, a weighing of ability against aptitude or of first love against the realistic consideration of later success or even of professional rewards. He will have some notion of the kinds of knowledge and method involved in the alternative branches of study and a general sense of the hemispherical outlines of the two faculties. At the outset neither will be for him a completely foreign continent. His classmates will not be dwellers on the opposite hemisphere of the mind with the thick of the world between them.

Even at the outset the alert student should have some questions about the posture of his college, its total programme. He may have enquired into the reputations of the several departments between which he had to choose. The canny student may even have raised the question of ' general requirements.' The serious scholar will have asked what kind of person will I be as a graduate of the college. What kind of mark will my

64

college have placed upon me after four years? What kind of education will I have received and how well will I be fitted both to earn a living and to live? Will I be a different person or merely a better informed person? Will I be trained to do some job well or do well in whatever I may reasonably undertake?

After the first starry-eyed days on the unfamiliar paths and in the strange corridors of his *alma mater's* estate, when he has recovered from the anesthesia of orientation oratory, some other questions are likely to occur to the student: Why do I have to take biology 101 and Chinese 101? What have these courses to do with business administration? Why should a chemistry student be required to study Plato? Why must the history student read Chinese poetry and study geography? What has mathematics to do with college biology? After the first term the question may be raised in anguish and anger: Why must all study English and philosophy?

The answer to all these questions begins not with the syllabus or the manual of academic procedures but with the idea of a university. The best analogy for this strange, new institution is to an organism, a highly complex, mobile organism with marvelous capacities for thought and feeling. Such an organism must have a skeletal structure providing strength for both stability and motion. In the university this skeleton is called the curriculum. Without it the university, like any advanced organism, would be an amorphous mass. We may, if we do not too far press our analogy, compare the departments to the organs of the body. I should prefer not to make precise analogical identifications of individual departments and specific organs, as for example the spleen or kidney or appendix. The experts in the anatomy of the university sometimes differ on such matters! The point of the analogy is simply

65

that each department, like each organ of the body, is a living part of the larger organism and that its own life and the life of the organism as a whole depend upon its vital relation to the other organs. The relation of departments in a university to curriculum is similar in some respects to that of organs to the skeletal structure. The total curriculum and the functions of the departments are vitally interdependent. Because the relationship is crucial for the organism the nature of curriculum is for all departments a matter of concern secondary only to their own internal functions.

It is important to remember that *universitas* is a body of scholars and masters, not a body of subjects or disciplines, and that the other term for the university, *studium generale,* also refers to a school as an international institution rather than to a programme of studies. But very early in their history medieval universities came to accord an equal or higher importance to the curriculum itself. In the fifteenth century the phrase *universitas scientiarum* —a university of sciences—was the widely accepted definition of the *studium generale.* At its founding in 1477 the University of Tübingen was described as " a *studium* devoted to all sciences human and divine." [1]

Curricula both anticipate and reflect the major intellectual revolutions of cultures. The greatest figures in the intellectual history of mankind have recognized the problem of curriculum as basic in the communication of knowledge, training of minds, and the renovating of society. Most of the few, first-rate minds of the world have themselves laboured at the construction of curricula—Confucius and Mencius, Plato, Augustin and Aquinas, Descartes and Bacon, Kant and Whitehead.

---

[1] Culler, *op. cit.,* p. 24.

In most universities the curriculum at any one moment represents, as presidents, deans and professors will tell you—sometimes in pride and at times in despair—the blood sweat and tears of the faculties. The meeting of faculties, academic boards or senates at which curriculum is decided recalls another institution of the gay middle ages: the grand tournament. On such solemn occasions the academic knights are in full array, carrying the colours of their first loves, astride their favorite hobby horses and eager for the fray, for fair jousting and skilled jostling with all the grace of medieval knights in iron clothing.

What all we who enter the lists of these tournaments as the duty and privilege of our profession as teachers want to tell our students in all seriousness, though we speak facetiously, which among us passes for speaking modestly, is that the devising of curriculum is a sober and honourable endeavour involving much sacred tradition and daring adventure, and that the criticism of our efforts is not by any student ' to be entered into unadvisedly, or lightly, but reverently, discreetly, advisedly, soberly and in the fear of God.'

THE MEANING OF CURRICULUM

Curriculum means disciplined study. It is a set course of study in a particular area that can be covered in a fixed period with predictable results. Both curriculum and course are terms of the race track. Both have the same root. The verb is *currere,* to run. The training of the mind is metaphorically expressed as the running of a race, running the greatest possible distance in the shortest possible time. It is a metaphor arising from the chariot races of ancient Rome which were run on a circular or elliptical track. The metaphor is apt. During the first years of his academic career, the student may feel that he is going round in circles, or as the competition for survival, particularly in the physical sciences, presses home, he may feel that university life is a rat race. But the student who is truly fitted for the university will have, at least at moments, the joyful feeling of participation in a circus—for ' circus ' too is a derivative of the Indo-Germanic root of the word curriculum. And it is a three ring circus; for the curriculum has three basic emphases: the literary, the historical and the scientific.

The self-taught run across rough country and must be prepared to stumble now and then over unseen rocks, and to change direction when the terrain ahead appears impassable. The university provides a smooth track over well explored ground. It circumscribes a circle of learning within which the student can run with the minimum of wasted time and risk of arrest. Ancient education afforded a graceful progress around a modest circus. The running was the sport of the free and the pastime of the rich, the avocation of freedmen who did not have to work for a living with their hands. They were free to cultivate an acquaintance with the arts, a liberal education for the art of life.[2]

The concept of curriculum is far older than that of a university. For the most part the medieval university inherited its curriculum from the cathedral schools which in turn had followed the programme of studies in the ancient academies. In major matters the curriculum of the modern university differs very little from that of the most ancient schools. There is an essential character of importance in education as there is an essential quality in what it is important for men to know. Learning to live in paleolithic times and in the twentieth century

---

[2] See N. Fehl, "Religion In the University" in the *Chung Chi College Bulletin* No. 26, April, 1961, pp. 8 ff.

involves the same circle of learning: man's understanding of himself in terms of his past and of his relation to his environment, spiritual, social and physical. The history of curriculum is the story of the shifting of emphasis and of method with respect to this great circle of learning. In one sense it can be said that education deals with that which can be acquired, that which is other than, but based upon, man's natural endowments. All education involves both skill and knowledge. It is interesting to note that the word which we now apply to those subjects of purest knowledge and aesthetic value that are furthest removed from practical skills is the word that was first used to describe such skills. By the 'arts' we now mean the faculty of a university that has as its proper concern language and literature. More precisely arts is not literature itself but rather the science of criticism and evaluative interpretation. Yet it was the Latin word *ars* that most literally translated the Greek *techne* (technique—technical skill). The original use described action; the present use describes thought.

We know very little about education in paleolithic times but we may assume that it emphasized the arts in their original sense. A recent satire on education entitled *The Saber-Tooth Curriculum* traces the changing notions of the classical tradition of education in the old stone age from a purely practical and technical instruction in the core courses of 'fish grabbing,' 'wooly horse clubbing' and 'saber-tooth tiger scaring' to a purely theoretical approach to these subjects after they were no longer practiced by the tribe and so had become classical and sacred.[3]

---

[3] H. Benjamin, *The Saber-Tooth Curriculum Including Other Lectures in the History of Paleolithic Education by J. Abner Peddiwell, Ph.D. as told to Raymond Wayne*, (New York: McGraw-Hill Book Co., 1939).

We do know that language and myth (interpretation and response to the basic issues of life) together with a knowledge of the things of nature and the skills of using them have always been the tradition that is handed down from one generation to the next. We know also that education has always been an introduction to the way of enjoying life, answering to a basic need of divertisement. In addition to myth, every culture has its fantasies and its fables, recounted either in exercise of the imaginative faculty pure and simple or for the enjoyment of teller and hearer who revel in handsome posturing and lofty nonsense. Myth, on the other hand, far from being a tissue of pleasant delusion, reflects the supremely earnest attempt to apprehend reality, to catch in the subtle and oft times splendid web of language, universal and mystic truth. In myth the sober and the serious is touched with tenderness. Here no fairy prince or monstrous clever fellow with high spirit sets aside the order of life, grim and sorrow-laden though it be. Replacing these bright phantoms of a lighter mood are the representative symbols of man and of humanity caught in the inevitable conflicts of life—of the individual over against society, of mortality over against the constant and abiding, of the powers of ill pitted against those of good. Man seeks a resolution that will go beyond the seemingly arbitrary denial of human values. What is found issues, therefore, not in escape but in moral orientation. What emerges from the true myth is thus a world view, a normative understanding of life and a right attitude toward its tasks and resources.[4] It is in keeping with this concept of propriety, with this notion of doing the proper thing cheerfully and with grace, that each culture has produced the figure of the educated

[4] Susanne K. Langer, *Philosophy In A New Key* (New York: Penguin Books, Inc., 1948) offers a classic study in symbol, image and myth.

70

man as the nobleman who lives fully and with dignity. Education from the beginning was the training of the hero, a training that fitted a man to live with grace and dignity and when occasion demanded to know how to do the proper thing.

To march in one's place with one's fellows in the morning sun upon some bright way, to share with them the traveller's joy and pain with a large heart, and then, without rancour or complaint, to go, though stooped and weary with measured step and mortal dignity, into that country through whose bourne no traveller has ever returned—this is the lot of man. The brave man, properly bred and fittingly trained will make this journey in high spirit, dealing fairly with the companions of his way, and he will pass on with no little glory.

Before the time of Confucius, the formal education of the hero consisted for the most part in archery and skills of riding and charioteering.[5] By the time of the Chou Dynasty (c. 1100 B. C.) the cultivated man had been instructed in five arts: music, archery, horsemanship, writing and arithmetic. And all of these were summed up in the art of arts, li 禮 , the basis of the rites and ceremonies of public and social life.[6] These were also the accomplishments of the Greek aristocrat. As late as the fifteenth century such aristocratic skills were a part of the training of the young nobleman in the West. Pius II in his manual on *The Liberal Education* addressed to a young prince, advises: " It will thus be an essential part of your education that you be taught the use of the bow, of the sling and of the spear; that you drive, ride, leap and swim. These are honourable accomplishments in

---

[5] Creel, *op. cit.*, p. 75.

[6] Purcell, *op. cit.*, p. 4. See also Legge, *Sacred Books of the East* vol. xxvii, p. 346 and Martin, *Hanlin Papers*, London, 1880, p. 56.

everyone and therefore not unworthy of the educator's care." [7]

Beginning with Confucius in sixth century China, there is a basic shift in curriculum from athletic skills to literature and to manners in the highest sense. It is said in the *Analects* that ' the master taught four things: literature, conduct, loyalty and good faith.' [8] By the time of the Han Dynasty the Confucian emphasis had won imperial acceptance and for the higher positions in the empire the older heroic arts were replaced by knowledge and literary skill. " Odes in praise of music and essays on the archery and horsemanship of the ancients " were required in lieu of a test of the skills themselves.[9] Art as skill had passed on to art as a knowledge of ancient skills and it was soon to become an acquaintance with books on such knowledge.

We can trace a similar development in Greece from *arete* as the honour and excellence of the nobleman in sport and war to the notion of *arete* as the excellence of mind and spirit. There is in general a parallel between the education of the nobleman of the Chou and Sophistic education; and a similar comparison may be made between the innovations of Confucius and Socrates. Both were concerned with what it means to be a man, what it is that makes human life worth living. But the contrast between them is equally significant. Socrates is the more analytical and critical, less sensitive to aesthetic values, less observant of the graces of the social life. His contribution to Western education is the persistent examination of opinions and an experiment with inductive argument for the sake of universal definitions. Plato makes this

---

[7] *De Liberorum Educatione* 2.
[8] See Creel *op. cit.*, p. 96.
[9] Purcell, *op. cit.*, p. 26.

dialectical approach to wisdom the final, formal discipline for his philosopher king. He regards it, however, as a queen of sciences which can be approached only after proper preparation. The way is through mathematics, and his ideal scholar must serve an apprenticeship of ten years in the study of arithmetic, geometry, harmony and astronomy.[10] Of least importance in the Platonic curriculum are the arts of literature and traditional knowledge. He recognizes that it is essential for the young student to learn language and he himself demonstrated the high use of imagination and literary skill when employed in the sober service of philosophic discourse. But he rejected antiquity for its own sake and insisted that even the most sacred heritage of the past (Homer) should be severely edited to conform to the greater moral sensitivity of the new age.[11] Plato emphasized mathematics and regarded natural science as superior to literature but his own way of thought is still poetic, intuitive—systematic only in terms of controlling issues. His greatest insights are expressed in the language of imaginative images, in myth. Much of Plato is lyrical in form. He represents the transition from myth to science. Ernst Cassirer has suggested that this movement can be traced through many ancient cultures and that within it several stages may be marked.[12] Myth passes into epic as in the case of Homer where the several mythic traditions are unified and woven into the huge tapestry of the heroic age of the past. The epic is too grand for individual expression: it is the consensus of a whole culture with respect to its past. It has still the objectivity of myth, the authority of a divinely

---

[10] *Republic,* 521 c-531 c.

[11] *Ibid.,* 376 e-392 c.

[12] See the chapter on "Myth" in his *Essay On Man,* (New York: Doubleday & Co., 1954).

inspired ancestral memory. When particular moments are chosen by later poets as subjects for the more intense response of personal feeling a new mode appears — the lyrical. It illumines and heightens elements of the ancestral memory, but it bears always the mood of poignant recall. It breathes the secret of a vanishing past, of heroic moments soon to be forgotten, of faces seen for the last time in the splendid light of a setting sun. Lyric is a modulation of the theme of a culture from the key of mythic expression toward individual selectivity and valuation, and it is followed by a new reaching toward objective truth in the discursive mode of philosophy. The seminal ideas of mythology characterize the philosophical orientation. They are the rock from which its structures are hewn, the pit wherein its stuff has been digged. Plato stands at this point in the culture of the West. Philosophy may seek an even more abstract language and move toward an ultimate generalization. Or it may, as in the case of Aristotle, seek a firmer ground in the scientific analysis of concrete things.

So far we have noted several important shifts of emphasis and method in the curricula of antiquity: from athletic skill to literature, from literature to logic, from logic to science. Aristotle valued all three. In his discussion of individual sciences, such as biology, he suggests that the first task is a review of the opinions of others, then by critical comparison to evolve principles of definition, and finally in terms of these to devise methods appropriate to the field and relevant to its peculiar problem.[13] This pattern of procedure is the first bond between the several sciences. It is as it were a science of sciences, the logic of enquiry. All things have several

---

[13] See Richard McKeon, "Aristotle's Conception of Scientific Method" in *Roots of Scientific Thought* ed. by P.P. Wiener and A. Noland (New York: Basic Books, Inc., 1957), p. 73.

74

causes or sources: *1.* the material out of which they are made, *2.* the form into which the material has been fashioned, *3.* the power or agent which has accomplished the making and *4.* the end or purpose which a thing serves. All four causes, but especially the last, lead in Aristotle's thought to an interdependent ordering of all things, for one thing is the material of another and each thing has its place in a hierarchy of purpose. There is thus a chain of sciences.

As Greek learning passed into the Roman world, largely through the Stoics who valued both tradition and discipline, it came to be associated with a body of literature. Both Greeks and Latins in the age of the empire were fond of manuals of various kinds of knowledge, sketches of the thought of the several philosophers, syllabuses of the different sciences. Such handy summaries were then called doxographies. By the British, who value examinations more than course credits, they are called swot books. One value of swotting is that it leads to the maximum organization of minimum knowledge. In this the Romans excelled, and it is probably to them, at the turn to the middle ages, that we owe the organization of learning into seven liberal arts as the curriculum of the schools. The king of swot was Boethius whose manuals of Plato, Plotinus and Aristotle in Latin translation provided the text books of the schools for over five hundred years. Curriculum then became not so much a programme of studies in general as a series of texts to be mastered. For each study there was a standard and authoritative text. A younger contemporary of Boethius, Martinnus Capella, in the early fifth century described the new curriculum in an allegory entitled *The Marriage of Philologia and Mercury.*[14] Mercury was the Greek

---

[14] See Graves, *op. cit.,* vol. II p. 16.

god Hermes reputed to be a clever rascal, though a messenger of the higher gods and hence a bringer of wisdom. Philology is literally 'love of words' which should have been enough of a warning to such a clever fellow as Mercury. Philogia arrives at the wedding with seven bridesmaids — Grammatica, Dialectica, Rhetorica, Arithmetica, Geometrica, Astronomia and Harmonia — and each of these damsels describes at length her ancestors and the knowledge that belongs to her while Mercury and the reader are left waiting rather impatiently. Toward the beginning of the sixth century Isadore, the learned Bishop of Seville, in a work entitled *Etymologiae* indicates that the seven arts have been divided into two courses; the first is called the *trivium* (the three) and includes grammar, logic and rhetoric, and the *quadrivium* (the four)—arithmetic, geometry, music and astronomy. It is significant that Capella speaks of the mistress of the arts as philology and that Isadore describes them under the title of *Etymologiae* (the study of words). Language is the foundation of all learning. This is, of course, as true today as it was then. But there is here another implication. All learning arises from books. Isadore can believe that his treatise is actually a compend of all knowledge and that anyone who reads it with under-standing is the completely educated man. There is the implication that all knowledge has been discovered and recorded. It is available to the student who has mastered the elements of grammar. The teacher is now called a lecturer (from the Latin *legere*), that is 'one who reads.' He may be the transmitter of all knowledge even to the illiterate. Both the early medieval European and Chinese regarded perfection as abiding in the past. To achieve it is to face backwards, and for this endeavour the ability to read the written word and to exegete its meaning is the fundamental discipline. Grammar rather than either thought or action becomes the essential tool and ' the processes of acquisition are more cultivated than those of invention.' [15] Rashdall marks this as the fatal defect of medieval education, ' a fatal indifference to facts ' not recorded in books and the tendency to put books ' in the place of things.' The study of the arts became the occupation of the book-worm whose whole educational career could be lived within the covers of books and upon the nourishment found therein. He could so easily become the receptacle for inert ideas which had the power to inspire neither questions of coherence or the testing of adequacy. Nature, too, was to be studied in a book rather than to be observed by the senses. This led, as Bacon was later to remark, to the notion of nature as simply a cycle of recurrence—the wheel of the seasons— or to the curious aberration and the calamitous deviation as the judgment of God. Science, too, was a traditional knowledge contained in an authoritative book for which grammar was the one thing needful.

One basic reason for the long sleep of the sciences in the middle ages both in China and in the West was the reduction of all knowledge to the mode of literature. Hence mathematics as the foundation of the sciences was either treated as the wisdom of the ancients to be found in their books or else as a sub-scholarly and wholly practical pursuit. An aspect of the enslavement of mathematics to literature was the notation system by Roman letters in the West and by characters in China. For the most part medieval science dealt with the practical and

---

[15] Purcell, *op. cit.,* p. 40. It is interesting to note that in Chinese tradition from the time of Chu Hsu (A.D. 1130-1200) the *Four Books* occupied the same place as the *Trivium* in the West, while the study of the *Five Classics* corresponded to that of the *Quadrivium*. See de Bary, *op. cit.,* p. 127.

the curious or the occult. These were combined in China. It is interesting to note that the characters for mathematics (算 suan and 數 shu) are derived from the prognostication of fates and the foretelling of the future. Needham observes that " when the Sung scholars are said to be ' expert in arithmetical art' they are just being skilled to predict the length of their own lives and those of others." [16] In both China and the West the major public function of the mathematician was the devising and correcting of the calendar. We must note also the interrelation of logic and algebra and the fact that medieval Europe had to wait until the twelfth century for the first fairly complete text of Aristotle's logic. The logic of the middle ages was the simple arithmetic of grammar but this too was almost lost sight of under the passion for names— the names of the parts of speech and their stylized definitions that could be reduced to a catechism. An example of the study of literature is the following extract from Priscian, the standard text book on the *Aeneid* of Virgil. It starts with the initial word of the *Aeneid*— *arma* and proceeds as follows: [17]

What part of speech is *arma?*	A Noun
Of what sort?	Common
Of what class?	Abstract
Of what gender?	Neuter
Why neuter?	It ends in *a.*

One almost shudders when he realizes that Priscian continued throughout the middle ages as the standard text book in the universities on the *Aeneid* and that after its death in Paris it was sent to Oxford. Whitehead has remarked that knowledge does not keep much better than

---

[16] J. Needham, *Science and Civilization in China*, (Cambridge: The University Press, 1959), vol. III p. 4. See also pp. 151, 153, 155, 163, 164.

[17] See Graves, *op. cit.*, II p. 19.

fish and this is precisely the state of the freshness of
grammar after five hundred years at the turn to the
twelfth century. One not insignificant aspect of the new
spirit of the twelfth century was the appearance of better
and more complete texts of Aristotle so recently translated
into Latin that the grammarians had not yet had time
to reduce them to embalmed corpses. The vital curiosity
of the Greek mind coupled with its demand for the
critical review of opinions leaped from these new texts
into the minds of alert masters, enabling them to respond
to the new challenge of an expanding Europe in the
twelfth century. Here, as we have seen, is the theoretical
cause behind the rise of the university. Latin grammar
continued to be the basis of the arts course but it was
now a preparation for something beyond itself. Logic
became the controlling discipline of the *trivium* and
philosophy as the unity of all arts became the science of
sciences. Hugh of St. Victor describes the new curriculum
in his *Didascalion:* philosophy is ' the knowledge of things
as they are ' and hence has many parts for there are
many ' different kinds of things.' [18] The kinds of things
are now organized into four categories: theoretical,
practical, mechanical and logical. The seven arts are
described as the several ways *(viae)* that converge in
philosophy as all roads lead to Rome. In most of the
earliest universities the study of these seven avenues
leading to the bachelor's degree as well as to philosophy
occupied the first six years of a scholar's career.[19]
Theoretically he was now a philosopher and might as
such proceed to those special sciences such as medicine
and law which were regarded as professional, i.e., they
were the technical application of philosophy to a practical

---

[18] See Newman, *Discourses* pp. 388 f.
[19] See Mullinger, *op. cit.,* p. 573.

field. Theology, the queen of the sciences in the thirteenth century, demanded a more rigorous programme, pushing upward from the knowledge of the universal truths of philosophy to the source of all truth in God. Theoretical studies for the theologian required four years of lectures on the Bible and two years on doctrine as expounded in Lombard's *Sentences*. The bachelor of arts after these six years of further study became a bachelor of divinity. For four more years he served as an apprentice teacher, first for two years in Scripture, concentrating on two books of the Bible, then for a year as a reader of the *Sentences,* and in the final year as an intern lecturer. After another period of four years he could apply for the chancellor's licence to teach as a regular master. One final year was spent as a probationary candidate for inception into the guild of doctors of theology.[20] The status of Reader in British Universities as a probationary Professor originated in the theology curriculum at Paris. The degree of Bachelor of Divinity was in the middle ages a much higher degree than that of Master in the other professions, and continues at the better schools today to represent a more rigorous programme than that of the doctorate in many fields. Few medieval clerics achieved the B. D. degree. Most left the university before receiving the arts baccalaureate. Available statistics indicate that only a third of the scholars headed for any profession ever graduated at all. Less than one half of these were accepted for the apprenticeship in a special art leading to the master's degree and the licence to teach. Only a few of those accepted completed the course and became Masters. Finally, of these few, only the best might proceed toward the baccalaureate in divinity.[21] Most clerical

---

[20] *Ibid.,* p. 572.
[21] *Ibid.*

scholars were satisfied to get enough Latin to pass the Bishop's examination for ordination which in the best of the dioceses seldom went beyond a simple exegesis of a passage from the Missal. Similarly in the other professions, most scholars were satisfied with the Latin necessary to the office of clerk in the government or of apprentice to a doctor of law. While strict laws limited the teaching of medicine to qualified grammarians, it was not considered that the practice of medicine required much more than a good stomach, a bag of herbs, a sharp knife and a brave patient.

Some time towards the close of the medieval period the technical faculties (law and medicine) declined in most universities and the faculty of arts supplied the whole of the university programme. This was the historical circumstance that led to the later division of the arts faculty into the literary arts and pure science.[22]

In China a century before the rise of the universities in Europe there was also an attempt made to reform higher education by the individual protest against inert ideas on the part of Wang An-Shih (1012-1086). As an official responsible for the examination system he deplored the exclusive emphasis upon language and the neglect of content relevant to the needs of government and the life of the people. One Chinese historian records that ' even the pupils at village schools threw away their text books of rhetoric, and began to study primers of history, geography and political economy.'[23] The reform was, however, short lived. Most of his colleagues did not share his opinions.

As the passage from the culture of ancient Rome to the middle ages is marked by the production of manuals

---

[22] Moberly, *op. cit.,* p. 173.
[23] Purcell, *op. cit.,* p. 15.

such as those of Boethius and Isadore of Seville so also the waning medieval culture produced systematic ency- clopaedia encompassing the whole of theoretical knowledge. For theology one such work was the *Sentences* of Peter Lombard. The most famous were the *Summae* of Thomas Aquinas. These had in their origin been brave and daring works attempting to reorganize the method and reshape the material of the great sciences in the new light of the rediscovered Aristotle. Soon, however, they themselves became authoritative textbooks treated as inert ideas by those who lectured upon them. Already in the latter part of the thirteenth century the great Oxford scholar Friar Roger Bacon can refer to such works as 'horse loads' of erudition lacking the liveliness of Scripture which deals not with stale and useless speculation but with the divine dramas of creation, providence and redemption.[24]

The revival of learning in the fifteenth century known as the Renaissance was again a shift from an all too exclusive emphasis upon one method and one discipline (philosophy) to a re-examination of the Greek and Roman classics. Professor McKeon has described it as the ' subversion of dialectic to grammar.'[25] It was not, how- ever, simply a return to the early medieval curriculum, to grammar as the key to commentaries upon ancient knowledge. It was a shift of interest to primary documents to be studied in their own right—not as compendia of knowledge but as insights into man as intellectually and artistically creative. Again we can better understand this shifting of emphasis by its parallel in ancient Greek culture: the shift from philosophy to the Sophistic educa- tion. We have seen that all basic changes in curriculum

---

[24] *Compendium Studii Theologiae* (Brewer's translation).
[25] See Harbison, *op. cit.,* p. 35.

are not isolated phenomena; they occur within a context that includes most of the important aspects of life—trade, discovery, political and social institutions. As in the case of the rise of the university in the twelfth century, so in the case of the Renaissance, action and thought provided mutual stimuli. The practical discovery of the magnetic needle led the way to new adventure which was made possible by an expanding economy. An interest in trying new dishes was a simple yet important aspect of the Renaissance. A new tool, the compass, a taste for new dishes, and a new spirit of adventure led to the discovery of America in 1492. It was the heroic individual, the richness of the concrete moment in history, the beauty of a single line of poetry appreciated by and for itself that characterizes the spirit of the Renaissance. And this is something new, not just a revival of the past, and it is something that could not have been without the experience of both phases of the middle ages. Adventure and creativity seem most often to arise out of the disciplines of the simple life, and insight seems quite often to be the gift of those who have laboured conscientiously under authoritarian teachers. It is so often this rugged apprenticeship that adds up to the kind of ' experience ' that is worth having, not the untidy escapades which beg that name. The Renaissance is a shift from logic to experience, and a most important aspect, so far as the history of Western culture is concerned, involved religious experience. The relation of the new interest in grammar (particularly Greek grammar) and the spirit of the Renaissance is found in the relation of Erasmus to Luther. A root of the Reformation is exposed in Erasmus' overthrowing of the old Latin translation of the Greek text of *Matthew* 3:2. The Latin had it 'do penance.' Erasmus translated it: ' return to your right mind.' This leaped at Luther who found in Erasmus' new Bible the head-on meeting of literature and life.[26]

A significant distinction is to be marked in the nature of the Renaissance in Italy and in Northern Europe. For the most part the former was a new insight into literature as the basic discipline in the study of man, particularly man as artist. It was a rebirth of the heroic and aristocratic tradition. P. Vergerius, an early renaissance educator, writes in the tradition of the Sophists and Isocrates: " We call those studies liberal which are worthy of the free man; those studies by which we attain the practise of virtue and wisdom; that education which calls forth, trains and develops those highest gifts of body and of mind which ennoble man and which are rightly judged to rank next in dignity to virtue only." [27] In northern Europe, where the Renaissance coincided with the Protestant Reformation, the emphasis shifts to the education of all Christian people. Luther's conviction that all men are called of God to serve Him in whatever occupation contributes to the general good, and that in the Bible God speaks to each man directly, led to a notion of education for life. Further, in the rediscovery of the Bible in northern Europe, there is a new interest in history both as the area of God's special self-disclosure and also as the discipline by which the pure religion of the apostolic age can be explored and the deviations of succeeding centuries exposed. A most important contribution of the Renaissance-Reformation era is the emergence of history as an essential discipline alongside literature in the curriculum of higher studies.

---

[26] *Ibid.*, p. 90.

[27] *On Noble Character and Liberal Studies.*

THE MODERN AGE

History and science have been the two controlling disciplines of the modern age. Each has been a locus around which the departments of the modern bi-polar university have clustered. Historical method has dominated the broad field of liberal arts. Scientific method has dominated the broad field of the study of nature. Social studies have developed with a dependence upon both. Broadly speaking history is the study of human affairs, the study of man, and science is the study of nature. Both were reborn at the threshold of the modern era, and both were related to a parallel revolution in Christian thought. The pre-condition of modern historical science was the renaissance study of ancient languages and documents, and this study was also directly related to the origins of Christian thought and life in the early church rediscovered in the Reformation. Luther's appeal to the New Testament and to early Christian origins had its parallel in Bacon's appeal to efficient causes.

In the year fifteen hundred, despite all the gains of the twelfth century and the Renaissance, there was less knowledge of nature to be found in European schools than there had been in the academy of Aristotle. Similarly, since the late Hellenistic age, Europe had produced no historical writing comparable to Thucydides. Then, within the span of a little over one century, modern science burst into flower in Europe. In 1560 neither Galileo nor Kepler had been born. By 1700 Newton had published his *Principia*. We speak now of the quiet growth of science over the centuries since the Renaissance and the Reformation. Actually the growth of scientific knowledge during the seventeenth century was dramatic and earth-shaking. A galaxy of geniuses shot across the European horizon:

85

Francis Bacon, Harvey, Kepler, Galileo, Descartes, Pascal, Boyle, Newton, Locke, Spinoza, Leibnitz. This was also the century of Cervantes, Shakespeare and Milton. Professor Whitehead has suggested that the new idea which gave impetus and direction to that century of genius was the "passionate interest in the relation of general principles to stubborn facts." And it is the wedding of these two elements, he believed, that " forms the novelty of our present society." [28]

When humanist education was at its height in the second quarter of the sixteenth century the fascination of stubborn fact began to be felt. In the 1530's it was recognized by one of the more daring writers. " On a rainy day," Rabelais tells us, Gargantua and his tutor " went . . . to see the drawing of metals, or the casting of great ordnance; how the lapidaries did work; as also the goldsmiths and the cutters of precious stones. Nor did they omit to visit the alchemists, money-coiners, upholsterers, weavers, velvet-workers, watch-makers, looking-glass framers, printers, organists and other such kind of artificers, and . . . did learn and consider the industry and invention of the trades." [29]

With all its passion for literature the sixteenth century, at least on the common level, had an interest in doing things better. The flowering of skills in the ordinary crafts preceded the age of scientific genius logically as well as chronologically. The scientific age began as a people's movement, the desire for tastier food, better and more attractive clothing, more comfortable lodging and more pleasing furnishings. Quite early in the sixteenth century, writers began to take notice of the improvements in the trades. The Spanish scholar, Vives, urges not only

---

[28] See A. N. Whitehead, *Science and the Modern World.*
[29] *Gargantua and Pantagruel,* i, 24.

a change of attitude toward the practical arts—scholars need not " be ashamed to enter into shops and factories and to ask questions from craftsmen "—but also the inclusion of the knowledge of crafts in general education. His interest is historical, technological and practical: " wherefore and how they were invented, pursued, developed, preserved and how they can be applied to our use and profit." Walter E. Houghton finds in Vives the precursor of Francis Bacon and of an idea that was the germ of seventeenth century science: the study of crafts as an important clue to a knowledge of nature.[30]

"How much wealth of human wisdom is brought to mankind by those who commit to writing what they have gathered on the subjects of each art from the most experienced therein. . . . By such observation in every walk of life, practical wisdom is increased to an almost incredible degree; those who make such observations should hand them down and let them serve posterity, for whom we ought to care as we do for our own sons." [31]

Those who work with the things of nature, materials and metals, have had to learn to work with nature itself. It is to the stubborn facts of the ways of nature that man must turn for a more relevant and adequate knowledge of his physical environment. Bacon draws this implication from the new interest of his age in technical knowledge, but he could have drawn directly from Vives the character

---

[30] "The History of Trades: Its Relation To Seventeenth Century Thought" in Wiener and Noland, *op. cit.,* p. 354. This dream of Bacon's has now been realized in Singer, Holmyard and Hall, *History of Technology* (Oxford: University Press, 1954), 5 Volumes.

[31] Vives, *On Education* p. 210. (A translation by Foster Watson of *De Tradendis Disciplinis*) Quoted from Wiener and Noland, *op. cit.,* p. 355.

of the importance of such knowledge—a practical ministry to human need.[32] In his life, Vives is a symbolic type of the transitional man—the humanist in passage to the modern age. He was born the year Columbus discovered America. He shared with Luther an interest in Augustin. Like Luther he was a friend of the great humanist, Erasmus. Like Erasmus he was attracted to England and for a while studied and lectured at Oxford. His critical study of education *(De Caucis corruptarum Artium)* anticipated Bacon's *Organon.*[33]

At the beginning of the seventeenth century, Bacon outlined a new science curriculum in his *Advancement of Learning.* He divides the kingdom of nature, like Gaul, into three parts: *1.* 'Nature in course or the history of creatures' and natural law; *2.* 'Nature erring or varying'—curiosities and marvels; and *3.* 'Nature altered or wrought'—man's control and reshaping of the powers and materials of nature. Greek science was almost exclusively concerned with the first, medieval science with the second, yet " History of Nature Wrought or Mechanical is by far the most important." Former studies of nature have been of the sort that " vanish in the fume of subtle, sublime, or delectable speculation." It is only the last that operate " to the endowment and benefit of man's life." [34]

It is important to note that shops and factories were the first laboratories and that Bacon had the wit to translate 'experience' with respect to science as 'craftsmanship.'

---

[32] See W. E. Houghton, Jr. in Wiener and Noland, *op cit.,* pp. 354 f.

[33] See Berthe Vadier, *Un Moraliste du XVI me siècle: Jean-Louis Vives et son livre de l'êducation de la femme chrétienne* (Geneva, 1892).

[34] *The Works of Francis Bacon,* ed. Spedding, Ellis, and Heath III pp. 332 f. (The passage is from *The Advancement of Learning*).

For him, science begins with a history of the mechanical arts: what men have learned in their work about the nature of raw materials and the processes by which these are transformed into articles of use to mankind. Such a "history of trades" is to become, in Bacon's dream of the new university, a laboratory manual for the controlled experiments that will lead to discovery of general methods and universal laws. The word *laboratory* itself indicates the first home of the scientist as the factory, and the importance of this place of labour as the foundation of learning is seen in the name Bacon suggests for it— Solomon's House, the house of the wisest of men. It is to be a new kind of college, not a school in which traditional knowledge is handed down from one generation to the next, but rather a society of research, a "college of inventors." Its library will include the history of trades but equally important will be its 'Inginary'—'work houses of all sorts' with furnaces and vaults and isolated rooms [35] With Luther, Bacon exalts the value of experience and the dignity of labour. Unlike Luther, he sees little value in grammatical studies. The Baconian scholar will no longer be occupied with the "reading of hard Hebrew words . . . where either (he) will trample upon or play with mysteries" nor will he "parrot-like repeat hetersclitous nouns and verbs" but instead spend ten or twelve years " in the study of things . . . rather than in a rabble of words." [36]

---

[35] J. Spedding, *The Letters and the Life of Francis Bacon*, p. 164.

[36] The quotation is from a young disciple of Bacon's, W. Petty, who in his middle twenties set out to produce, according to his outlines, a monumental 'History of Trades.' See *The Advice* (of W. P. to Mr. Samuel Hartlib for the Advancement of Some Particular Parts of Learning) in *The Harleian Miscellany*, VI, p. 146.

We can not overestimate the significance of this shift from the ideal of liberal and aristocratic education to the study of trades and the training for non-academic and non-clerical professions. The most obvious differences between the medieval and the modern university arose with this shift in emphasis. Previously knowledge enabled a man to rise above the miseries of the mundane life by the cultivation either of aesthetic faculties or of the reason which led ultimately to religious contemplation. Bacon, with his journalistic sense of cultural change, speaks of knowledge as power—not the power to transcend the world but the power to transform the world, the power to remake nature. "Men must know," he declares, "that in this theatre of man's life it is reserved only for God and the Angels to be lookers on." [37] The new age asks more than " the pleasure and dignity of a man's self " for such an ideal has not the power of improvement. Contemplation and action must " be more nearly and straitly conjoined and united together than they have been." [38] Bacon's man of science is a knight on crusade. His chivalry is loyalty to truth, his honour is the excellence of patient labour, his gallantry a devotion to all mankind. He has been given a mighty sword and a stout buckler, the new weapons of science. Before these weapons were forged men could not carry out the solemn obligation which the Christian religion had laid upon them. Bacon's own prayer is like the offerings made by a knight in his lord's chapel before undertaking his errand of mercy.

"Wherefore, seeing that these things do not depend upon myself, at the outset of the work I most humbly and fervently pray to God the Father, God the Son,

---

[37] *The Advancement of Learning,* VII i.
[38] *Ibid.*

90

God the Holy Ghost, that remembering the sorrows of mankind and the pilgrimage of this our life wherein we wear out our days few and evil, they will vouchsafe through my hands to endow the human family with new mercies." [39]

Prior Moody's summation of the spirit of Baconian science clearly exposes the pedigree of the seventeenth century mind: " the identification of scientific truth with use and therefore with charity, with power and therefore with pity, is fundamental to . . . (the new) conception of true learning." [40]

The university curriculum which Bacon proposed shows how completely the faculty of arts had absorbed the other faculties of the middle ages. Bacon provides for only two: arts and theology. Theology is a superior faculty with its own field and method related to divine science and dealing with the knowledge that comes by revelation.[41] The faculty of arts has three divisions—poetry, history, and philosophy. History and philosophy are of major importance. Poetry is little more than an adornment. History provides continuity and unity to the curriculum as the mediator between poetry and philosophy. These are fundamental divisions based upon the faculties of the human mind: imagination, memory and understanding.[42] The natural sciences are subsumed under philosophy with its three divisions of mathematics, physics and metaphysics. History, as the store of human knowledge, serves the needs

---

[39] Bacon himself entitled this 'The Student's Prayer.' See *Works* XIV, p. 101.

[40] Quoted from Moody E. Prior, "Bacon's Man of Science" in Wiener and Noland, *op. cit.,* p. 389.

[41] See Robert McRae, "The Unity of the Sciences: Bacon, Descartes, Leibnitz," in Wiener and Noland, *op. cit.,* p. 390.

[42] See R. G. Collingwood, *The Idea of History* (New York: Oxford University Press, 1946), p. 58.

of philosophy understood as science. The unity of science is presupposed in the unity of the world of nature, or more precisely the world of matter.

Science can, however, deal only with the measurable causes that are wholly within the natural world. Bacon's metaphysics is strictly limited to the generalization of scientific knowledge, the summary of the working of nature as seen within the circle of nature. Creation and divine providence, the ultimate causes and their agencies, lie outside both the scientific and metaphysical realm. They belong to theology. Nature, says Bacon, can in no sense contain God. " God is completely outside nature." [43] Philosophy as the unity of the physical sciences and theology as the science of revelation are completely independent disciplines. In part this sharp distinction was for the protection of the integrity of scientific studies from any external authority. In part it was to safeguard the Christian faith to which Bacon himself adhered without reservation from encroachment by science. But for the most part it was an inheritance of the renaissance mind and a naive notion both of the implications of science and theology. Bacon did not see that the speaking of God in nature and in history and in human experience involves the dialogue of science and theology, of history and science, and of history and theology. We must note in passing the influence of Bacon upon Kant in the latter's attempt to safeguard faith by the destruction of philosophy as the vital link between science and theology. Many of the ills of the modern university both with respect to science and philosophy on the one hand, and the study of religion on the other can be traced to this ' illegal ' ontolectomy. [44]

---

[43] *De Principiis atque Originibus,* Works, V. 291.
[44] See N. Fehl, *A Case For Systematic Theology* (Sewanee: University of Sewanee Press, 1959), pp. 9 ff.

Although Bacon preserved the dignity of theology as a separate and superior faculty he had little to say about it as an academic study. It is, in his programme, cut off from philosophy, and hence could be in no sense the "queen of the sciences," i.e. an interpretation and organization of man's knowledge of nature. Again Bacon anticipated Kant in finding the heart of religion to be moral obligation, the moral imperative. "The conquest of nature is dictated by religion, for all questions of moral ends belong to religion and the end of science is the fulfiling of the Christian obligation of charity." [45] Religion formulates, and urges the divine imperative. Science devises the ways by which man can effectually discharge the duty that is laid upon him. "It is an excellent thing to speak with the tongues of men and angels, but . . . if it be severed from charity, and not referred to the good of men and mankind, it hath rather a sounding and unworthy glory than a meriting and substantial virtue." [46] Bacon was the prophet of modern Protestant liberalism and Kant was its philosopher. The concept of the Christian religion as a gospel of social ethics exercised a powerful influence upon education in the West. On the one hand it exalted education as a chief means whereby the kingdom of righteousness (the fatherhood of God and the brotherhood of man) might be established. It furnished the impetus to found many colleges and universities, especially in the new world. Its weakness lay in its inability to understand the business and the importance of theology as *the* theoretical discipline: the task of interpreting the speaking of God in nature as well as in history and in human experience. [47]

---

[45] *Advancement of Learning* I. See McRae In Wiener, *op. cit.,* p. 396.

[46] *Ibid.*

[47] See N. Fehl, *op. cit.*, pp. 11 ff.

Descartes, like Bacon, distinguishes the disciplines of the faculty of arts as poetry, history and philosophy, and relegates theology to a separate and superior faculty. He also divides philosophy into the special studies of mathematics, physics and metaphysics. Unlike Bacon and Liebnitz, however, he does not regard history as a serious or fruitful discipline and is inclined to associate it with poetry rather than philosophy. In his *Discourse on Method* he doubts that history is a science and he warns against the evils of escapism which he finds inherent in its study

"I thought by now that I had spent enough labour on the study of ancient languages, on the reading of ancient authors, and on their histories and narratives. To live with men of an earlier age is like travelling in foreign lands. It is useful to know something of the manners of other peoples in order to judge more impartially of our own, and not despise and ridicule whatever differs from them like men who have never been outside their native country. But those who travel too long end by being strangers in their own homes, and those who study too curiously the actions of antiquity are ignorant of what is done among ourselves today.

Moreover these narratives tell of things which cannot have happened as if they had really taken place, and thus invite us to attempt what is beyond our powers or to hope for what is beyond our fate. And even histories, true though they be, and neither exaggerating nor altering the value of things, omit circumstances of a meaner and less dignified kind in order to become more worthy of a reader's attention; hence the things which they describe never happened exactly as they describe them, and men who try to model their own

94

acts upon them are prone to the madness of romantic paladins and meditate hyperbolical deeds." [48]

While Bacon emphasized experimental science and inductive method, Descartes found the centre of science in mathematics and in the deductive method of seeking wider applications of general principles. For Bacon the unity of the sciences was found in the unity of nature or the uniformity of matter. For Descartes the unity of the sciences derives from the unity of the mind or the integrity of thought. Descartes' science of sciences was thus mathematics and what he sought as the key to a new age of science was a ' Universal Mathematics.' [49] Between Bacon and Descartes the early seventeenth century had formulated the two basic methods of modern science (inductive and deductive) and the two basic principles—the observational order and the conceptual order. To emphasize either one as the more important is to ignore the mutuality of the two in the subsequent history of advance in the sciences. Modern science is both Baconian and Cartesian. Leibnitz followed Bacon in the dream of a great encyclopaedia of useful knowledge as the basis of further discovery and invention.[50] The history of knowledge as the foundation of the university curriculum, in Liebnitz' programme, raised history to a place of equal honour with science. These are the poles within which the curriculum as a field of force has operated in the university since the seventeenth century. But this field of force is also a field of tension. Leibnitz defended the classical tradition, Descartes the new learning.

---

[48] From the *Discourse On Method* i. An almost too perfect parallel to Descartes is from F. Sanchez (1581) quoted by H. Butterfield, *Origins of Modern Science* (New York: Macmillan, 1957.), p. 98.

[49] See McRae in Wiener, *op. cit.,* p. 401.

[50] *Ibid.* p. 404.

" Wisdom," Leibnitz wrote, " is a full knowledge of the sciences and of the art of applying them." [51] Such universal knowledge or even the desire for it, Descartes described as folly. Not knowledge itself but a capacity to form sound judgment was his ideal of the new university education. Bacon's ideal scholar was the knight scientist, Leibnitz' the man of universal knowledge, Descartes was satisfied with ' the man of good sense.'

The seventeenth century revolution in science, apart from the quiet working of the fellows of several colleges on their own, did not substantially affect the university curriculum until the eighteenth. Similarly the renaissance of historical studies in the eighteenth century had to wait well into the middle of the nineteenth before attracting the serious notice of dons and tutors. In the early part of the eighteenth century Vico of Naples set himself to formulate principles of historical method parallel to those of scientific method devised by Bacon. Vico substantially altered Bacon's theory of the division of human knowledge. For Bacon's poetry, history and philosophy, Vico substituted art, religion and philosophy.[52] The point to be noted is the shift from physical sciences to history; for in Vico's scheme the major philosophic discipline is history. As God created the world *ex nihilo* so Vico sees history as the creation of man. The task of the historian is to expose the pedigree of contemporary society. History is thus not Bacon's or Leibnitz' store of useful knowledge but an evaluative study of basic social institutions in terms of their origin and development. History is the story of *our* past. It is to contribute to our understanding of ourselves, of our contemporary society and its institutions. Vico commends without qualificafion

---

[51] *Ibid.* p. 402.
[52] See R. G. Collingwood, *op. cit.,* pp. 63 ff.

the study of language. He sees, as the renaissance historians did not, the historical value of mythology, sagas, fables and legends. In these the past speaks to us of its spirit. Tradition cannot be discarded or neglected by the historian simply because it distorts details. Within tradition is the kernel of truth which the historian seeks. But even the husk is important. It reveals both self-interpretation and also the accepted interpretation of a later age with respect to events.

With Hume the arts are dropped completely from the ideal curriculum. He proposes the three faculties of mathematics, natural philosophy (science) and natural religion (history as the discipline concerned with value judgments). History for Hume is self-criticism. It enables man to look upon his past and observe his errors. While he was a librarian at Edinburgh he employed these principles in writing his *History of Great Britain* from James I through Charles I, and demonstrated his impartiality by offending everyone. In general eighteenth century historiography viewed itself as the pivot of a slanted see-saw. Standing at the fulcrum the past pitched downward toward the 'wretched ages of superstition.' The future pointed upward toward man's unlimited future supported by the sure strength of rationalism. As the rationalist theory of history was an inversion of the Christian in which reason took the place of the Gospel, so the Romantic theory was an inversion of the Hebrew linear view of history in which the historical process as Divine Providence was replaced by the process of man's own self-development. Romantic history in the latter part of the eighteenth century is the record of man's irrepressible forward thrust, the expression of his creative spirit. Rationalism at the beginning of the century had related man to nature. Natural science rather than the arts was regarded as the proper basis for the study of man. Romanticism, on the other hand, distinguished man from his physical environment. Man was seen in contrast to nature, and history defined in contrast to science. Nature was the realm of necessity, and science an account of nature's rigid laws. History was, on the other hand, the description of events in the realm of freedom, the diary of the human spirit. Romantic interest seized upon the unique moment and the passionate enjoyment of the passions of the past.

We have been reviewing the advanced thought of the seventeenth century philosophers with respect to the re-organization of curriculum from the side of natural science and of the eighteenth century historiographers from the side of history. Actual changes in the universities on the Continent and in England came quite slowly. Milton as a Puritan, and hence with Luther, a critic of Aristotle, was still not prepared to welcome the overthrow of the classics as the core of the university programme. He appears, indeed, as a defender of the older education but argues that the function of classical education must be redirected from the purely grammatical and aesthetic to a concern for the great ideals of mankind. The ancient authors are to be read for another purpose as well: to teach mathematics, agriculture and the ' science ' of trades. It seemed to him axiomatic that they should continue to be the basis for all education in politics and law.[53]

The major problem exercising the English universities in the seventeenth century was the ecclesiastical question of conformity to the beliefs and practices of the Church as defined by the Crown. Cambridge tended to be Puritan, and Oxford too had its non-conformists. It is interesting to note that the Puritans sided with the scientists in favour

---

[53] See Ulich, *op. cit.*, p. 82.

of a reorganization of the curriculum in terms of the overthrow of Aristotle and an openness to the Baconian point of view. The master of Caius College, Cambridge, William Dell, actually proposed the abolition of both universities " as hopelessly pledged to antiquated and obsolete methods." [54] Then Oxford's Chancellor, Cromwell, by a pledge of compromise saved both institutions with a reform of studies and of the discipline of the students and the morality of the masters. Toward the end of the seventeenth century both universities responded to the new scientific development. Newton had been at Cambridge from 1669 to 1702 and was succeeded by Whiston. Oxford established a readership in chemistry in 1704, and Cambridge inaugurated the Plumian Chair of Astronomy and Natural History in the same year. Newton's emphasis upon " the mathematical way " to the sciences had its effect upon Cambridge. Early in the eighteenth century mathematics was an inescapable hurdle in the newly established *tripos* or honours examination. The word *tripos* at first referred to the three-legged stool upon which the examiner sat on Ash Wednesday when he determined the fitness of candidates for distinction. It then was applied to the successful candidate and later to the papers, on which the student's Latin poems previously submitted to the examiner, were inscribed on the reverse side with the list of names of successful candidates.

Provision was made during the first half of the century for scholars who were not seeking a living in the Church. In a small volume, published in 1730 under the title *Advice to a Young Student*, Daniel Waterland lists some of the books to be read by those in philosophy who did not aspire to theology. Such students were either those who planned to make a career of their nobility or those

---

[54] See J. B. Mullinger, *op. cit.,* p. 771.

who sought government posts for they were required to read Grotius on political institutions. They also read Newton on optics. [55] For the most part, however, Oxford and Cambridge continued to be universities in the tradition of a Christian interpretation of Graeco-Roman classics till the latter part of the nineteenth century. Their main purpose continued to be the training of gentlemanly priests for the Church. The education of the nobleman followed the same curriculum. This was the ' idea of a university ' which Newman loved so dearly. Throughout the eighteenth century and for most of the nineteenth, the major programme of studies continued to be the classics and Euclid's mathematics.

We need but note how recent is the rise of the red brick universities of England, indeed of all the seats, with few exceptions of higher learning in the Isle apart from Oxford and Cambridge, to mark the strong bonds of that well-nigh indissoluble and monogamous union of the aristocracy (lay or clerical) and the university. While it lasted it was a happy union, and it was fruitful. It produced what now we most cherish of the English past: a liberal mindedness, perceptive, mellow and insightful, a graceful reason and a reasonable graciousness. It was in many respects the best possible education for the art of life. From the beginning of the Christian era, the ideal of wisdom was the marriage of the arts and theology. Theology as a field of scholarship and as a force in culture lived by that love which the arts so freely and so fully gave it. And that love was a mutual love, and the arts lived also by the love of their beloved. Theology mourns the decline of the arts in the university. It can recall only with moist eyes the " Greats " that prepared

---

[55] See Ulich, *op. cit.*, p. 90.

a man to be a gentleman and a scholar; and of such, in those days, was the kingdom of theology.

That gracious, happy land is now, indeed, Utopia— nowhere, and both arts and theology must in the new order accept the status of commoners, yea even of servants in the university. They are now service departments. And this is in the best and highest sense, their vocation and their reasonable service. The failure of the "Greats" was their failure to serve the culture as a whole. The failure of theology in that day was its failure to believe that God could do a new thing in the university, that He who spoke in times past in Hebrew, Greek and Latin could in these days speak in the language of chemistry, biology and physics, of sociology and even of psychology.[56]

The new age has burst outward the confines of the older circle of learning all along its course. The demands of the twentieth century have made more crucial than before the problem of the greatest possible distance in the shortest possible time. Plato could allow in his ideal republic leisure to the age of eighteen for primary education, to thirty for his mathematicians and to fifty for his philosophers. Students today must have mastered by the age at which Plato's scholar began his arithmetic (20) far more mathematics than the latter was expected to learn in the next ten years. Chung Chi science students today must pass more rigorous courses in maths than Macaulay failed in the recent past at Cambridge! Leisure as an important aspect of education and of university life has been banished by the harsh demands of even minimum competence in contemporary university studies. And in this importunate departmental devouring of leisure something else has been devoured as well: the capacity to

---

[56] See N. Fehl, "Religion In The University," *Chung Chi College Bulletin* No. 26 (April, 1961), pp. 10 f.

101

respond to the arts, the capacity to cherish the liberal ideal, the capacity to desire wisdom.

The mastery over a three year period of twelve books or less only a short while ago would fit a student for honours at Oxford and Cambridge. A final observation must be made with respect to this neat curriculum. The books were well chosen both for content and style. They were and remain great books. The teaching of them had been perfected over centuries. There is probably no study which is sharper in outline yet with greater insights than that of Greek culture in the English university of the nineteenth century. Why is this so? We must answer that school boys read their Homer and university students read Plato, Euclid and Aristotle, Aeschylus and Sophocles in depth. All that they assimilated in their common room discussions and from the wide ranging interests of their tutors, they read back into these studies and still were forced to maintain a sacred sense of faithfulness to the text. Next to this in perfection of discipline came the study of the Old Testament. The poverty of other programmes in comparison to these is apparent in the papers written by Oxford students in the new sciences during the last century.

The really significant difference between the curriculum of the university today and that of Oxford or Cambridge in the recent past lies in the immaturity of the new fields. The selection of important matters in the arts curriculum from the Renaissance to the twentieth century was made with the mellow wisdom of masters who knew their field with breadth and in depth. Wise selection and effectual organization comes only with that kind of wisdom. In the new sciences, physical and social, no such wisdom has yet been gained. The simplest solution to obvious gaps and weaknesses in the teaching of the new disciplines appears to be the addition of extra courses. The modern university curriculum consists for the most part of corrective and supplementary courses largely because the basic core has not yet been determined and crystallized. We add courses in the new maths to the old, and courses in frontier areas in biology, physics and chemistry like coaches to a train. Some of the latest courses to be added are a long way from the engine. Perhaps in another hundred years the teaching of mathematics and the physical sciences will achieve that mastery and unity of perspective and method that will make a precise selectivity possible. The eight to twelve books assigned to the Oxford student of the former century accomplished the purpose whereunto they were appointed to be read. He was in his time a cultivated gentleman. The forty books read by the science student today do not make him a scientist. He is a rank amateur in his field and almost illiterate outside it. He has less knowledge of the principles of mathematics than did the Cambridge student who knew so little beyond basic algebra in the eighteenth century. The latter part of the nineteenth century was an era of specialization and hence of creation, sometimes quite artificial, of new disciplines each claiming to be the key to the new scientific age. One gets the impression from the sociology of Comte and or the psychology of Watson and Freud that these new kinds of enquiry can solve even the problems relating to the theory of light by case studies, the plotting of neural synapses and psychoanalysis. And there is enough truth in these pretensions so that they cannot be lightly brushed aside. The growth of knowledge in the past century has been too great to be assimilated by the university as a whole. Until such organization is possible, the university must continue to live by emergency programmes, changing its curriculum as a small craft adjusts its sails to every change in wind and sea. There is no care free sailing in the modern university either for teachers or students. We run at a perilous speed simply to keep from being swamped by the mountainous following seas of new knowledge. But it is a welcome wind that blows so hard upon us. Whitehead has commented upon " the curious illusion that a more complete culture was possible when there was less to know. " Surely," he writes, " the only gain was, that it was more possible to remain unconscious of ignorance. It cannot have been a gain to Plato to have read neither Shakespeare, nor Newton, nor Darwin." [57]

---

[57] *Aims of Education,* p. 57.

Confucius discussed with Lao-tsze concerning the fundamental principles of Art.

CHAPTER IV

A PROGRAMME OF STUDIES:
THE THREE CIRCLES OF LEARNING
THREE MEANINGS OF KNOWLEDGE

OUR survey of the history of curriculum has shown that education has to do with certain basic kinds of study that are perennial. We have noted the shift from grammar to dialectic that formed the curriculum of the first universities in the twelfth century. Universities in the Renaissance were organized under the movement from logic to literature. Seventeenth and eighteenth century university studies reflected the new modes of experimental and mathematical science. Since the last century two organizing principles have dominated the curriculum: the new mathematics and the historical-comparative method. In general it can be said that university education has of necessity to encompass three circles of learning and that these circles are intersecting to the extent that in each a portion of the other two is included. They may be described as the circle of literary or aesthetic knowledge, the circle of history, and the circle of science. These

105

three circles of learning are epitomized in three words, one Chinese, one Greek and one Hebrew. These words are also seminal ideas in the cultures of the East, the Near East and the West.

The ideograph for learning 學 pictures two scholars in a forest above the character for son, the boy under the roof. There is here the connotation of study in a place of seclusion in the setting of nature and of the transmission of knowledge from one generation to the next. The same ideograph 學 occurs in the word *chüeh* 覺 and is otherwise rare indeed as a component of Chinese characters. In *chüeh* it is associated with the character meaning to see 見. Originally the picture was that of an eye with an eyebrow above and with both brow and eye enclosed in an oblong. Later the eyebrow was placed below the bottom line of the oblong and took on the form of the character for man 人, *ren*.[1] *Chüeh* means to see in the sense of 'to feel' and thus has a relation to *wang* 望, to gaze, to view, to contemplate. Here *yueh* 月, the moon, is an important component and 望 can also mean the fifteenth day of the month or the full moon. 望 to look, to see, or more precisely moon-viewing or seeing in the light of the moon recalls the feminine principle, *Yin* 陰, and the goddess of the moon who has as many phases as there are moods of womankind. Li T'ai Po, the most famous poet of the moon goddess, exalts her as the supreme object of aesthetic contemplation. As her light takes 'the sleepless by surprise' so the aesthetic apprehension comes suddenly upon the poet and the artist, possessing him in a flashing moment of intuitive awareness.[2] The moon also is the remembrancer who

---

[1] 說文解字詁林 VII, 3857.

[2] Li T'ai Po, *Ode to the Queen of the Night* 夜 思. See Bredon and Mitrophanow, *The Moon Year* (Shanghai: Kelly & Walsh, Ltd., 1927), pp. 391 ff.

induces in the mind poignant memories of past moments, the 'thoughts of home.'[3] She is the mistress of the discrete, concrete moment upon which the artist seizes for the stuff of his creative dreaming. Our word *chüeh* most simply translated 'to see' has many of these nuances. It can mean 'to awaken' or 'to be aroused' or 'to become aware of' or 'to be illumined.' It means to see in the sense of an inward perception, to grasp suddenly, in a flash of illumination, an intimate understanding of a moment, an idea, a form. The character for learning is related to the character for 'seeing' not only morphologically but also in classical literature. To learn is suddenly to realize what you have never known before 學之爲言覺也，以覺悟所未知也 .[4] To learn is to become aware of, to feel 覺.[5] The cultures of the East have emphasized the art of living. China especially has viewed life as art and has valued harmony and enjoyment of the aesthetic in the propriety of relationship and the balance of experience. The Chinese language developed a special capacity to convey the richness of the concrete, the precisely refined richness of the specific, individual moment of awareness. Chinese characters are themselves pictures. They are pictures to be painted, not letters to be scratched. Writing as painting is done with a brush and the first discipline of the Chinese painter is to master the art of brush strokes.[6] The model for the strokes is the symbol of mobile, delicate strength—the bamboo leaf

---

[3] See the last line of Li Po's most famous poem.

[4] From Pi Yung in *Pai Hu Tung.*

[5] Cf. The *Works of Mencius,* Bk. v "Wan Chang".

[6] F. S. C. Northrop, *The Meeting of East and West* (New York : Macmillan, 1946), p. 317.

as an art form.[7]   The second discipline of the painter is
'to grasp immediately apprehended aesthetic factors in
purity of concrete expression.'[8]   Chinese culture arises
from the art of language and the Chinese language is the
language of art.   It is so thoroughly adapted to poetic
expression that it is in consequence poor in abstract or
analytical denotation.[9]   China has produced very little
prose of comparable excellence.[10]   F. S. C. Northrop
characterizes the genius of Chinese culture as a concern
for the 'aesthetic object rather than the external physical
object' and cites in this connection a famous whimsey
in the poetry of Li T'ai Po:[11]

> I lift my wine-cup to invite the bright moon,
> With my shadow beside me, we have a party of three.[12]

Certainly what the Westerner feels as an immediate
response to the cultures of China and Japan and to the
variants of these elsewhere in South East Asia is the
appeal to his capacity to respond to the offerings of
spiritual peace and the lure of beauty in its humblest
expression.   Many Western students of Eastern culture
have found in the latter the Chinese substitute for religion.
Religion has dominated Western culture in its passion
for science as well as its artistic expression.   The peace-
fulness of beauty has in the same way dominated Eastern

---

[7] See William Willetts, *Chinese Art* (Harmondsworth: Penguin
Books, 1958), vol. II pp. 562 f.   For an interesting example of
a painting that is very close to calligraphy see *Bamboo Shoots*
attributed to Wu Chen (A.D. 1280-1354).   It is printed on p. 53
of the illustrations in Willetts.

[8] Northrop, *op. cit.,* p. 328.

[9] *Ibid.,* p. 319.

[10] See Lin Yutang, *My Country and My People* (New York:
Reynal & Hitchcock 1935), pp. 231 ff.

[11] *Op. cit.,* pp. 322 f.

[12] 月下獨酌

culture.[13] The capacity of the Westerner to respond to the excellence of the Eastern development of the aesthetic circle of learning demonstrates the fundamental character of this circle. It is an essential part of the world of culture which man everywhere and in all ages has created to express himself.

A second seminal word which also means to see is one Greek term for knowledge: *theorema:* a sight or spectacle, an object to be examined, and hence, something contemplated by the eye of the mind as a theorem in mathematics. This describes a kind of knowledge that is called ' theory.' Theoretical knowledge—science—was the Greek way of apprehending the world. The Greek way was to contemplate a thing, especially an idea, an image of the mind, to see it in the context of its relations, to know the ' what ' and the ' why ' of it, to understand it in principle. *Theoreo* (I see) means to look at something as a spectator watches the games, to stand off from it, to stand at a distance and to view objectively.[14]

Our third word is Hebrew: *yada^c*. It is in the Greek text of the Old Testament sometimes translated *oida,* to see in the sense of knowledge. The root *vid* of the Sanskrit word *veda* is a cognate of the Greek *eid* and means knowledge in the sense of that which has been found, discovered.[15] But the Hebrew *yada^c* is not directly translatable into Greek because it is a seminal idea of Hebrew thought and bears a distinctive meaning defining

---

[13] Lin Yutang, *op. cit.,* p. 242.

[14] See N. Fehl, "Logos Theology In Buddhism and Christianity" in *The Chung Chi Journal* (Hong Kong: 1961) vol. I, No. 1. July 1961.

[15] Alan Richardson, ed., *Theological Word Book of the Bible* (New York: Macmillan Co., 1959) pp. 121-122. Key passages are *Deut.* 11:2 ff; *Is.* 41:20; *Amos* 3:2; *Jer.* 1:5. Cf. *1 Cor.* 8:2 and *Gal.* 4:9. See also G. Kittel, *Theologisches Wörterbuch zum Neuen Testament* (Stuttgart: Kohlhammer, 1945).

our third circle of knowledge. It is not primarily a knowledge of things but rather of happenings. It is not aesthetic insight nor theoretical understanding, not a knowledge of principles, but rather a divination of the significance of events. Again *yada^c* is not so much associated with sight as with sound, not with seeing but with hearing. It is not a knowledge for which a man can search or that comes with research. For the Hebrews, reality was not an elemental substance. Reality was what happened, and *yada^c* was the awareness of what had happened, of what God had done.[16] *Yada^c* is a hearing of the speaking of God in events, recognizing the fact and purpose of His mighty acts, hearing in them the imperious demand upon man to serve. *Yada^c* is the knowledge of history as vocation.

To hear is different than to see. We cannot search out God. He is truly the *Mysterium tremendum et fascinosum.* He is Holy and thus in a sense ' wholly other.' But in His speaking the distance is bridged. Man is confronted with a speaker. To see is to observe, to stand at a distance and look on, to be an onlooker. But in speaking and hearing there is an encounter. The speaker lays a claim upon his hearer. Speaking and hearing is an I-Thou encounter. Here the subject that knows is not simply a passive instrument, an observer, an onlooker. And the object that is known is not only an independently existing reality, not only an object but is itself a subject, a Thou, who confronts the knower. And the knower thus confronted is not a mind alone but the whole spiritual being of man. And the context of this encounter is that of ' internal history,' the story of what

---

[16] See Rudolf Bultmann, *Primitive Christianity In Its Contemporary Setting,* transl. by R. H. Fuller, (New York: Meridian Books, 1956), pp. 22 ff.

happened to *us,* the living memory of the community.[17]
This kind of knowledge cannot be described as an opinion
or even as a belief about the nature of things. What is
involved is a fundamental value judgment and a response.
Philo distinguished this circle of knowledge from that of
reason *(scientiae)* and from ' sensation ' *(videndi)* by a
third organ of knowledge which he identified as the
' heart.' This third circle he calls ' prophecy ' and its
special sphere is history.[18] " The holy books . . . (of the
Hebrews) are not monuments of knowledge *(scientiae)* or
of vision *(videndi)* but the divine command and the divine
word." [19]

Probably the most fundamental symbol of Judeo-
Christian culture is the *Word of God.*[20] For primitive
man language was sacred. It was in and of itself
powerful, magical. Mythologies trace back the origin of
language to a mighty gift of gods to men.[21] A word is
a charm : it awakens power. Whoever utters words sets
power in motion. There is in the culture of primitive
and ancient peoples no notion whatsoever of ' mere words,'
' empty words.' Mere words in contrast to deeds, empty
words in contrast to charms, appeared only when men
committed the sacrilege of profaning the sacred power of
speech. This sense of sacrilege lies behind Confucius'
conviction that no society could survive the improper use
of names, that fundamental to all social reform was the

---

[17] See N. Söderblom, *The Nature of Revelation* and Richard
Niebuhr, *The Meaning of Revelation.*

[18] See H. A. Wolfson, *Philo* (Cambridge : Harvard University
Press, 1948), vol II pp. 3-10.

[19] *Quaestiones et Solutiones in Genesin.* iv 140.

[20] No one has explored more extensively the significance of
this symbol than Karl Barth. See the first volume of his *Church
Dogmatics, The Doctrine of the Word of God* (Edinburgh : T. &
T. Clark, 1936), vol. I part I.

[21] See G. van der Leeuw, *Religion In Essence and Manifestation,* (New York· Macmillan, 1938), pp. 403 ff.

' rectification of names.' [22] In biblical symbolism the power of God is His Word. The analogy is to be found in the command of the sovereign. The sovereign has the power (authority) to speak.[23] What he commands is done. Knowledge is awareness and response with respect to the sovereign's will. It is not propositional truth but command. The foundation of Judaism is the proclamation: " *Hear O Israel,* the Lord thy God is one Lord; and *thou shalt* love the Lord thy God with all thy heart and with all thy soul and with all thy mind and with all thy strength." It was through Moses that Israel came to know of Yahweh; and Yahweh disclosed Himself to Moses in His command: " I send you now to Pharaoh that you may bring forth my people." The knowledge that came to Isaiah was essentially not a vision but a vocation, a calling, a command: " Whom shall I send and who will go for us." When the word of the Lord came to Jeremiah it was a command: " To whom I send you, you shall go." Biblical knowledge is in terms of imperatives: send, go, do! [24] The key passage in the Old Testament to the distinctive ' wisdom ' of Israel is *Deuteronomy* 30: 11-14: " For this commandment which I command you this day is not too hard for you, neither is it far off. It is not in heaven, that you should say: Who will go up for us to heaven and bring it to us, that we may hear and do it. Neither is it beyond the sea, that you should say: Who will go over the sea and bring it to us, that we may hear it and do it? But the word is very near you; it is in your mouth and in your heart, so that you can do it."

---

[22] See also *Hsün Tzu* 22.

[23] See G. E. Mendenhall, *Law and Covenant In Israel and the Ancient Near East* (Pittsburgh, 1955).

[24] See Wright and Fuller, *The Book of the Acts of God* (New York: Doubleday & Co., 1957), pp. 27 ff.

In these three words, *chüeh, theorea* and *yada*[c], are the centers of the three circles of man's knowledge, art, science, and history. We have now to trace the circumference of each circle and to observe the common areas that are in each instance enclosed.

THE CIRCLE OF POETRY (LANGUAGE AND ART)

That Poetry as learning constitutes a circle with an inner integrity of scope and method has never been seriously questioned nor has the importance of this circle in successful university education been in doubt for very long in any age. Universally the key to literature is language. The written word had its origin both in Egypt and China in the magico-religious, pictographic representation of things. The written language in China was in antiquity regarded as a gift of heaven. Long after the magic of speech was forgotten the written character retained its sacredness. Characters ' make Heaven rejoice and Hell tremble; ' they ' capture the rhythm of the universe and put men in tune with its music.' [25] We have already spoken of the power of the word in speech. Cassirer suggests that the spoken word was originally the instrument of man's power over his world.[26] To speak is to command, to name is to control. The Sumerian myth, preserved in the symbolic theology of Genesis, which tells of Adam's naming of the animals and the plants of the Garden of Eden, reveals this aspect of the power of words. But experience did not always prove the efficacy of this first science—the science of the magic

---

[25] See Arthur de Carle Sowerby, *Nature in Chinese Art* (New York, 1940). Appendices *A* and *B* are by H. E. Gibson on Shang pictographs.

[26] *Essay On Man* (New York: Doubleday & Co., 1954), p. 144.

113

word. And when words lost their magic they were in a sense set free from science, delivered from the obligation to do something and thereby endowed with the opportunity to mean something.[27] They were freed from a menial task to serve thought. It has been said that the first philosophy was the philosophy of language as the bearer of meaning. Certainly one of the earliest basic problems in Greek philosophy was that of the relation of words to things, of meaning to being, of thought to reality, of mind to the world. And the first basic answer still remains the liveliest option: the human mind and the world, thought and reality participate in a common principle, a common ground. Heraclitus called it the *Logos* (word). The most recent term found both in ' field physics ' and the ' philosophy of organism ' is *process*.

One important function of language is that it reveals the nature of the relationship of man to nature as conceived in each culture. Humboldt spoke of language as a magic circle which each culture draws around itself. What is truly distinctive in any language is not the sound of its words or the rules of their use (grammar) but rather " the world perspective " which each language reveals.[28] Each language has a personality, a characteristic way of understanding and responding to the world.[29] This char-

---

[27] *Ibid.,* pp. 144 f.

[28] Quoted by Cassirer, *op. cit.,* p. 156. from Humboldt.

[29] Whitehead draws from Herder and Humboldt in his description of language as 'the incarnation of the mentality of the race which fashioned it. Every phrase and word embodies some habitual idea of men and women as they ploughed their fields, tended their homes, and built their cities.' (*op. cit.,* p. 74). He goes on to observe (p. 75) that 'the languages of heaven will be Chinese, Greek, French, German, Italian, and English, and the blessed saints will dwell with delight on these golden expressions of eternal life.' My own comment would be that if the mastery of Chinese is one of the joys of heaven, the span of eternity is appropriate.

acteristic sense of what is important is indicated in each language by the connotations of denotive words.[30] Thus in Latin the word for moon is ' the measuring one.' In Greek and in Chinese it is ' the shining one.' A man belongs to a culture—or to say the same thing in other words—a man is cultured when he has acquired a feeling for language, an appreciative sense of its connotative contours and colours, and when he comes to cherish the mutuality of his thought and his words.

Language reveals a perspective but in and of itself it cannot penetrate nature. It cannot of itself give assurance of a valid relation between names and things, between thought and being. The chief cultures of the world have known the despair of this scepticism. It arose in the West with the Greek world and continued in the middle ages in the controversy over nominalism (names) and realism (beings). Confucius had occasion to warn that empty words—names that did not accurately and honestly denote the objects to which they were applied—could cause cancer in a culture. Yet even in the sceptical ages words have value. When they can no longer describe things they can describe experience. The power of words both to represent and to recreate human emotion is vital to culture. Words prompt and persuade. 'Mere rhetoric' is still the catalyst of social action. Arthur Waley has noted the force of language as the weapon of diplomacy in *The Book of Songs*.[31] The Sophists emphasized this aspect of language and in Roman culture rhetoric was the queen of the sciences. In forceful speech, in oratory, the magic of language appears again. Man's speech

---

[30] See S. Langer, *op. cit*. on the connotative aspect of language.

[31] Arthur Waley, the *Book of Songs* (translation and notes) pp. 335 ff.

directed to nature may return unto him void but words will quicken human hearts.

Literature is determined by language and language is renewed in literature. Both are living, not mechanical things. Language to live at all must live a restless life. Grammar no more than physical science is proof against genius—the genius of a Dante or a Shakespeare, a Luther, a Li Tai Po and a Goethe.[32] But like all living things language too must have its structure. A culture is not only a way of looking at the world. It is also a way of thinking about what is seen. Language is not only perspective. It is also logic. Grammar is the structure of thought, the skeletal framework that provides stability and thereby supports growth. A hundred years ago John Stuart Mill observed that ' the structure of every sentence is a lesson in logic.' [33] Bertrand Russell has more recently observed the patterns of the new mathematical logic in ' the significance of a sentence.'

The rules of grammar as well as words are involved in expression—in the way in which something is said. Art is the living union of thought and expression. It is not divisible into parts: thought and expression, content and form, meaning and style, what is said and the way of saying it. The way in which something is said tells us something about what is said. To get at the thought of the artist we need also to ask what insights are implied in the literary structure of his work.[34] Newman defined style as a ' thinking out of thoughts into language,' and

---

[32] See Luther's address *To The Councilmen of All Cities in* Germany. See also Graves, *op. cit.,* II p. 183, and Cassirer, *op. cit.,* p. 284.

[33] See Cassirer, "The Influence of Language upon the Development of Scientific Thought," *Journal of Philosophy,* xxxix 12 (June, 1942).

[34] See my "A Reading of King Lear" *infra* pp. 294 ff.

literature as 'thoughts expressed in language.'[35]   Similarly the Great Preface 詩大序 to the *She King (Book of Poetry)* defines poetry as 'the product of earnest thought.' "Thought cherished in the mind," it continues, "becomes earnest; exhibited in words, it becomes poetry. The feelings move inwardly, and are embodied in words."[36] The art of literature is to express the meaning of a moment. "To express it, and to express it well," Collingwood noted, "are the same thing."[37]   Shakespeare's random hints at the secrets of the artist's soul have provided the stuff of which have been made the serious definitions of poetry in the West. First, poetry starts with a sensitive but sharp and objective awareness of the life of a passing moment.

> The poet's eye, in a fine frenzy rolling,
> Doth glance from heaven to earth, from earth to heaven,
> And, as imagination bodies forth
> The forms of things unknown, the poet's pen
> Turns them to shapes, and gives to airy nothing
> *A local habitation and a name.*

The poet gives concreteness and precision to experience. He stops the cinematic rush of life that passes by unnoticed in the crowded traffic of our congested souls and lifts up sharp, brilliant and clear some one thing that really matters. Art involves limitation. Brilliance and clarity involve selective focus. Because the artist's 'eye is single' his whole 'body is filled with light.' He deals in *disciplined* imagination or as Shakespeare himself said 'imagination all compact.' And his imagination

---

[35] Newman, *op. cit.*, p. 68.

[36] James Legge, *The Chinese Classics* (Hong Kong: University Press, 1960), vol. IV *She King*, p. 34. See *infra* p. 274.

[37] *Principles of Art* (Oxford: Clarendon Press, 1938), pp. 279, 282.

serves not to distort but to verify the posture of humanity. These several hints are best explored in Professor Preston Roberts' definition of poetry as "an effort to tell the story of man's life that is so concrete in manner of expression that the telling appears to reflect as in a mirror or to heighten as in a dream the very concreteness of life itself."

The function of poetry is first of all to stimulate and channel man's capacity to respond emotionally to life. This is an aspect of education to which all ages except our own have given serious attention. It is avoided today for several reasons. One is that all cultures and communities have lost the essential homogeneity that characterized human society before the industrial revolution. No one is sure that he knows what form such education should take. We are no longer sure of the character of virtue in our culture. We tend to be satisfied with the negative concern for adjustment and social conformity. The ancients were more positive. All classical civilizations and especially the Chinese and the Greek regarded the development and careful shaping of the emotional life not only as important as the cultivation of the intellect but also as an elemental and interrelated discipline without which no other training could be expected to succeed. The only book which Confucius explicitly commanded his students to read was the *Book of Poetry* and he appears to have associated the value of poetry with his central principle of education, the discipline by means of *li*.[38] Both Plato and Aristotle were aware of the importance of nurturing the emotional life.

Greek experience expressed a wide range of solutions to the problem of emotion. Plato feared the emotions for

---

[38] See Creel, *op. cit.*, p. 96.

he found them, perhaps in his own life, to be the enemies of reason. His programme was therefore to subdue them and hence he banned the great poet of Greece from his curriculum. The way of Aristotle was to govern the emotions by ' reasonable indulgence.' There was a third way as well, the way of Dionysius, the god of unlicenced passion whose devotees could resist anything but temptation. Aristotle who spoke for the common mind of Greece was nearer to Plato than to Dionysius: human passion must be purified or the soul purged of excessive and malignant emotion.[39] Art is the agent of purgation. Aristotle used the medical term *catharsis*. To witness the passions writ larger than life upon the stage in the lives of the great ones of earth is to purge one's own emotional life of petty passion, of meanness. It is to win through to health by the elevation of these forces beyond subjective experience. The artist enables us to see ourselves objectively. For the spectator at great drama the deep wound of his own tragedy is no longer so deep.

There is more wholeness and hence wholesomeness in the Chinese understanding of emotion. In the *Four Books* and in the later philosophers, emotion is seen as the dynamic of life. In the education of the whole man this power is harnessed and directed toward its proper end: the sustaining force of character.[40] In the shaping of man's instinctive tendencies, virtue is produced. Harnessed emotion supplies the power for the operation of the mind. " It is because man has a living body that he has a mind." [41] What is the true and the good " does not depart

---

[39] See F. L. Lucas, *Tragedy in Relation to Aristotle's Poetics*, (London: The Hogarth Press, 1928), pp. 30 ff.

[40] See *The Works of Mencius*, Kung-Sun Ch'ow Part I, ii 9-16. See also the *Analects of Confucius*, 4:5; 6:25; and 12:15.

[41] Tai Chen, *Yüan Shan* 2. See Creel, *Chinese Thought From Confucius to Mao Tse-Tung* (Chicago: University of Chicago Press, 1953), p. 185.

from human nature. If what is regarded as truth departs from human nature, it may not be regarded as truth." [42] Emotion is therefore to be cultivated and refined. " My children," Confucius once said to his disciples, " why do you not study poetry? Poetry will stimulate your emotions, help you to be more observant, enlarge your sympathies, and moderate your resentment of injustice." [43] Lin Yutang explains to his Western readers the place of emotion in Chinese culture by contrasting the English idiom for thought—' a man ransacks his brain '—to the Chinese—' he ransacks his dry intestines.' Chinese poetry at its best, he suggests, begins in the intestines (the seat of sympathy and emotion) and travels upwards to issue finally in delicate sentiment and 'rhythmic beauty informed with spiritual grace.' [44]

Throughout the history of education in both East and West this concern for a humanizing of the sensual life remained paramount until this century. The English Public School was, and in some instances still is, primarily an attempt at civilizing the vitalities of young gentlemen— sometimes by some quite uncivil means. For the most part parents were satisfied to have their sons come home from public school prepared upon occasion to behave properly. Modern education has suffered from a ' failure of nerve ' both of parents and of schools. The development of a capacity for emotional response to life has been in large part left by default to commercial enterprise —the comic book business, the cinema and the advertisers of cosmetics. And the evils of these should be charged not so much to the greed of the hucksters or to the

---

[42] Translated by Lin Yutang in *The Wisdom of Confucius* (New York: Random House, 1938), pp. 123 ff.

[43] *Analects* 17:10.

[44] *My Country and My People* p. 244.

depravity of human nature, as to the failure of education on all levels to stimulate and channel the emotional life.

As in China, so also in the West, the cultivation of emotional adequacy has always been the function of the classics—the function of art as a field and a force in the university. Wordsworth defined poetry as ' emotion recollected in tranquillity.' Great literature relates thought and passion. It shows us the power of passion in life— the dynamic of passion in the dimension of greatness. It reveals the horrible capacity of passion to destroy and the pitiful plight, even of the great ones among us, whose passion has failed of purity and piety. Art does what oft times life cannot do: it draws the poison out of passion so that we can enjoy its power to exalt and exhilarate without injury to our souls. Art enkindles without inflaming. Cassirer observed that in the theatre of Shakespeare " we are not infected with the ambition of Macbeth, with the cruelty of Richard III, or with the jealousy of Othello. We are not at the mercy of these emotions; we look through them; we seem to penetrate into their very nature and essence. . . . The great dramatists show us the forms of our inner life . . . (so that we) feel . . . the infinite potentialities of life." [45] In art—literature, the theatre, poetry—we participate in passion without being subject to compulsion, immune to the pressures of passion in life. ' The tragic poet is not the slave but the master of his emotions; ' and ' he is able to transfer this mastery ' to us.[46] And in this experience our own emotions are purified, our capacity for humane sympathy and unfettered love increased. Our hearts are lifted up. Purified passion ennobles. We are strengthened by its might in the inner man so that we come to behold

[45] *Essay On Man*, p. 189.
[46] *Ibid.*

with poet and painter the heights and the depths of the human spirit, the humane vision that surpasses knowledge.

But the artist also knows that the varieties of human experience are too vast, too complex, too ambiguous for tragedy. Tragedy demands neatness, clarity and simplicity. The tragic drama allows for only a few actors, for one specifiable tragic flaw, one inexorable working out of the movement from fortune to misfortune, from pride to perdition. Comedy allows a wider stage, a longer span, a larger scene and a cast that includes all sorts and conditions of men. The structure of comedy can be less precise. It has time for laughter. To laugh without scorn, to smile without sneering is to be humane. The grammarian or the mathematician, the chemist or the theologian who cannot laugh at his work as well as at himself, even though he finds his colleagues highly amusing, is not a humane man. University halls should resound with laughter as well as learning; for laughter is learning and even the highest learning is a 'praise of folly' as well as a praise of God because life under God is a ' divine comedy.'

Art has also another function which is to free us from bondage to our lesser self, that self which binds us to the humdrum routine of getting and spending, performing our wretched little sacrifices to the puny gods of prophylactic propriety and puerile pleasure. President Shuster came down upon the importance of the circle of art in the university because liberation of the human spirit is more crucial in our kind of civilization than in any former age.[47]

The average chemist will become a member of some chain gang of scientists marshalled like a posse for ferreting out a new explosive or antibiotic. And the

---

[47] Quoted from *Education in the Age of Science, op. cit.*, p. 28.

political scientist, fresh from the study of the arcana of government, will be fortunate if he can pass a civil service examination and proceed daily to chores with the Housing Authority or the Bureau of the Budget. But if somewhere along the road such a student has caught a glimpse of the ' city ' as seen by a man for whom the span between Plato and Quincy Wright does not exhaust the vision of that ' city ' as it has been or may be, he will not sleep without dreams.

Confucius told his son that if he did not study poetry he would be ' like a man standing with his face to a wall.' [48] There is no more reason now than then to doubt that any education approaching excellence would be possible ' apart from the habitual vision of greatness.' And Whitehead warns that ' if we are not great, it does not matter what we do or what is the issue.' [49]

There is one further claim for his right to be heard which the poet lays upon the university. He speaks for man and of the essentially human, and so his testament is as sure in our age as in the past. He teaches us to care and yet not to care for the moment of perfection, to hear the echo of the perpetually perishing as harmony rather than dissonance. In this the poet is the sublime interpreter of faith, drawing from death its sting and winning from the grave its victory. Here we are dealing with the deepest and oldest concern of mankind, the concern born of the religious quest. What man as man has ever sought in his religion is some assurance of permanence in nature, some hope of survival against the risks inherent in all endeavour and some sustaining faith against the dissolution of all effort in the paralysing consciousness of the awful fact of death. Whitehead

---

[48] *Analects* 17:9.
[49] *Op. cit.,* p. 77.

expresses this ground of religion in the thought that the world " craves for novelty and yet is haunted by terror at the loss of the past, with its familiarities and its loved ones. . . . The ultimate evil in the temporal world is deeper than any specific evil. It lies in the fact that the past fades, that time is a perpetual perishing." [50] This is the theme of poetry, the cry of the poet.

> Blow, bugle, blow, set the wild echoes flying,
> And answering echoes answer, dying, dying, dying.

And yet poetry itself is an answer to the echo.

> The music in my heart I bore
> Long after it was heard no more.[51]

Man is a civilized and a humane creature when he can witness the ' cracking of a noble heart ' and answer: ' Goodnight, sweet prince, And flights of angels sing thee to thy rest!'

And by the poet's magic, nature too is made human; for man—for all that he is a monstrous clever fellow with his mathematics and his gadgets—has need in the twilight to be to nature also son and lover. The poet as well as the scientist transforms and reshapes nature, and nature apprehended as human is no less essential to man's spirit than nature apprehended as rational is to man's mind. All poets have civilized nature but none with such delicacy and humour as the Chinese. Tu Fu made poet's peace with the inexorable law of change by seeing the charm of courtesans in the turning seasons.

---

[50] *Process and Reality* (Cambridge: Cambridge University Press, 1929), p. 481.

[51] These couplets from Tennyson and Wordsworth are quoted by Whitehead in his *Principles of Natural Knowledge,* p. 200. See the comment on this passage in Bernard Meland, *Seeds of Redemption* (New York: Macmillan, 1947), pp. 52 f.

I deeply rue the passing of the spring
And on a cane I pace the scented isle.
Before the winds dance wanton willows
And on the water petulous petals smile.[52]

And Yeh Li teaches us a humane harmony in which nature's moods complement rather than determine our own.

Pair by pair, little swallows on the bookshelves hop.
Dot by dot, little petals on the ink-slab drop.
Reading the *Book of Changes* I sit near a window
Forgetful how much longer spring will with us stop.[53]

---

[52] From *Quatrains on Sundry Moods*. With very slight modification this is the translation of Lin Yutang.

[53] From *A Scene in Late Spring*. Translation by Lin Yutang.

Confucius undertook with his students to write the History of Lu.

THE CIRCLE OF HISTORY

History is the middle circle of learning. Its circumference touches the centers both of the circle of poetry and the circle of science. History stands between poetry and science not in the sense of an intermediate discipline but as a mediator and interpreter. It has at various times been closely identified with the social sciences as the fundamental discipline upon which these are built—as mathematics is the foundation of physical science. From the middle of the nineteenth century, history and social science have developed together. The new disciplines of archaeology, philology, anthropology, sociology and psychology have been the helpmeets of history *(hilfwissenschaften);* and history, in turn, has been the method basic to social studies. Comte at the middle of the nineteenth century described ' positive philosophy ' as consisting of five sciences: astronomy, physics, chemistry, physiology and *social physics.* The term is significant. Societies—social institutions—in Comte's view have also a nature which can be observed and measured and described as well as, and in the same way as, physical phenomena. Social physics, no less than physics, is in Comte's words

126

to be a ' subject henceforth reducible to definite laws, enabling us to base action upon sure knowledge.' [54] Thus the two poles of university education in the age of science are clearly marked. Science is the study of nature. History is the study of human affairs or of the human significance of things. Science studies man as a part of his physical environment. History views man as distinct from his physical environment. History studies man as a being that seeks not only to know and to live but to express his life—to create, to act not only in accordance with his environment but upon it, to create for himself in the midst of the perpetually perishing and over against the inexorable laws of nature a dimension of immortality and freedom. Over against what nature is, stands what man has done. It was the insight of the Israelites that the real distinction between man and all else in creation was that man has a history. It is his history more than his nature that provides the significant data for the study of man. His destiny is a function of his history as well as his nature. His nature is the goal of his history.

Greek thought, on the other hand, regarded history as a function of human nature, the function of the substance that is man. History could then also be the poetry of the past, not in the Cartesian sense of fiction, but as the concrete instance of universal law. But the poetry of reason was always more important for the Greek than the poetry of event.[55]

---

[54] *Course of Positive Philosophy: General Considerations Concerning the Hierarchy of the Positive Sciences.* ii.

[55] See Aristotle's *Poetics.* The Judeo-Christian notion of man is more profound. It does not deny a nature to man. He is created bearing the *imago dei* but this image has been qualified or distorted as suggested in the myth of the fall. The myth of the flood indicates God's plan that man shall recover his nature but that this recovery belongs to the drama of redemption which is history.

History, however conceived, has always exhibited an inner tension between the demand that it be a descriptive science and the demand that it be an interpretive discipline. R. G. Collingwood distinguished history from myth in that the latter has a story to tell whereas history begins with the asking of questions. The word itself *(h)istoria* names that knowledge that comes from enquiry —the answer to questions: what happened, how did it happen, why did it happen? There is here the notion that the historian, quite contrary to what is allowed to the examiner of a witness in the courtroom, asks questions without any previous theory to which the answers may be responsive. He is simply curious. He has no thesis to establish or no opponent's case to demolish. He asks no leading questions. He organizes the answers he obtains into ' presuppositionless,' descriptive accounts; and thus he tells precisely what happened in exactly the way that it happened.[56] In so far as Comte had any place for history in his social physics, such scientific history would have been his ideal. Some concern for accuracy, for faithfulness to facts and for the impartial criticism of evidence is a basic presupposition of history as a discipline. But history is also interpretive. It is also thought—the kind of thinking done by historians. Historical thought always involves a response. Leopold von Ranke (1795-1886) who has been called the father of modern scientific history became an historian, he tells us, as a young man, because the past summoned him to discover ' the works of God displayed in the history of the human race.'[57] It is because, von Ranke insisted, the chief competence of

---

[56] Leopold von Ranke, *Geschichten der romanischen und germanischen Völker* in the Leipzig (1874) edition of the *Werke*, xxxiii p. vii.

[57] See Hans Liebeschutz, "Ranke" in *Historical Association Pamphlets,* 1954, pp. 4 ff.

the historian is judgment that his chief virtue must be integrity. ' Joy in detail ' does not make an historian of the man who is lacking in an ' eye for generalities ' or a ' passion for humanity.' [58]

Dilthey, the younger contemporary of von Ranke, recognized the tension in the study of history as a tension in university education: the polarity of art and science. History as mediator could not escape this tension but it must understand its own orientation. He distinguished the subject matter of history as the study of concrete events and individuals from that of natural science as the search for abstract generalizations; and the knowledge of history as an inward experience from the knowledge of science which has to do with the external environment.[59] The closer that history approaches to science the closer it comes to being merely a statistical report, chronologically arranged. Such a report may be significant when it deals with a limited and controlled reaction of a thing to other things. As such it may be highly useful knowledge. But chronology in history is ' the corpse of the past!' [60] It is less than the corpse; for a corpse has still the flesh. The embalmed can ' look natural.' It is only the skeleton which does not even reveal what the corpse looked like, let alone the living past! The task of the historian is not to record but to revive, to re-present the spirit of the age.[61] History is therefore, for Dilthey, an art which depends upon but cannot be subsumed under science.

---

[58] The quotes are from Ranke's *Uber die Epochen der neueren Geschichte* pp. 15-21. See H. Butterfield, *Man On His Past* (Cambridge: The University Press, 1955), p. 104.

[59] This is the theme of his *Einleitung in die Geisteswissenschaften,* 1883.

[60] The phrase is from Croce. See R. G. Collingwood, *The Idea of History* (New York: Oxford Univ. Press, 1956), p. 203.

[61] See Croce, *Zur Theorie und Geschichte der Historiographie,* (Tübingen, 1915.).

The Italian philosopher, Croce, one decade after the appearance of Dilthey's major work, *(Introduction to the Science of Mind,* 1883) discussed the relation of history to science in an essay entitled: *History Subsumed Under the Concept of Art.* It might have been called ' The Portrait of the Historian as a Young Artist.' Like Dilthey, Croce was critical of the notion of scientific history. Science bothers with the individual only as an instance typical of all other individuals within a class. What is unique in the individual interests the scientist only as a challenge of generality, as a test of abstraction. Art on the other hand is ' the intuitive vision of individuality.' Art seeks knowledge of the individual. Science seeks knowledge of the universal, the general. History is thus closer to art, or, as Croce at first believed, it is itself a kind of art. The artist reveals what he sees in the individual form or the individual moment. The historian similarly describes the individual and the unique but he is under the further demand to ascertain that what he has seen corresponds to what did happen. Art then is the larger circle of the possible; the narration of what actually did happen is the inner circle of history.

In these views of Comte, von Ranke, Dilthey, and Croce three notions of history appear: history as art, history as method (scientific control in the testing of evidence and the scientific report of investigation) and history as judgment. The first observation to be made here is that history is indeed all these, and it is for this reason in part that it is the mediate circle of learning in the university. And the second observation is this; the excellence of art and the excellence of science do not, however, depend upon the degree of isolation which they may be able to achieve with respect to each other. The artist is not the greater artist because he is religiously ignorant of science or because his thought processes have

130

the least in common with those of science. Nor is the scientist the better chemist or physicist because he has carefully filtered out of his working mind all artistic sensitivity and insight. Both artist and scientist are observers whose capacity for alert attention has grown with discipline, and in some notable instances the physicist and biologist have found in poetry and painting a significant detail of form or behaviour which they had themselves previously missed. Neither artist nor historian deals with a different set of the general laws of thought than is in force in science. We may in fact observe that the painter and poet were aware of the need to create for their own media symbols of the relation of relations before science had developed its post-Euclidian mathematical symbols to describe the relation of relations in the physical world. In all circles of contemporary learning a new concept of fact and hence a new concept of being and of the relation of fact and thought to being has replaced the former center. The center of each of these circles until the very recent past had been the notion of being as substance. The irreducible things of science, the atom as the elemental substance, could be compared to the irreducible fact— the hard, objective stuff of history. And the artist dealt with the essence of substances.

Yet the basic difference between scientific and historical fact remains. A physical fact is the interpolation of statistical averages based upon observation either direct or controlled (experiment). When the physical events observed are of significance for science—that is, when evidence points to the conclusion that they may generally be expected to happen in a certain way—this knowledge is most precisely and adequately presented in the language of numbers and mathematical symbols. Historical fact, as Cassirer has pointed out, is of a different kind and is

discovered in a different way.[62]   The historian has no
laboratory in which an apparatus can enable him to
observe with greater precision the events of the past.   The
most characteristic aspect of the past is that it is gone—
gone forever.   The chemist works with all the necessary
materials at hand and with his apparatus he can reconstruct the event in which he is interested.   If he is a
competent chemist with reliable equipment his experiment
will result in an accurate reconstruction of a physical
event.   The historian cannot so reconstruct the past.   He
can only remember it.   With the aid of all documents,
artifacts and other materials at his disposal he can picture
what may have happened.   An historical event is a
million times more complicated than a physical event.
Historical events are too complex to yield to scientific
control.   The historian can only remember as best he can
with the incomplete aids available.   And his conclusions
will always be of the nature of memory which is partial
and selective.   Memory reveals not all that happened, or
indeed what did happen or the way something happened,
but rather the character of the importance of the past.
Memory is never a reconstruction.   It is a re-creation—a
resurrection from the dead involving if not a new spirit
at least a new body.   Even contemporary history can in
no sense be scientific.   A fact in the realm of human
affairs is never a mere occurrence.   Something occurs and
somebody responds to the occurrence and this response
is the stuff of an historical fact.   Historical fact is always
occurrence *and* reception.   But the historian is himself
not the receiver.   He works with the testimony of others—
people whom he has never known, with whom he could
not speak, whose ways of life he has not shared.   Ancient
languages no longer spoken are no longer languages of

---

[62] *Op. cit.,* pp. 221 ff.

direct communication, and the things of history are no longer things. They have ceased to be physical objects. They have ceased to be facts. They are the material of symbols. The world of the historian is, in Cassirer's words, a symbolic universe.[63] The 'laboratory' work of the historian is thus not an analysis of molecules but an analysis of symbols. And symbols have life—they are meaningful only in so far as they participate in the life of the historian himself. He breathes into them the breath of his own experience. The English historian, Michael Oakeshott defines history as 'a seeing of the world from a fixed point in experience.' It is the latter phrase that is important. Every object is seen from a perspective. Perspective is ingredient in history. "We cannot separate what has come to us from our interpretation of it." History then is what the past means to us at this moment and from this perspective. And so there is no 'fixed and finished past.'[64]

Is history then simply the mirror in which we see ourselves or, to be more cynical, only the mirror in which the historian sees himself? In a very real and important sense this is true. The past is such a mirror. This is the word used by the famous Chinese historian of the eleventh century, Szu-ma Kuang who called his work *T'ung Chien*, the *Mirror of History* and spoke of his efforts as the attempt 'to view antiquity as through a mirror.' History as the mirror of the human face and the posture of man in the world means just the opposite of subjective portraiture. History objectifies human experience. It shows us man as creator and victim and sinner. History is, in Cassirer's paradoxical phrase, 'objective

---

[63] *Ibid.*

[64] *Experience and Its Modes* (Cambridge: University Press, 1933). I consider this an important book in part because it led me as a college student to an interest in history.

anthropomorphism.' It is not simply a series of snap shots of individuals either candid or contrived but the portrait of man, the portrayal of what man is in terms of what men have done. History objectifies in that it corrects the distortions of the partial data of individual lives and of particular times, and the final work of the historian is not a series of generalizations about the average man or the conventional group picture but the ' real man '—man in terms of the potentialities of the species evidenced by what, across the ages, men have done. Without history, which reaches over the broken arches of our generations and our institutions and our cultures to span ' the opposite poles of time,' we would be simply creatures of a day. History enables us to see ourselves and to criticize ourselves at a distance. It is a kind of cultural introspection and psychoanalysis which goes deeper than individual experience could tolerate and plumbs such depths as the single layers of particular ages cannot provide.

So far what has been said of history binds it to art not only in terms of interest and of method but also of function and effect. History as a circle with the integrity of its own field and purpose seems to have become absorbed into the circle of arts so that it is itself not a whole circle but only that common area of the intersecting circles of art and of science. Its distinctive aspect is hence to be sought elsewhere. We have already spoken of the word that describes the uniqueness of historical knowledge—the Hebrew word yada^c—the knowledge of event as judgment and as vocation. Friedrich Schlegel described the historian as ' *einen rückwärts gekehrten Propheten* ' or as Cassirer translates, a retrospective prophet.[65] Both Schlegel and Cassirer mean by this the

---

[65] *Op. cit.*, p. 225.

prophecy of the past as ' revelation of its hidden life.'
The historian as prophet can reveal a significance in men
and movements which were not seen by their contemporaries. But this is not all, nor is it the important work
that the historian does as prophet. History is the meaning
of the past for the present and thus ' all history is
contemporary history.' The ' facts of history are present
facts.' The Hebrew prophet found in history God's way
of pointing to the alternatives in the insistent present.
History is not only a mirror in which we see ourselves
in the depth and fullness of historic time. It is a word
that is spoken to us. History supplies and supports the
human sense of heritage and responsibility, of commission
and stewardship, of command and destiny. The great
historians have in every age sensed their vocation as
a calling to prophesy. The poorer historians are those
who speak without having been spoken to. The naive
historians are those who have mistaken their sermons for
objective accounts of what actually happened. Gibbon
was an excellent example of the apostle who preached
with fervor the gospel of those liberal virtues to which
he had been so fully converted before he found them in
the Antonine Age. All history is judgment. It is first
of all the judgment of what shall be studied; what are
the questions to be asked and of whom shall the enquires
be made. It is judgment with respect to the kinds of
evidence that shall be sought and the kinds of criticism
to which collected evidence shall be submitted. It is
judgment with respect to how evidence, so proved, shall
be used. It is judgment in terms of interpretation, and
it is judgment in terms of conclusions. And all this
judgment, whether it be of matters small or great, follows
from the historian's fundamental conviction as to the
character of the importance of human life. History is

the realm of the divination of goodness, the circle of the conscience, the science of the prophetic word. And this is also the oldest as well as the most persistent notion of history as a discipline. The *Han Shu (History of the Former Han Dynasty)* so describes the purpose of the *Spring and Autumn Annals:* It " passes moral judgments on events and is the symbol of good faith." [66] In the West from the Hellenistic through the Medieval ages the most frequently quoted definition of history was ' that philosophy that teaches by examples.' For Lord Acton history was ' the record of truths revealed by experience.' [67] Herbert Butterfield, latest of the great Cambridge historians, is somewhat more straightforward: " Our final interpretation of history is the most sovereign decision we can take, and it is clear that every one of us, as standing alone in the universe, has to take it for himself. It is our decision about religion, about our total attitude to things, and about the way we will appropriate life. And it is inseparable from our decision about the role we are going to play ourselves in that very drama of history." [68]

---

[66] *Han shu* xxx 12. An excellent brief summary of historiography in the Han dynasty can be found in W. T. de Bary, *Sources of Chinese Tradition* (New York: Columbia University Press, 1960), pp. 266 ff.

[67] From *Cambridge Address,* 1895. For comment on this address see R.L.P. Milburn, *Early Christian Interpretations of History*—Bampton Lectures 1952 (New York: Harper & Bros., 1954), p. 2.

[68] *Christianity and History* (London: G. Bell and Sons, 1949), p. 39.

Confucius forecast a rainy day by observation of natural phenomena.

THE CIRCLE OF SCIENCE

In describing the circles of art and of history we have dealt with some portions of that circle which is science; for it has never been an isolated circle but has at least up to the present period been related to other university studies not only by tangencies but also by intersection.

The first thing to be said about science is that it, too, is a human activity. In part because it has drawn a sharper line between its officiants and its laymen in its early stage as alchemy and astrology as well as in its modern form as a new mathematics, science has preserved its aura of mystery and magic long after art and history have suffered disenchantment. Nonetheless, science, too, is a human activity, and it is like art and history a construction of the world in terms of human intelligence. What distinguishes the scientific way of viewing the world from that of art and history is that a different language is used. Science is a viewing of the world from the perspective for which mathematics is the best way of describing what is seen. Two misconceptions can easily arise from this fact. The first is that the language of

137

numbers is purely descriptive and not conceptual. The second is that because a numerical language is different from and more abstract than a verbal language, it must therefore express a superior kind of knowledge. Bertrand Russell, who was a very competent mathematician, observed that " physics is mathematical not because we know so much about the physical world, but because we know so little; it is only its mathematical properties that we can discover." [69]

When Huxley defined science as sitting down before the facts like a little child he was nearer to the truth than he deserved to be because his misunderstanding of science was cancelled out by his misunderstanding of children. Science is not a carbon copy of nature and children are the most imaginative and creative people. The scientist like the artist and like the historian creates a world in the image of human understanding. The truth of Huxley's aphorism is not that nature speaks for itself or even that the ' facts ' of nature are any less the raw materials of science than the data of sense perception or the ' facts ' of the past are the raw stuff of art and history. All knowledge is both an ordering and an interpretation of facts. Arthur Koestler, who has studied the scientific mind especially with respect to the kind of temperament that leads to discovery, sheds some light on Huxley's phrase ' like a little child ' when he writes, " every creative act—in science, art or religion—involves a regression to a more primitive level, a new innocence of perception liberated from the cataract of accepted beliefs." [70] Science began with classification but its classes are categories that reflect man's mind as much as they do ' nature.' And even ' nature ' itself is a human idea. It is a construct

---

[69] *An Outline of Philosophy*, p. 163.
[70] Arthur Koestler, *The Sleepwalkers* (New York: Macmillan, 1959), p. 519.

of the human mind. The classification of plants by Linnaeus, the father of modern botany, was proudly described as ' artificial '—a work of art.[71]

It is the art of order which the scientist imposes upon the profusion of the individual things of nature. The scientist observes but he also postulates. He inspects but he also conceives. He measures but he also theorizes. The notion that science is simply a photograph of nature is as far from the facts as the notion that history is a photograph of the past. And the notion that science proceeds solely by inductive reason is equally in error. If this were so we would, by its history, be forced to the judgment that it had behaved very badly, and that it was just at those points where the greatest disparity between its principle and its practice occurred that it made its greatest leaps forward. A strictly inductive method would have led to a gradual but steady accumulation of knowledge which in turn would have provided for ' a continuous and organic ' progress. All historians of science, but none in stronger language than Koestler, have noted that the pattern of advance in science has been one of circuitous route and uneven pace. " The great discoveries which determined (the course of science) were sometimes the unexpected by-products of a chase after quite different hares. . . . At other times the process of discovery consisted merely in the cleaning away of the rubbish that blocked the path, or in the rearranging of existing items of knowledge in a different pattern." [72] In no field, we would believe, could science be more itself, less affected by the chances and changes of art and history, more sure of its foundation and more certain of 'irresistible progress' than in mathematics. But the theory of numbers comes

[71] See article "Linnaeus" in *EB* 11th.
[72] Koestler, *op. cit.*, p. 513.

to a virtual stop with Euclid and the next great advances which logically and potentially could have come within a few generations simply did not occur until quite recent times. The implication, that would be hard to ignore of this typical fact about science, is that, as a way of viewing the world, it is not a method or a form of thought which proceeds independently of other methods and other forms, and hence that it is neither purely quantitative in content nor inductive in method.

It is, to be sure, the most systematic of all human disciplines for it cannot allow a single datum to defy its classifying categories. And it is systematic also in the sense that it demands a precision of order and an exactness of description which a verbal language cannot provide. Words are connotative as well as denotive, and, in part because of their concrete richness, have no inherent systematic order. Such an order is available only in numbers which are applicable to everything that can be measured and hence can serve to express the measurable relationships between things. Planck spoke of the two tasks of science as ' the measuring of all things measurable ' and the discovery of new methods whereby ' to measure what had been previously unmeasurable.' The new physics is built upon the implication of a new kind of measurement—a new way of systematizing and of expressing the ' relation of relations ' among things, or more precisely, ' the relation of relations ' among activities.[73]

In crossing this threshold in the nineteenth century, science ceased to be simply ' organized common sense ' and it ceased to be mainly an inductive reasoning, operating upon the data of sense experience. The frontiers of the studies of the last century have made clear, what was

[73] See Cassirer, *op. cit.,* pp. 261 ff. and his *Substance and Function* and *Einstein's Theory of Relativity* (Chicago, 1923).

140

probably always the case, that science cannot properly be described as a ' common sense ' discipline, distinct, in simple Baconian terms, from the imaginative circle of art and the speculative circle of philosophy. Science became essentially conceptual as the new mathematics passed beyond the ' rational numbers ' of the ' things ' observable by the senses or conceived as functioning in mechanical relations. The new instruments such as Michelson's interferometer were not an extension of human sense organs and the new data they provided resulted in the overthrow of common sense notions.[74]

We speak of the scientific revolution of the seventeenth century but that age seems from our vantage point a fairly peaceful advance within the confines of common sense compared to the revolution of the nineteenth century. It was only when three centuries of science came to fruition in the three revolutionary ideas of the nineteenth century (the modern notion of atomicity beginning with the chemist, John Dalton, the idea of organic evolution beginning with the biologist, Charles Darwin, and the notion of ' field physics ' with its many contributors) that the importance of what was begun in the seventeenth century could be rightly judged. Looking backward, Butterfield can criticize the notion held by historians, in the very recent past, that the modern world was the product of the Renaissance. What was begun in the seventeenth century, he sees as an altogether new kind of civilization, one that " could cut itself away from the Graeco-Roman heritage in general." He concludes his essay on " The Place of The Scientific Revolution In the History of Western Civilization " with the judgment that

---

[74] See Whitehead, *Science and the Modern World* (New York: Pelican Mentor Books, 1948) pp. 115 f.

" since the rise of Christianity, there is no landmark in history worthy to be compared with this." [75]

[75] H. Butterfield, *The Origins of Modern Science*, (New York: Macmillan, 1957), p. 190. See also Chauncey Wright, "The Origins of Modern Science" in E. H. Modden, *The Structure of Scientific Thought*, (Boston: Houghton Mifflin Co., 1960).

Confucius listened to the proposals of Yang Hoo but did not fully accept them.

CHAPTER V

A PROGRAMME OF STUDIES:
CURRICULUM AND EDUCATION
SCIENCE AND THE UNIVERSITY

IN so far as Professor Butterfield is right in his judgment of the historical importance of the scientific
revolution, the circle of history in the modern university
must include within itself a large portion of the circle
of science. On the surface, the new kind of civilization
of which Mr. Butterfield speaks is the culture of inventions—a new way of life based upon gadgets. The use
and manufacture of gadgets have altered the whole
topography of our existence. Household appliances and
the mass production of prepared food and clothing have
reduced to insignificance the traditional role of women as
automation of industry has minimized the role of men as
craftsmen. The vast circulation of printed material, radio,
the cinema and television have reduced the significance
of the individuality of the common man. In this culture

143

of gadgets, and the economy appropriate to their manufacture and sale, basic social structures have been forced to change. The consanguine family has had to give way to the conjugal as a unit more readily adaptable to the culture of industrial cities. The Church in the West, the Uma in the Near East and the Sangha of Buddhism, which were, before the revolution, organizing and directing institutions in their respective cultures, have become voluntary societies of peripheral significance. The status and role of individuals in terms of birth, sex, training and occupation have undergone a series of radical readjustments. Communication media involving the travel of news, goods and people have altered not only the structure but also the concept and strategy of international relations. All this belongs to the surface, to the topography of the rise of that new kind of civilization that is, in Butterfield's words, the only ' landmark in history worthy to be compared ' with the rise of Christianity. The amazing fact about all this change is that it was an unplanned, sub-rational adjustment to diverse practical pressures that arose in the attempt to make use of the gadgets of applied science. Almost without exception, and in the exception only to a slight degree, were any of these changes the result of new scientific theory. They were the result of applied science—the adjustment to the pressures of action not of thought. It is a fact of sober and of somber import that the popular meaning and the miracle of modern science denote the invention of magic gadgets not the discovery of a new understanding of the universe. And I must go on to the judgment, which of course is personal, that one reason for this reversion of twentieth century science to primitive magic is the failure of the university to deal with science as a university subject. The seventeenth and the nineteenth centuries were the time of theoretical advance, centuries of scientific

144

discovery and thought. Our generation has been almost exclusively a time of invention—of applied science—and university science has been largely a making of engineers. With the tremendous breakthrough on all fronts in the nineteenth century, the twentieth should have been alive to the implications for thought of the work of Dalton, Maxwell, Michelson, Becquerel, Rutherford and Thomson as well as to the application of theoretical discovery in the interest of invention for commerce and military technology. It is of course the valid complaint of the university that its funds for science have been limited to the dictates of commercial and government benefaction. But it is here that the university must be the university— not a collection of " Research institutes " for meat packers, electrical appliance manufactures, the pharmaceutical and cosmetic industries or the government. It is the university alone of all the institutions of contemporary society that can sustain and develop scientific thought. If the university fails in this we can enter another dark age, and we shall be as blind to our predicament as was the tenth century; for in the so-called Dark Ages men thought they were advanced. They were aghast at the ingenuity of their ' scientists ' who could predict eclipses and concoct pain killing drugs and aphrodisiacs.

As a theologian my deepest fear is that science in the university can so easily abandon its high calling as a theoretical discipline. That the peace between religion and science should be the failure of science to have anything to say that provokes the theologian to realize that God speaks through his prophets Dalton and Darwin and Michelson and Planck and Einstein as well as in the Bible and the Eucharist, leads to the conclusion that He has lost confidence in our culture. Another way to put this is that the twentieth century may be the classic instance of man's ' failure of nerve.' [76] And yet in no century had science the greater reason to be the intellectual center of the university than it has in this. Now as never before our science departments should be alive to the meaning for man of this new civilization of which they are the architects. And this is so in respect to some scientists. But the disturbing fact about the science faculty in general is not that it keeps the other faculties in the travail of painful re-appraisal and re-conception of the motifs of contemporary life and thought but that it does not. It is the posture of contented insularity, the willingness to study and to teach their subjects in such a way that they are neutral to the university as a whole that is disturbing.

By its very nature, science enforces upon its devotees a hierarchy of function which does not permit easy trespass and yet binds all together in a kind of closed society. Thus there are many ' scientists ' who are technicians of a quite low order but who have been taught to do a simple job in a workmanlike manner even though they have little knowledge of the principles of their own speciality and less of modern science as a whole. There are other ' scientists ' who are specialists with a thorough working knowledge of a limited field and who are gifted researchers, and yet excluded from the general colloquia even of their own sciences by the barriers of language both mathematical and descriptive. There are other scientists who know their own discipline as the historian

---

[76] Experiment and invention on a high level are essential functions of pure science. Rutherford's splitting of the atom was an important advance from Thomson's theory of electrons. The first chain reaction at Stagg Field at the University of Chicago was a further advance of theoretical as well as practical significance. Some scientists insist that no theory has won its place in the history of science until an invention has appeared which could not have been previously devised except by some fool like Edison.

knows his field; and, while enjoying a high competence in a chosen area, are capable both of understanding and contributing to the interpretation of frontier studies along a fairly wide sector. Finally, there are a few scientists who can speak about the circle as a whole, and not only envision the breakthrough that may alter the whole perimeter but also are concerned to note the bearing of scientific discovery upon human wisdom. Modern science is a very large enterprise, and it must of necessity organize its research with the greatest possible division of labour. But this is a circumstance of significance to education in an age of science. There is no other faculty in which competence involves greater specialization and hence such substantial barriers to communication. There are many scientists—some of them in the university—who are convinced that science is essentially not thought but action.[77] They are, therefore, inclined to doubt that there can be any such thing as a philosophy of science, and are sincerely vexed at the efforts of their colleagues to interpret scientific thought. There are others who have come to this conclusion unaided by their knowledge of science. Biologists, physicists and chemists are men who are as likely and who have as much right as historians

---

[77] An interesting historical footnote to this question is Bacon's allegory in the First Book of his Novum Organum (1620): "Those who have handled sciences have been either men of experiment or men of dogmas. The men of experiment are like the ant; they only collect and use: the reasoners resemble spiders; who make cobwebs out of their substance. But the bee takes a middle course; it gathers its material from the flowers of the garden and the field, but transforms and digests it by a power of its own. Not unlike that is the true business of philosophy; for it neither relies solely or chiefly on the powers of the mind, nor does it take the matter which it gathers from natural history and mechanical experiments and lay it up in the memory whole, as it finds it; but lays it up in the understanding altered and digested. Therefore, from a closer and purer league between these two faculties, the experimental and the rational, such as has never yet been made, much may be hoped."

and philologists to be pious positivists. A conservative positivism passes so nicely for a scientific attitude.

These are some of the more obvious problems involved in the relation of the arts and the science faculties in the modern university: the demands of any adequate under- graduate science syllabus upon the curriculum of the university student, the barriers of communication between departments within the science faculty and the iron curtain between science and arts lecturers, the serious question whether science ought to involve itself in philosophy, and the bigger problem of how, should science so desire, effectual dialogue between arts and science could be implemented. But the alternatives to such a dialogue are not appealing. Arts education in isolation from science in our time would provide less than a ' finishing school ' training. Science education on no broader foundation than middle school arts would be frightening. And yet the problem of implementation is basic. How can arts courses be more than extra curricular for the science student and how can the arts student do anything worth- while with one laboratory science course? It is here that the real language problem exists for the Eastern university and for the Western. The basic language problem for the Chinese university in the Commonwealth Association is not the difference between the Chinese language and English. It is between both English and Chinese on the one hand and mathematics on the other. In the Western university the student may be led to the self deception that because no other language than his native tongue is required for his arts programme, he has therefore an easier road to education than the Eastern student. If so, he is easily deceived.

Modern mathematics is, however, not a formidable study. It is a good example of what can go wrong in education when practice is thundered into the place of theory. In this I can speak from personal experience. I did not learn any mathematics either in high school or in college. In both instances my teachers were interested only in answers, in the set procedure of solving a certain kind of problem. Given a problem and instruction in the steps involved in its solution, the student was expected to repeat these steps in examination with the same problem involving only different numbers. I was never taught the theory of which any problem was an application. What mathematics I have learned, I have acquired as a teacher in theology who is concerned with mathematics as the new language for reading in science. As one who has studied both Latin and mathematics I am convinced that the study of basic algebra is no more difficult than the study of ancient language, and that it is far more important to the curriculum of the modern university. Latin was once the key to the knowledge that was important. This is no longer so. Whatever is important for our time in Latin literature has been ably translated. What was important in Latin as one foundation of European languages, lives on in the modern aspect of those languages or else it can be readily reviewed in the dictionary or in Waldo-Porkorny. Mathematics has replaced Latin as the portal through which an educated man must pass, and the learning of this language in secondary school is essential to competence in history and philosophy as well as in science. The failure of communication between arts and science in the university is not to be charged to the barbarism of the scientists alone. It is a function also of the ignorance of the other faculties of the only language in which some of the most important knowledge in our age can be expressed.

149

SCIENCE AND HISTORY

On the theoretical frontier there is in our time, as in all great ages, a more considerable possibility of communication between the circles of learning than in the times of that kind of dogmatism that results from insular and, therefore, inert ideas. The problem of a university is whether the relation of its circles of learning goes beyond tangencies and is more crucial than superficial penetrations. The historian may take account of the technological bearing of science upon sociological, economic and political structures and functions. He may go on to interpret the impact of these factors upon ideologies. The artist may supply samplings of man's spiritual response to life in a scientific age. But ideally the university seeks an organic relation of the circles of learning as ways of viewing the world: the interrelation or interaction of science as theory with art and history. It sustains an organic structure of faculties in order to discover if there be any significance in the relation of the nature of humane insight to historical and scientific fact and whether the dialogue on a conceptual level of poet, historian and scientist can lead either to mutual enrichment or to a fundamental unity of perspective.

The university is justified by faith in the possibility of such a unity. From the time of the Greeks to the end of the eighteenth century, science and history appear for the most part to have been two different and opposing ways of looking at the world. The classical study of nature cancelled out what Christian faith understood to be the soul of history, and Christian thought for the most part chose history rather than nature as the area of God's significant self disclosure. The physical world was in orthodox theology little more than the stage upon

150

which the divine drama of salvation was enacted.[78] The
conflict of religion with science that arose in the seventeenth century continued in part to be the conflict of
history and the study of nature, the opposing emphases
upon the general and the specific, the mass and the
individual, the inevitable and the unique, necessity and
freedom. History guarded the notion of the unique occurrence conceived either in humanist fashion as the miracle
of human creativity or in religious fashion as divine
intervention. Seventeenth and eighteenth century science
reinforced the notion of nature as a fixed and unalterable
order after the analogy of fate in Greek thought and
the structure of primitive folk society in general. The
philosophy of nature continued through the eighteenth
century as a projection into the physical universe of the
closed system of tribal society with its unalterable custom,
its denial of individual expression. The concepts of
eighteenth century science centered upon the immutable
and the static and were not essentially different in
perspective than the cosmological myths of primitive
man.[79] The philosophies of Plato and Arostotle were
profound treatments of primitive mythology which pictured
the universe as a two-storied building: earth and heaven,
the home of men below and the abode of the gods above,
the fate-bound, tragedy-laden realm of human existence
and the eternal perfect realm of absolute truth, beauty
and goodness. Primitive science pictured the unit of
reality as some irreducible substance, imperishable and
unchanging, out of which all things were made. For the
most part romantic history in the latter part of the
eighteenth and the first half of the twentieth century
developed the concept of the unique, the highly individual,

---

[78] See Raven, *Natural Religion and Christian Theology,* I,
p. 20.

[79] See Fehl, *Essay On Natural Law* pp. 18 ff.

the unpatterned and the irrational, expressed in images of the heroic individual and the spirit of the age. Since von Ranke and Croce, history has come nearer to science not only as method but also conceptually. A good deal of the best contemporary historical writing could be described as a thinking out of Croce's mature conclusion that " the universal must be incarnate in the individual " and that it is this divination of the structures and dynamics of process incarnate in individual events which is the real task of the historian. But science also has moved nearer to history. In the work of Dalton, Becquerel, the Thomsons and Rutherford, of Planck and Einstein the notion of the universe as consisting of masses in a static pattern in space was overthrown. The new physics deals with the atom not as substance but as event. Next to mathematics the most appropriate description is poetic: "An atom is a tiny planetary system, a merry-go-round in miniature." [80] And these tiny planets, the electrons, are not themselves substances. They have been pictured as ' particles of negative electricity,' as 'points of energy or response.' The description of an atom is an interpretive report of activities in relationship, and that of a molecule is the story of a larger event involving the relation of relations of activities.

The hypothesis of organic evolution undermined the notion of a static two-storied universe from another perspective. Biology was the first of the physical sciences to devise the notion of emergence and novelty as a necessary explanation of some stubborn facts of science. The concept of relativity and the Quantum theory in the recent past have pointed to an open-ended universe in which natural law becomes simply statistical averages and in which the position of viewing anything is as

---

[80] See Meland, *op. cit.,* p. 78.

significant as the object to be viewed. The definite boundary between nature and history exists neither for the historian nor for the theoretical scientist. From the point of view of these new hypotheses nature is something happening—nature is history. Whitehead presses the notion of event as the unit of natural occurrence toward universal applicability for all circles of learning in his philosophy of organism. Instead of separate entities in space and time or of a split universe with colourless and soundless bits of matter set against colour-and-sound-creating minds, " the world shows a creative forward movement where each event exists for the prehension or inclusion of all others, and where each in turn, is the growth in a new way of feeling the rest of the universe." [81] Here there is no divorce between nature and life, nature and man or the circles of art, history and science. The ideal opposites which in the twelfth century occasioned the shifts in curriculum from grammar to dialectic and in the Renaissance from logic to literature and in the seventeenth century from humanities to science and finally in the eighteenth from science to history, are from this view operative in each circle of learning. The tension between meaning and being, thought and action, contemplation and participation, past and present, permanence and evolution, ultimate and concrete—the abstract and the individual, wisdom and discovery, wholeness and specialization, imitation and inspiration, that have arisen in man's conceptualizing and valuing of his world are polarities that characterize to some extent the special concerns of the several faculties; but in any strong faculty they are internal tensions, and for the university they

---

[81] *Process and Reality* (Cambridge: University Press, 1929), pp. 484 ff. See also "Lecture Eight: Nature Alive" in *Modes of Thought* and *The Principles of Natural Knowledge.*

point up the fact that a body has many members and that the members of a body are organically related.

CURRICULUM AND THE DEPARTMENTS

It is here in the relationship of the many members, the departmental pattern of organization, that we encounter what may well be the crucial problem of the modern university. Before the eighteenth century the basic structure of the university was in terms of faculties. In general, the division of faculties reflected the medieval pattern according to which foundational studies—the seven arts—constituted the major faculty, and under it the specialized studies of law and medicine were organized into graduate schools. Theology at Paris and elsewhere in the *universitas magistrorum* type of *studium generale* was the ' superior faculty '—the queen of the sciences. With the gradual degeneration of the graduate school faculties and the division of the arts faculty into classics and science, the modern departmental structure arose. The specialized studies underwent a transition from graduate, theoretical disciplines toward the technical professional schools of law and medicine that were associated with the university, for the most part, only in a geographical sense. Theology in England ceased to be a university faculty, superior to the faculty of arts. Either it was studied as an undergraduate subject within the arts curriculum or in a professional school apart from the university. The English university thus became a one-faculty institution of higher education, and the baccalaureate programme was accepted as its chief task. Against the background of this history, the curriculum discussion in the seventeenth century led by Bacon and Descartes is significant. The programme is by both divided into three departments—poetry, history and philosophy. Poetry and history were what we would

154

call 'minors' although Bacon considered the latter an important subject. The major was philosophy which in turn was divided into mathematics, the several physical sciences and metaphysics. Philosophy thus included, in Bacon's words, the 'circle of the sciences' of which the highest discipline was metaphysics—the integrative and interpretive 'science of sciences.' Similarly in Descartes' curriculum, philosophy was the 'major' but the several sciences were to be studied as applications of the 'universal science of mathematics!' Metaphysics as the chief discipline of philosophy was to relate the world seen as extension (nature) with the world seen as thought (mind), and for this task 'universal mathematics' was to be interpreter. Descartes, as a fairly good Catholic, proposed that theology be continued as the superior faculty of the university—a kind of graduate school without any vital relation to the undergraduate programme. To Bacon, in part in the interest of the Anglican Faith, a sharp distinction between philosophy and theology seemed desirable. The significant feature of both curricula was the motif of a science of sciences. The goal of the physical sciences as university subjects was metaphysical truth. The 'scientist' was called a 'natural philosopher,' and the studies in biology, physics and chemistry were described collectively by the phrase 'the new philosophy.' Throughout most of the nineteenth century, although the term 'natural philosophy' had been replaced by the term physical science, biology, physics and chemistry were studied as theoretical disciplines essential to critique and construction in metaphysics. It may have been the case, as Newman believed it was true in his Oxford, that the breakup of natural philosophy into separate departments of physical science marked the loss of the essential character of the university as a society of masters and scholars devoted to the integration and systematic inter-

155

pretation of various kinds of knowledge. Certainly by the beginning of our own century, with the rise of the social sciences, each of which claimed by the word of Comte to be *the* interpretive discipline, and with the abandonment by the physical sciences of the high calling of natural philosophy, departmentalization had in fact if not by intent radically altered the idea of a university and its function.

For the first time in the history of higher education there is no organizing motif structurally written into the programme of studies. There is no higher discipline toward which all others contribute and which is the crown of every student's university career. Many emergency programmes have been devised to ameliorate the depressing results of education in the modern departmentalized university. Some schools have required students to take courses or write examinations in specified areas outside their field of concentration. Other schools have preferred a wide offering of elective courses and encouraged the student to choose an avocation in addition to his major. Others have, like Chung Chi, instituted an integrative and interpretive sequence of courses as a general requirement. None of these 'corrections' of the departmentalized university has been an unqualified success. The departmentalized teacher and student is as much an aspect of the modern university as is the 'organization man' of the business world. The organization man may just do in business, though he is a rather sad figure even there, but the departmental mind will not do in the university. I want to illustrate this observation in respect to the physical sciences because I am convinced of the prime importance of these disciplines. Scientists themselves may be—and usually are—citizens with deep convictions on some of the more crucial matters of the modern world. They may be men who are constrained by conscience to speak out on political issues, social morality and academic freedom. I know some scientists who feel they have a special vocation to witness to their Christian faith and their involvement in the programme of their parish. But it is so seldom that one hears a scientist speak *qua* scientist on anything academic. It is so tragically seldom that one hears a chemist or physicist demand to be heard because he feels he has something to say in terms of his science that has a bearing on human thought—upon philosophy.

C. P. Snow has urged the greater use of the scientist as counselor in social institutions and particularly in government because he is convinced that from him may be expected the wisdom of insight and foresight.[82] What one misses entirely in Snow's portrayal of the ' new men ' is any insight or foresight whatsoever in respect of the implications of scientific theory itself for the shaping of the modern mind. By breeding they are liberals or they are conservatives in politics, they are passionately human both in their relation to their colleagues and wives and to their research, but they are as much as the cadres and the industrialists, men of action and not men of thought—as least not of thought arising from their special knowledge.

Snow concludes his Godkin Lectures at Harvard with the judgment that " It would be bitter if, when this storm of history is over, the best epitaph that anyone could write of us was only that: The wisest men who had not the gift of foresight." [83] It is because he is right that his *Masters* and *New Men* are ' bitter ' books—the bitter tale of the brilliant scientist who has failed us where we need him most as philosopher and theologian. At least in the university the man of science must be responsibly

---

[82] *Science and Government*, (Cambridge: Harvard University Press, 1961), pp. 80 f.

[83] *Ibid.* p. 84.

aware that the most crucial impact of science upon our world is not just the cultural implications of its technology. He should be sensitive to the philosophical implications of its theory. It is *qua* scientist that he must speak. The real danger in our age, and in part, because of the departmentalized school, is that science could so easily become the servant of government in its military technology and the servant of industry in its commercial ventures rather than the servant of the university, devoted to the task of the education of minds and the enlightenment of man. For too many institutions, it is the bitter fact that science is *in* the university but *not of* the university. The university can thrive on hot wars but it cannot survive cold wars. The inherent frictions between art and science can find an expression that is the healthy sign of a school's inner growth.

There is a good deal of thinking out loud as well as speaking out of school in any discussion of the contemporary university. The very difficulty one feels in getting down on paper what presses on his heart in these matters is a reminder that every view is a partial one and that no one speaks purely as spectator. It is where he stands as well as at what he looks that determines what a man sees. Probably more often than others the theologian is constrained to ask the scientist " Is there any word from the Lord? " The historian as well as the scientist can urge upon us the caution against a premature canonization of new hypotheses. We have, however, not only the right but the duty to think as well as to act with the courage of our concepts. It is not right that our way of life should be altered so radically by the technological side of our new science and that our former ways of thought should be dissolved by negative inferences while we remain indifferent to the positive implications for re-conception in its theory. The university lives by the

158

faith that theory matters. It is this kind of wager—not some sort of covering insurance—about which Pascal and later William James were concerned. It is the kind of commitment that gives us the boldness to venture what we are and what we have on the faith that a university is worthwhile—that when the chips are down, we should rather be wrong with Whitehead than right with Russell.

CURRICULUM CONSIDERATIONS

When we are quite realistic about these circles of learning in terms of the classroom and the study—when we consider the day to day business of the university in tutorial and laboratory—we remember that what we have to deal with is the functioning of the human mind itself. The insights of literature and the uses of historical evidence are subject to the same kind of testing as goes on in the physical sciences. The same principles of logic are involved in reaching an historical judgment as in formulating an hypothesis. In each instance alternative explanations must be taken into account, and in each the usefulness of the conclusion determines its significance. Serious work in literature and history is no less responsible and no more arbitrary than in science, for it is the same human reason that directs the critical and constructive efforts in all three. Nor is there in any field the danger that breadth of knowledge will diminish specialized competence. The well informed and versatile mind has proved to be thereby better equipped for critical thought. It is the teacher or student who lives between two stacks in the library or on one bench in the laboratory who creates in himself and for others the illusion that competence in his field has made him what he is. The science an arts student can learn in one laboratory course will probably not amount to very much, but it will temper his admiration for anything that appears in print. If his distrust of the lab manual leads him to a more critical appraisal of books in general, he will not have wasted his time. And if the science student can be chased out of his cozy laboratory into a rough and tumble seminar with unbelievers for whom ' research ' is neither a sacred nor a magic word, he may become a better scientist. W. B. Gallie tells of one shocking word of Lindsay's at Keele that started a science professor on the climb upward from demonstrator to lecturer. The professor pleaded that research was the life of science. Lindsay asked quite simply, " Why? " An apocryphal version has it that Lindsay shouted: " For God's sake, stop your damn researching for a while and begin to think! "

If these two chapters on curriculum have proved nothing else, they have shown that while the term refers to the running of the academic race in the shortest possible time, the discussion of curriculum does not. Most of this discussion can be summarized in two principles and a word about method. The first principle is that the survival of the university in the modern world demands a stricter sense of the limitation of subjects to be studied within a faculty and an even more severe limitation of the courses required in the study of a subject. The first implication of this principle is that unless all three circles of learning are interrelated in the undergraduate curriculum, there is no university. The health of the university is in its wholeness. But health and soundness do not mean fat. Indeed, fat in any department is as surely a danger signal for the university as fat around individual organs is for a man. Universities tend to accumulate fat. Long after Terence and Plautus ceased to speak to anyone except the antiquarian, they continued to be ' literature ' in the university. Dead ideas and modes of expression are no more eloquent than other

160

corpses. They do not even make good ventriloquist's dummies. There should be no space wasted in the arts departments for morgues or museums. Even for the arts major there is no time for anything but the best—and by the best is meant the kind of literature which, though it may be very old, is contemporary. Great historical writing can be good literature but too often the history of literature is neither. The kind of poetry that speaks to a student only after he has exhausted his patience and his wits on complicated discussions of meter or arguments on dating, has probably very little to say. Poetry deserves its place of great honour in the university, but only in so far as it is poetry. Criticism in its broadest sense there must be. Why something is good is needful knowledge. Looking through criticism at a single phrase or theme, the structure of a plot, the heart or mind of a character, as one looks through a microscope, the student will see pattern, movement and life that would otherwise go unnoticed. The laboratory manual that guides the student in examining the significant specimen is as necessary to the study of the arts as of the sciences; but the arts can do strange things with their microscopes and their manuals. Little more can be said for the memorization of one kind of manual than of the other. Several years of courses on the microscope itself could indicate a curious kind of thoroughness.

The problems for curriculum in this area may not be essentially different than they were in the middle ages. In a sense the university emerged from the cathedral school when men like Abelard insisted that a notion of what was not learning—not literature or philosophy—was the essential thing. There could not have been a university in the twelfth century without this strict sense of the limitation of time and effort to lively studies. Now we tend to be overwhelmed by the extent and variety of accumulated knowledge, but the problem is still the same: a judgment of the character of importance. It is probably true that our egalitarian, departmentalized structure complicates the problem for us. This structure, rather than the growth of knowledge, is likely to present our chief hurdle. One curious feature of the mind of the modern university is that its concern for wholeness leads to the proliferation of departments and by this very circumstance is self defeating. The most carefully devised programme of studies in the interests of wholeness and balance may only prove the fallacy of a well rounded curriculum taught by narrow experts. I am sure this is a factor in the failure of inter-departmental programmes. So often it is the trivia of both arts and science that comes to the surface in such ventures. The scientist is quite likely to illustrate his preoccupation with the latest project and the interpreter for arts is often ' imbued with the culture of the day before yesterday.'

The second principle stems from the observation that an age has a Gestalt—that there is a fairly significant convergence of studies that reflects lively interests and determinative concepts underlying the chief thrusts of the several faculties. We have noted the converging of science and history in the new concept of event and the convergence of both with contemporary literature in the exploration of the wider context of human relationship. The articulation of such natural unities lies within the capacity of the university. Though we may not aspire to the grand unity of all things human with the Divine as did those brave schools of the middle ages, we shall have served no mean vocation if we can interpret to our age the inner bearing of its ideas one upon another, and assist in bringing to clearer expression the murmurs of its disquietude and the whisper of its hopes. Certainly, university subjects should be pursued as responsive to ' the insistent present:' for

162

they can lose nothing academic by the deepening of the sense of responsibility. Furthermore, it is just these ideas and just these yearnings that furnish the relevant issues for research and study. Issues become ripe for solution and new areas are opened up to research because they are relevant to the destiny of an age. The university, as much as the Church, must not only live with its history but also it must live intensively the life of the present. There should be no question of confusing such a demand to respond to the present with the modern notion of adjustment. It is, in fact, through the intensive exploration of seminal ideas as they relate to all three circles of learning that their true worth is assayed.

The comment to be made on method is a fairly obvious conclusion. Efficiency is an obsession in our time. Progress is a word we have come to use in speaking of production, of producing more things more quickly. If a student is to acquire more knowledge today than was required a century ago, and yet he completes the course in the same time, we may attribute his success to the progress of education. A carefully planned curriculum and better ways of teaching and study should improve the management of learning. But the university is not a factory, and the processes involved in educating a mind are of a different order than those of manufacture or the teaching of a subject or the training of an expert. Even during the war and even in the United States it still took nine calendar months from conception to delivery, and it is probably true that one's *alma mater* is similarly immune to progress. It takes time for a mind to mature, and a simplified or streamlined programme of concentration in one specialized study is not university education. The two English universities made no attempt until quite recently to provide specialized knowledge in any field. They attempted no more than to train a man to be

163

a scholar by an intensive reading of a few books. A man so trained, they believed, should be able to acquire on his own whatever knowledge he needed; and that curriculum worked fairly well until it was felt that university graduates should know something as well as be fitted to learn something. The Redbrick programme is almost the opposite of eighteenth century Oxford. It is designed to supply the required knowledge for a particular position, and in some instances does a reasonably good job of insuring that its graduates are shielded from learning anything else. Such efficiency can be fatal when the graduates show up in government and particularly in the Education Department.

American education is closer to the aims of the 'Oxbridge' tradition, but it seeks to prepare a student for learning by exposing him to a fairly wide range of studies. It is believed that a college education is a larger venture than mere study, and that the student should not be over-burdened with academic tasks during so important a stage of his development. There is, however, a wide freedom in the American college, and no student is denied the right to major in academic pursuits. Graduate study then becomes the serious business of the university, and American standards are usually higher and the programme more systematic than in either the British or the continental university.

The obvious comment is that a combination of British and American programmes would better serve the cause of modern education. We ought not to be satisfied with narrow specialization on the baccalaureate level. Neither should we be satisfied with a haphazard or relaxed attitude toward the undergraduate curriculum. Even with exclusive concentration in a departmental programme, it is no longer possible to turn out in four years either a competent historian or a competent chemist. It must be taken for granted that professional competence will demand graduate study. The proliferation of departmental courses does not produce a better graduate student. Advanced subjects are better studied on a graduate level. If the student is to go out from the college into immediate employment, his career will be best begun with some breadth beyond his field in place of semi-graduate knowledge in his speciality. This is particularly true for those who go from the university to teaching positions in the lower schools. Not only do they need breadth beyond their subject but a semi-graduate knowledge of advanced studies is precisely that little learning which is a dangerous thing. The undergraduate curriculum has therefore to give its largest place to basic courses pursued intensively, and to methodological procedures. Where the core course in college chemistry must be hurried through in order to get in a host of 'advanced' courses in Electrochemistry, Petroleum Reservoir Analysis, Colour Chemistry and Ceramic Engineering, it will become a cram subject leading the student toward efficient memorization but teaching him very little science. That kind of chemistry can, of course, have little bearing upon art or history. The student subjected to such a programme will be a prisoner in his department, herded into a corral from which the only exit is by a forced march into some dreary industry. If, on the other hand, he can study his chemistry with the leisure to ask questions and participate in the romance of repeating great experiments, science can come to mean for him a venture of the free mind. It will be a liberal subject.

We have described history as the mediating circle between those of art and science. Historical method structures the studies of several departments, and history in any field is a significant way of seeing theory in perspective. Historical study is thus a community effort.

Equally important is the role of history as pontiff—the bridge builder between science and art. There can be no liberal education in the modern university that does not take account of science anymore than it was possible for the faculty of arts in the thirteenth century to ignore Aristotle. The student in literature who ignores either the technological or the theoretical implications of science is as limited in his treatment of contemporary writers as he would be without a knowledge of Calvinism in his treatment of Milton or Melville. The student in history requires a broad knowledge of science in both its aspects, not only in his telling of the story of human affairs since the seventeenth century but also in understanding himself, his own perspective and the point in time from which he must view the whole of the past. And the science student needs history. There are several facets to the insight with which Collingwood concludes his *Idea of Nature*—"that natural science as a form of thought exists and always has existed in a context of history, and depends on historical thought for its existence." [84] History is the key to an adequate grasp of scientific theory. It is also the key to an understanding of experimental science and that essential attitude toward laboratory procedure that makes physics and chemistry and biology university subjects. The student who knows nothing of the history of the great experiments which he repeats in the laboratory does not really know what he is doing and why he is doing it. Apart from history his lab work is little more than a higher grade of manual labour performed in a factory that produces nothing.

History in the Eastern university is even more important than in the West. For the modern East, living at random under the impact of technology, Western science,

---

[84] *Op. cit.*, p. 177.

taught apart from its history, is indeed a dangerous thing. It is then all that the East has feared of it, a new white magic at every moment threatening to turn black, a harsh thing, giving so little in reparation for so much that it has destroyed.

From medieval times into the very recent past, Aristotle's logic served as the meeting place in the university for doctor and lawyer, mathematician, philosopher and theologian. For the modern university that meeting place is the history of science.

Confucius was always followed by his youthful though grey-headed disciple Yen Yuan.

CHAPTER VI

A COMMUNITY OF MASTERS AND SCHOLARS

THE COMMUNITY OF MASTERS

THERE is no other aspect of the nature and history of a university that is so essential to an understanding of its unique character as its origin as a guild. The university is a guild—a society of masters and scholars. It is not a programme of studies or an organization of departments or an examination syndicate. The first universities—and some of the best from the twelfth century to the present—regarded these things as secondary to the fundamental concept of the *universitas magistrorum et scholarium,* the guild of masters and apprentices in the art of learning and the communication of knowledge. A guild master is one who has attained to a recognized standard of excellence in his craft—who is capable of producing a masterpiece. An apprentice is one who is committed to learning a craft, to working with a master and under a master's guidance.

168

The university is a special and peculiar kind of guild. It is not a club, it is not a government bureau, and it is not a church. That which binds its members together into a fairly intimate kind of association is not any common trait of mind or temperament. If there is one trait common to all, it is that of a strong bent toward individuality. Some of the best men in the university from the twelfth century onward came to it because they could not easily adjust to the demands of conformity, either superficial or essential, imposed by other professions. The university has offered a life worth living to some who could not fulfill their purposes in the military or the parochial ministry, the business world or the diplomatic corps. What the outsider might, after his first week in the academic community, interpret as a preference for comfort and licence—that informality of dress and manners sometimes a trifle overdone nowadays—has for some a sacramental significance. It may be an outward and visible sign of an inner conviction that each individual has a right to devote himself to what he considers important. The university is an association of men and women who exhibit a wide variety of opinion on the issue of what is important!

Some university people are by nature men of action— clever, practical men who would have made their ways toward greater heights of visible success than the academic world can offer. Some are by nature contemplative men and women of deep feeling and an occasional profound insight who could never have managed that modicum of organization and shrewdness that is essential to survival in business or government. Some are brilliant, quick, decisive. Others have minds built for the test of endurance in a life-long struggle with stubborn facts. Some are ambitious, driven by an appalling singleness of purpose toward a particular notion of accomplishment. Some live

169

abnormally free of anxiety, child-like in their enthusiasms, naive in their worship of colleagues and students and beautiful ideals. Some are bitter, sophisticated to a pitch of horrible tolerance of the enemies of their deepest loyalties. Others are curt and harsh with any deviation from their notion of the academic sanctities.

To people from the outside, this community must seem strange indeed; for while the relations of its members have a deeper quality than those of most occupational associations—the probing of thoughts and the weighing of insights and foresights do not allow much mental or spiritual privacy—university people are likely to be more diffident than others and apart from their colloquies, more inclined to live apart, less than ' men of affairs ' given to maintaining the social amenities. A good master is often by choice a lonely man. Certain disciplines demand, at least at times, a withdrawal which the business world could not readily either understand or tolerate. University life has rather more polarities than other professions. The role of tradition may be more obvious and yet less determinative in some things, yet in others be openly flaunted while inwardly served. The senior common room, no more than the academic board room, is a place of sweet reasonableness. A reasonable compromise is, in fact, harder to compose in faculty than in a business, not only due to the difficulties involved in dealing with issues on the level of principles—principles do of course generate more passion than do facts—but also because the university community does not value agreement as highly as do other institutions. It tends to be distrustful of consensus and inclined to get along with as little formalized agreement as possible. One insight into the university is that it is a community based upon other loyalties—only those can be members who have a prior obligation.

Most university people are religiously sensitive to their concept of the holy even though it be the most secular of idolatries. Actually traditionally religious people tend to be more tolerant, more perceptive in respect to the *sacra* of others, perhaps because they are more realistic, less judgmental than the secular apostles of righteousness. The moral fervour of the positivist can sometimes throw the puritan fundamentalist off balance.

University people are, moreover, more likely to be confidential in their sarcasms than in their evangelism, more shy and diffident below the surface of their fervours, more critical than others of their own beliefs, less sure in their inner selves of the groundlessness of their opponents' opinions. They live within closer range of deep experience. Their nerves are near to the surface of their impersonal demeanour.

Neither the community of masters nor the community of scholars is a community of saints. Both will exhibit all the human foibles, virtues and vices of any group of human beings. Nor is the university a gathered group of geniuses or of sages. To picture the ideal university as the society of the reasonable and the wise is to miss the point of what it is. Obviously the university is not ' one big family.' It may be less obvious that the university does not, or at least should not, regard itself as *the* institution of the society that is to preserve or to reshape the culture. It does not and ought not to take the place of the Church or the state or the family. The wise medieval architects planned *three* piers for their notion of society: the *Sacerdotum,* the *Imperium* and the *Studium.*

All three foundations were inter-national or, more precisely, pre-national. For the Church and the Empire, the rise of nationalism was an axe laid to their roots. For the *studium* the ideal of universalism was no less essential. The University of Paris, in its finest hour,

171

drew its glory from the foreign doctors. From Italy had come Thomas Aquinas and Bonaventura, from Belgium, Siger of Brabant, from Scotland the famous Duns, and from England, Roger Bacon and William of Occam, from Germany, Albertus Magnus. Budinszky remarks the absence of Frenchmen at Paris, though the University was for France as much a symbol of national pride as the Vatican for Italy and the Empire for Germany.[1] Salerno too had its foreign masters of world renown such as the Christian Jew, Constantinus Africanus, who brought to the study of medicine in Italy not only the learning of the great Arabic authorities but also the 'secrets' of Babylonia and India.[2] Scholarship knows no national boundaries and the members of a faculty who share a common speciality are likely to find in their studies as strong a bond as race or fatherland. The Holy Roman Empire has ceased to be, and the ecumenical Church is a hope of the future. The *studium* is the one great universal institution of the middle ages that has survived and is in reality a *commonwealth* of nations. Even the most virulent nationalism cannot ignore without peril to itself the knowledge of foreign scholars.

University scientists are far less credulous than government on the issue of science secrets. They know how short the life of such secrets is likely to be, and they are critical of strictures upon the interchange of knowledge as a national policy. Provincialism in the arts is no less dangerous. When it is nationalistic it can be pernicious, a sinister corruption of the very purpose of studies in literature and in history. It was deplored by Matthew

---

[1] *Die Universitat Paris und die Fremden an derselben in Mittelalter,* (Berlin, 1876). See also Etienne Gilson, *Medieval Universalism and Its Present Value,* (New York: Sheed and Ward, 1937). See also Ulich, *op. cit.,* p. 22.

[2] Graves, *op. cit.,* II p. 77.

Arnold a century ago as "a serious, fierce, narrow misconception of the whole relative value of one's own things and the things of others." [3]   Max Müller's observation made on the occasion of his inaugural lecture in the new chair of comparative philology at Oxford-*Wer eine religion kennt, kennt keine* (who knows one religion knows none) was a prophetic word which led those who heard him gladly to a far deeper understanding of the relations of cultures and of the element of discontinuity of the Christian religion not only in respect of other religions but also in respect of Western civilization.   Max Weber, coming to America from Germany, encouraged American studies in sociology and enabled Americans to see their own social structures from a new perspective.   Because there are now many Chinese in the faculties of American colleges and a number of sound sinologists in the faculties of Eastern universities, we can look toward a new era in Chinese studies.   The visiting foreign lecturer may stimulate and provoke.   He may be an ambassador of goodwill but what he has to offer that is of real value to the university is that which he can give only as a member of the university, as a working master doing his study in the community.   One working sinologue, drawn into the research of his colleagues and assisted by their knowledge in his own, is worth more than a fairly long procession of sinophiles bearing greetings.

The community of masters has to-day its fundamental justification in the need for colleagues both in one's own and in other fields.   Scholarship proceeds by stimulation and inspiration on the level of the masters as well as on that of the students.   The master needs those with whom he can think out loud and who can be casually critical and informally helpful just as he needs to hear the

---

[3] Quoted from Moberly, *op. cit.,* p. 60.

173

thinking out loud of others. No one who has lived in this kind of community would hazard the chance that he could for long do without it. He knows the importance of the day to day exchange of ideas, the benefit of the new angle, the suggestion of a book he had not come across, the fraternal criticism of a judgment where his own competence had blinded him to other alternatives. His colleagues are an *alma uxor,* patient with his recognized idiosyncrasies yet mindful of duties to him. To whom else can he go? These needs of the individual are understood within the community because they are shared. The community is elastic in its responses, or to use a theological term—forgiving. The unique quality of the *universitas magistrorum* is this elasticity. In it mature men of stature can disagree with each other sometimes with great vigour because they have retained the resilience of the relationship of fellow students. Here disagreement can produce deeper sympathies—not because of sentiment in the popular sense but in its best sense—sentiment for the vocation itself, for the enterprise of the community as a whole. Such a compact between men is quite different from the tolerance expressed in the motto of Saki's cat: ' sleep and let sleep '—though in a poor university the sleeping arrangements do become rather too sacred to be discussed, especially by junior staff. The medieval guilds developed a compact of free-masonry among competitors in an age rather more violent than our own. Realistically that compact established the right to compete and the basis upon which competition could be engaged in without fear of reprisal. In the living up to that compact the quality of honour emerged—the honour of guild members and the honour of the guild itself. The university has, over the centuries, prized that sense of honour—the honour of a profession and the honour of its members who, though they may be cordial enemies and destined by

174

conviction as well as temperament to disagree and to oppose one another as occasion offers, are determined to be fair. In lieu of Christian charity, which is a grace that God has not indiscriminately conferred, even upon all bishops, priests and deacons, the honour of the guild and of its members is no mean virtue.

Confucius sometimes left his disciples and wandered about by himself.

THE RELATION OF MASTERS TO SCHOLARS

No 'better head and hand' than those of Newman have joined perception and expression to describe what it is that the community of masters in respect of its own peculiar life has to offer to a community of scholars. The university he defined as a meeting of excellence and unity—a community " in which the intellect may safely range and speculate, sure to find its equal in some antagonist activity, and its judge in the tribunal of truth. It is a place where inquiry is pushed forward, and discoveries verified and perfected, and rashness rendered innocuous, and error exposed by the collision of mind with mind and knowledge with knowledge. It is the place where the professor becomes eloquent and is a missionary and a preacher, displaying his science in its most complete and most winning form, pouring it forth with the zeal of enthusiasm, and lighting up his own love of it in the breasts of his hearers. It is the place where the catechist makes good his ground as he goes, treading the truth day by day into the ready memory, and wedging and tightening it into the expanding reason. It is a place

176

which wins the admiration of the young by its celebrity, kindles the affections of the old by its associations. It is a seat of faith, an Alma Mater of the rising generation. It is this and a great deal more, and demands a somewhat better head and hand than mine to describe it well." [4]

What essentially binds together masters and scholars is their common vocation as students. The university undergraduate is an apprentice and a student, not a pupil. He should have passed his pupilage before coming to the university, having won in middle school a vision of freedom through the mastery of discipline. Otherwise the university is likely to seem to him the poorest of schools, slovenly in its serving at a meager table. He will miss the services of his middle school teachers who had so painstakingly determined just what and how much he should learn each day, and had prepared that daily fare in such nourishing morsels as were of the proper size and shape to be swallowed without chewing.

The relation of master to student is not primarily that of teacher and pupil. In the university there are older students, experienced in the art of learning, drawing with grace and ease from a large store of knowledge in their daily studies. There are younger students, so recently top form in the lower school, who must strain with all might and main to drag out some tiny particle of knowledge that could be of use in their assignments. For the freshman, the reading of every book will at first seem a rugged march through an alien and hostile country— every paper a Herculean task demanding a fierce struggle with awkward facts and cruelly elusive ideas. And in both instances the results can seem so crushingly disappointing. For every moment of exhilarating discovery —every thrill of things falling into place with a snap in

[4] *University Subjects,* p. 12.

177

the construing of a passage or the performing of an experiment—there are a thousand moments of vexed frustration to be suffered daily in the tribulations of undergraduate study. The very poise and ease of the older students—the professors and lecturers—and the ' luck ' of their results can quite naturally become for the Freshman and even for the young graduate student a pitfall into despair. Yet in fulfilling the task which has been set for him to do in the library or laboratory the Freshman is transformed from pupil to scholar. He becomes a true apprentice learning as he works with the masters at their common trade.

One of the harder lessons that is learned in the Freshman year is the discovery and acceptance of a fact which may astonish parents and laymen and even members of boards of governors or of the Education Department: the fact that it is not the exclusive purpose of a university to teach. Its prior purpose is the uniting of young students and older students in the pursuit of common studies. The *studium generale* is a *universitas magistrorum* structurally related to a *universitas scholarium*. It was never the understanding in any of the crafts that the major function of a guild master was to teach his apprentices. His prior obligation was the pursuit of his craft. Nor was it the sole duty of an apprentice to prepare himself to become a master. His prior obligation was to serve a craft and in and by his service, if he were a competent worker, he became a master craftsman. The university which considers teaching its only proper business is most likely to be a place where there will be very little learning and very little justification for learning. The younger students must be encouraged to develop from the outset of their college careers both the skills of independent study and the responsibility for discipline and learning by which

178

alone they can become full-fledged members of the university community. Without these skills and without that responsibility they can go to the best university, and, though they are successfully carried over the course by some well meaning tutor, they will have received nothing more than a post-secondary education. The responsible student who has by his own efforts in a poor college converted middle school perseverance into the power of a competent scholar will have received the best education that a good university can offer.

A second astonishing fact about the community of masters and scholars is that it is not its purpose to mould character. The very idea is appalling! This does not mean that the university is irresponsible or that it is not concerned about the character of its members. But it is sheer fiction or self-deception to suppose that every master is or should be personally concerned with the life and character of each of his students. That would be pernicious nonsense. He is concerned about working with his students in the study of a subject. He should be concerned with the educating of minds as well. But if he got involved in the life of every student, he would be of limited usefulness as a member of the university. Of course a master is a human being, and usually he is more intelligently sensitive than the average businessman or the average government official to the personal side of relationships. His humanity is in a real sense a function of his scholarship and of his vocation to study and to share in a community of learning, but counseling is not his proper function. Worthwhile human relationships are built upon common interests, and in the pursuit of these the master often proves to be one of the most effective guides in many aspects of the younger student's development as a person as well as in his career as a scholar. But the master does not set out to be a foster

179

parent. It is the university, not an individual professor, that is properly addressed as *Alma Mater*. Further, the master's essential orientation is to the community—the *universitas magistrorum et scholarium*—and not to individual students. He may rightly consider that this commitment is a means toward the end of a ministry to the young, and he will probably serve them better because his prior obligation is to the university as a whole.

Some subjects have their place in the university because they relate to the interior resources of the spirit and to those aspects of man's environment that are of social and religious significance. In the exploration of these subjects lies the chief duty of the university with respect to the training and the nurture of the spirit. The Church and the home have their special ministries. The university is not the extension or the auxiliary of either in terms of their proper ends and of their proper methods. The university has its own proper end and its own appropriate method and it is in respect of these that its best service is rendered.

Since its earliest days when both masters and scholars were in clerical orders the university has sought to allow the greatest possible freedom in the deportment of its members consistent with the demands of getting on with the job. It has always accounted itself a society of adults whose behaviour was a function of the discipline and the thrill of scholarship. From all that we can gather, university life in the middle ages was rather more colourful than it is to-day. It appears to have been expected that the high spirits and aristocratic feelings essential to the good scholar would sometimes find expression in non-academic ways. University authorities were then, as now, mindful of the value of property so that at Oxford and Cambridge in the thirteenth century, just as at Chung Chi to-day, the few regulations imposed upon the students were in the interest of safeguarding funds and buildings from abuse. As at Chung Chi now, so also at King's College, Cambridge, in the middle ages, there was a statute forbidding scholars to share their lodgings with lower animals. Unlike Chung Chi, King's College found it necessary to impose this regulation upon its fellows and chaplain as well. The imagination of the medieval Cantabrigian led the college to enumerate a larger list of pets and pests than would occur to the members of a residence committee to-day. Expressly forbidden are ferrets, falcons and hawks. "Nor shall they in any wise have or hold within our Royal College singly or in common, any ape, bear, fox, stag, hind, fawn, or badger, or any other such ravening or unaccustomed or strange beast." [5] The reason given is that since the fellows and students are enjoying the benefaction of the King the keeping of animals would be a misuse of food and funds. But there is also a Scriptural (apocryphal) injunction cited in support of the statute: "Woe unto those in sin, that take their diversion with the birds of the air." [6] Cambridge clerics were inclined to regard as purely frivolous any sport which was not attended with the serious concern of those who had made a wager. The king, however, was unwilling to trust his gifts to the college to the hands of such inexpert gamblers. Hence a second statute appeared to safeguard the King's monies: "We forbid and expressly interdict the games of dice, hazard, ball and all noxious inordinate unlawful and unhonest sports . . . which afford a cause or occasion for loss of coin, money, goods, or chattels of any kind

---

[5] Heywood and Wright, *The Ancient Laws of the Fifteenth Century for King's College, Cambridge.* See also A. A. Leigh, *King's College*, pp. 7-16. and G. G. Coulton, *Social Life in Britain from the Conquest to the Reformation* (Cambridge: University Press), p. 73.

[6] *Baruch* 3:17.

whatsoever whether within King's College or elsewhere within the University." [7]

On the matter of college property the regulations were similarly severe. " It is our will firmly and expressly to prohibit all of the aforesaid fellows (graduate students) etc. (scholars and the chaplain) from shooting arrows or casting or hurling stones, javelins, wood, clods, or anything whatsoever, and from making or practising singly or in common, in person or by deputy, any games or castings whatsoever within the aforesaid King's College or its enclosed precincts or gardens, whereby directly or indirectly, the Chapel or Hall or other buildings or edifices of our said College may suffer any sort of harm or loss in the glass thereof." [8] Many a cassock both at Oxford and at Cambridge covered lively limbs for one statute fairly commonly adopted by the Colleges inhibits the scholars and in some instances even the chaplain from engaging in dancing or wrestling or other incautious and inordinate sports within the Chapel.[9] Even ball playing in the chapels at King's, Cambridge, and New College, Oxford, is prohibited. But in both instances the statutes are explicit in the reasons given. No puritanical piety (Puritans had not been invented by then) is involved. The reason is a sound and solid concern for property so carefully itemized that one suspects the list of things thereby endangered was supported by instances: walls, stalls, paintings, glass windows and carved reredos.[10]

---

[7] Leigh, *op. cit.* In most instances these statutes had their origin in the older continental universities. This particular rule at King's College was in imitation of the earlier prohibition against 'unhonest games' at New College, Oxford.

[8] *Ibid.*

[9] Again the statute is a copy of one at New College which has been traced to 'the stern Bishop of Winchester,' William of Wykeham. See Rashdall iii 421. and Coulton, *Medieval Panorama*, p. 405.

[10] Coulton, *op. cit.,* p. 405. See Rashdall III 422, and *New College Statutes,* p. 100.

One rule that appears on the statutes of all colleges and on those of the universities as well enforces the keeping of *curfew*. The word is Norman, and was in use both in Middle English and Old French (M. E. *courfew;* O. F. *cuevrefu*) combining *covrir* (to cover) and *feu* (fire) for the covering or extinguishing of the fires at night. When the hearth fires were covered in the common room, fellows and students were ordered to bed. In part the regulation was in the interest of saving fuel. Only on holy days did benefactors allow for an additional hour or two of fire and candlelight, " in honour of God or His Mother or of some other saint." [11] On such festival days " a decent tarrying in Hall for recreation's sake " was permitted with the provision that " songs be sung and chronicles of the realms and wonders of this world, consistent with clerical propriety," be recited. However such singing and reciting were to be " in no spirit of levity." In these statutes we can see a major difference between university life to-day and the daily routine particularly of scholars that continued without substantial change from the twelfth century well into the nineteenth. The modern student depends upon the long stretch from dinner to mid-night or beyond for his serious study. Neither the medieval scholar nor the eighteenth century Oxonian spent much time in the library. For both undergraduate study was limited to a few works either dictated in lectures or, after the invention of printing, put into their hands. There is little evidence of interest in university libraries in England until the seventeenth century. The Bodleian was founded at Oxford with less than 2,000 volumes in 1602. The earliest list of the University Library at Cambridge, complied in 1425, numbers only 52 volumes. In the latter part of the

---

[11] *Ibid.* 408. See *New College Statutes* p. 42.

eighteenth century—nearly six hundred years after the founding of the University—it contained less than half the number of volumes in the Chung Chi College Library at its tenth anniversary.[12] The largest of the medieval libraries, the Sorbonne, in 1338 listed 1,700 books and pamphlets.[13] A limited number of these could be circulated among the fellows and masters. Scholars were in some instances permitted to examine books chained to the reading desk.

These few statistics point up a major difference in student life between the old universities in which learning was confined for the most part to vocal communication at set hours of the day and the modern university where the reference rooms and the circulating libraries constitute the heart of the *studium*. Some light is thus shed on the importance of the early curfew statutes. They were directed against the night-walkers—those who stalked abroad in the town intent on mischief. The discipline was not harsh and a far wider range of youthful indiscretion was allowed for centuries to the clerical scholar than is permitted to the secular ' young man about town ' in the modern university. It was, as the book of Common Prayer so neatly puts it, a ' superfluity of naughtiness ' that was discouraged. Frivolities within the university were indulgently regarded, but stalking abroad put a greater strain on the non-academic tolerance than it could reasonable be expected to bear. Hence with due regard to the tender conscience of townspeople, an Oxford student was given twice the fine for night-walking than for shooting a proctor with an arrow within the university premises.[14] Coulton remarks the reasonableness of the authorities at Bologna who charged a student who used his sword in

---

[12] See article "Libraries" by H. R. Tedder *EB* 11th.
[13] Rashdall I p. 491 (Powicke's *additional note*).
[14] Quoted from Coulton, *op. cit.,* p. 401.

the classroom a fine based on a fair return for missing that part of the lecture which the master was rendered incapable of delivering.[15]

There is a third category of university statute which appears from the evidence to have been both last and least: the enjoining upon scholars of a due regard for the needs of others. One instance from King's College, Cambridge, is typical: " We strictly and expressly ordain that no dweller in the aforesaid upper rooms . . . whether in washing his head or hands or feet or any other thing, or in any manner whatsoever, do spill water, wine, beer, or any other liquor whereby those in the lower rooms may be grieved in their persons, goods or chattels, or in any way molested." [16]

Sitting here in Ma Liu Shui with the ancient statutes in Latin of King's College, Cambridge and one mimeographed foolscap of ten " Dormitory Rules " of Chung Chi College in Chinese side by side before me, I am impressed by two facts. There has been very little change in university disciplinary regulations from the twelfth century to the middle of the twentieth. In both documents the same concerns are expressed: 1. that the funds of the college shall not by impropriety or negligence be diverted from its central aims, 2. that property shall be respected, and 3. that students shall not misuse their time, and that they shall, on a minimum basis, be mindful of the needs of others. In general the ancient statutes are more specific and legal, revealing a response to particular instances of damage or complaint. With less than three hundred characters the Chung Chi ' Rules ' cover the same general issues for which the King's College statutes require many

---

[15] Quoted by Coulton from C. H. Haskins, *Studies in Medieval Culture.*

[16] Coulton, *Med. Pan.,* p. 407.

pages. The other fact is the more important. The regulations derive from the special business of the university. There is the implicit recognition of the common vocation to a life of learning of masters and scholars. Implicit also is the reluctance to go beyond what is absolutely necessary in proscriptions. Had certain problems not arisen there would probably not have been any rules at all. Almost explicitly the university renounces any attempt to invade the privacy of its members. On the matter of individual rights, the ancient statutes are substantial and detailed. Neither masters nor students shall be accountable to the conventions of the town. They are not to be subject to civil courts. Their naughtiness, even when in superfluity, shall be judged by the university in terms of its special character and function, or the offenders will be cited to the ecclesiastical courts where provocation and intention were given greater weight than the indictment itself. The point was well taken and should to-day, when occasion demands, be reaffirmed. University discipline is founded in the disciplines—in the studies—of the university. It cannot be something imposed from the outside or something arbitrary with respect to the university's inner life. Individual discipline is a function of academic discipline. In the navy a taut ship is a happy ship. A strict command will be accepted, and afterwards applauded by the men, if the enforcement of duties is clearly in the interest of a more efficient operation—a more effective unit. If, on the other hand, the discipline reflects the personal preferences of the old man on matters that are indifferent to the ship as a fighting unit, even though he has adopted them from Lord Chesterfield or from his favorite cinema star, it is an imposition upon the ship of purposes which are not its own. A taut university is a happy community but its discipline must be that of the standard of excellence expected in the studies of its masters and its scholars.

Where the craft of learning differs from that of manufacture is in the nature of its masterpieces. The carpenter and blacksmith do their work for others and their creations are valued by their patrons in terms of utility and beauty in the service of something distinct from the craft itself. A table must be well designed and carefully fashioned to serve the special purpose of the man who has commissioned the master to make it. It must belong to the room where it will stand, and its use will depend upon the habits of that household. The work of a university master is in the service of his craft itself. It is for local consumption—for the benefit of the guild, the community of masters and scholars. In this sense it is the business of the university to teach, or, more precisely, to provide the conditions under which the work of the masters of the several faculties can be communicated and thus appropriated by the guild as a whole.

Of the several forms of communication, the most common and the oldest in the university, is the lecture. Unfortunately, the word appropriately describes too much of the ' teaching ' in the university. It is from the Latin *legere* (to read) and was first used in the *studium generale* to designate a function of masters in an age when the essential works were available only through oral communication. Hand written copies of standard texts were rare and costly, and had, therefore, to be read to the students. Even then the better masters added commentary, and simulated a discussion with the author by raising and answering questions on his treatment of the subject. An instructive fragment from Odofredus who came to Bolonga in 1228 as a master of civil law indicates an early departure from the lecture as simply the dictation of a text. " First I shall give you summaries of each

187

topic before I proceed to the text; secondly I shall give you as clear and explicit a statement as I can of the purport of each Law (included in the topic); thirdly, I shall read the text with a view to correcting it; fourthly, I shall briefly repeat the contents of the Law (to be extracted from the passage), and any distinctions or subtle and useful problems arising out of the Law with their solutions." [17]

There is evidence in early statutes that some lectures were simply a reading of required texts whereby the students could have in their own hands a copy in the form of abbreviated lecture notes. In some statutes a rapid or indistinct reading is forbidden.[18] The master is to be supplied a chair and a reading desk (lectern) of appropriate size for supporting his opened lecture book and of a suitable height for reading from it. A very early division of lectures into *ordinary* and *extraordinary* (Bologna) or *ordinary* and *cursory* (Paris)[19] may have in part taken into account two kinds of procedure: 1. the reading of essential texts at a pace suitable for dictation, and 2. a summary of important sections or of detailed material with commentary. At Bologna, however, by the middle of the thirteenth century masters were inhibited from reading at dictation pace during the ordinary lecture.[20] It may be assumed that here the students were able, through their control of the stationers (where copying was done) and of the booksellers who also lent out copies on an annual rent, to acquire the written text, and, therefore, resented the expenditure of lecture fees for the

---

[17] The proposal was preserved in the lecture notes of his student, Petrus Peregrossi, afterwards master at Orleans. Rashdall's source was von Savigny, the 19th century German historian of jurisprudence. See Rashdall I 218 and notes 1 and 3.

[18] See Graves II p. 91.

[19] See Rashdall I pp. 205-207.

[20] *Ibid.* 219 (*Bologna Stat.* p. 105.)

dictation of manuscripts otherwise available. Paris as a *universitas magistrorum* soon had its own statute on lecturing.[21] Here the intention is to prevent the student from taking full notes—to prevent the publication and distribution of the masters' property. A later statute indicates the reaction of the students: scholars who throw stones at masters who speak too rapidly are to be fined.[22]

Extraordinary lectures were given in the afternoon and could be offered by the junior masters. They dealt either with a review of important sections of the essential texts expounded in the ordinary lectures of the morning by the doctors (professors) or with the lesser or advanced texts—what is now called collateral reading. Presumably such books would be more difficult to obtain and hence the students at Bologna were willing to have them read at dictation pace. For the most part, however, by the middle of the thirteenth century the extraordinary lecture had become less formal. Questions were encouraged from the student, and the master regarded the session as affording a wider range for special problems and interests. Generally, medieval university texts were more provocative than the standard books to-day. They were written in the form of dialogue directed toward the solution of problems. Lombard's famous *Sentences* and the *Summae* of Thomas Aquinas are like the record of the debate on important issues of the great masters with a final determination by the author himself. They arose from the classroom—the exchange of questions between masters and scholars and the meeting of live options in the debates between the doctors.[23] The morning *lectio*, given as an exposition of the text, was a kind of dialogue on questions raised by the author together with those of

---

[21] See Curtis, *op. cit.* p. 106.
[22] *Ibid.*
[23] Rashdall I pp. 492 f.

189

the master and his scholars regarding the author's answers. It was in the case of Thomas, and later of Luther, a lively proceeding in which something really was happening. During these 'lectures' the doctors' own books were being written. Many of the passages in Luther's comments on Aristotle (his earliest lectures) and in his exegesis of the *Psalms, Galatians* and *Romans* reflect the excitement of lively debate—the thrust and parrying of a skilled and brilliant mind with the questions and opinions of eager students. Aquinas, though he lacked the wit and pithy style of Luther, was not, in his grave earnestness, a dull lecturer, ponderously weighing the merit of the authorities. "The end of philosophy," he taught his students, "is not to know what men have thought, but what is the truth of things." [24]

The more recent studies of the early universities point up the larger place that was given to discussion and dialogue than Rashdall had seen in the documents at his disposal.[25] Since there were few books to read, much of the time of masters and scholars was spent in discussion. There were weekly hours given to the *Repetitiones* (*Resumpciones* in the German *studium*) when the bachelors questioned the scholars on issues rising out of recent lectures or dealt with the questions of the scholars themselves on passages of the text and the expositions of the doctors. The great days in the community were those of the formal *Disputatio.* Several days in advance, the question for the debate was circulated throughout the faculty. The debate itself occupied two days. On the first a bachelor was appointed to receive the various contributions of scholars and masters. It was his function, during the day in the presence of the participants, to

---

[24] Commentary on *De caelo* bk. i lect. 22.
[25] See Powicke's *additional note* on Rashdall I v (pp. 490 ff.).

arrange these into a logical sequence of questions, comments, and objections. At the final session of the first day the bachelor (assisted by his master) presented a brief for the affirmative answer to the question or the thesis implied in the question. On the second day there was the determination by the Master who was obliged to defend his position against the questions of the whole faculty.[26] The Paris statutes required the masters to hold disputations during each term. Thomas Aquinas is reported to have given two mornings a week to the disputations of the various masters as well as those which he held himself. Even during his most creative period, when his chief duty was the writing of his *Summae*, he held a disputation at least twice a month.[27]

Student disputations were scheduled on holidays of which the medieval calander had rather more than were needed. In addition to these every Thursday was a holiday in the university. Student disputations, presided over by the master with his bachelors, were quite as common as lectures. Twice a year—during Advent and Lent—the penitential days were enlivened by a kind of free-for-all debate, the *Disputationes quodibetales,* which served as an open forum on whatever questions anyone was pleased to ask.[28] A manuscript (Assisi MS 158) lists over two hundred such questions that were disputed by sixty-five Oxford scholars during the ninth decade of the thirteenth century.[29] It now appears that repetitions and disputations were the real work of masters and scholars, the masterpieces of their craft. In them doctors and bachelors and scholars worked together. The skill of the scholar—his competence as a candidate for the

---

[26] See Curtis, *op. cit.,* pp. 107 ff.
[27] Rashdall I p. 219.
[28] See Curtis, *op cit.,* p. 109.
[29] Rashdall I 495.

baccaluareate—was measured by this daily working at the special craft of his faculty. Bachelors demonstrated in their daily performance, both as arbiters in the scholars' disputations and as participants in the masters' debates, their progress toward the goal of becoming master-craftsmen themselves. The heavy-weight bouts between the doctors kept open the relation of challenger and champion and encouraged the conviction that, on the highest levels of learning, new issues were constantly emerging and old questions were never answered with finality. Unfortunately, the attempt to preserve the best often leads to something rather bad. Whitehead would remark that this is as true of great ideas as it is of big fish. In the latter part of the thirteenth century there began to appear abstracts of the great debates and syllabuses of the best questions. The masters became instructors and the scholars were degraded to pupils. The disputations were reduced to a catechetical recital of set questions and expected answers. One of the symptoms of a dying university is the shift of emphasis away from the crafts-manship of lively discussion among the masters, and between masters and scholars, to the examination of pupils.

For well over a century the first universities maintained the ideal of the working community of masters and apprentices with the bachelor serving as journeyman. The scholar by his participation in the daily life of the guild gained the working competence of the journeyman, and the bachelor, through his daily tasks, was prepared for the making of a masterpiece as the proof of his fitness for full membership in the guild. German universities still retain the tie with the medieval guild by the use of the term *Arbeit* (Work) for the graduate masterpiece—the doctoral dissertation.[30] As soon as examinations,

---

[30] Graves II p. 92 n. 2.

external to the daily working of apprentices and journey-
men, became important, a host of new statutes began to
appear. The scholar must pledge that he will not seek
to compromise the rector by unsuitable gifts or overlavish
entertainment.[31] On the other hand, he will be assured
that the passages he is asked to construe and exegete will
be taken from a fairly small list, and that his final coaching
will have been to the point.[32] Following the lecture he
must give upon the two passages chosen, he must submit
to questions by his master's colleagues. They are by
statute required to swear that they had not previously
advised the candidate of their questions.[33] At Bologna
there was a statute in defense of the candidate at this
" rigorous and tremendous examination." The examiner
is required to treat him " as his own son." [34] At Leipzig
it was necessary to add a special statute inhibiting the
vice-chancellor and the dean from complying with the
student's request for a preview of the examination questions.[35] It was also necessary there and elsewhere to
secure a solemn oath from the candidate of safe passage
for the examiners from the hall to their homes. Many
continental universities were obliged to protect their masters
by a secret ballot in the decision of the fate of candidates,
while Oxford and Cambridge in modern times protected
both masters and scholars with the English pleasantry of
the pass degree.

The discussion of lectures, tutorials or disputations and
examinations belongs within the larger and theoretical
notion of the university as a community of masters and
scholars rather than to the more particular and practical

---

[31] Rashdall I p. 224.
[32] *Ibid*. p. 225 see also notes 2 and 3.
[33] *Ibid*. p. 226.
[34] *Ibid*.
[35] *Ibid*. p. 469.

concept of teaching. These activities are the work of the community—the corporate action of masters and scholars in the service of a common craft. University action cannot be divided into research and teaching nor can the community be divided into teachers and pupils. The life of the student, whether he be the Doctor *Invincibilis, Mirabilis* or *Angelicus* or the scholar *Bejaunus,* involves investigation and reflection and in both of these communication is essential. Research grows out of teaching and teaching is the communication of research. The seamless robe of learning should not be rent in respect of its activity anymore than in respect of its knowledge. This is, I believe, the deeper implication in the wisdom of Wang Yang-ming (Wang Shou-jen, 1472-1528) which David Nivison has summarized as an insistence upon the truth " that there is no knowing, to be recognized as such, which does not involve some kind of doing . . . that knowing must actually be doing. . . ." [36] It is not, I think, an impiety to believe that neither Dewey nor contemporary educational theory on the mainland of China need be the authoritative interpreter of this insight. There is another sense in which knowledge (*chih* 知) and action (*hsing* 行) may be integrally united in the life of the university. Thought and action may be related to acquisition and reflection and also to that dialogue " starkly between the self and reality—the scholar in his study, the monk in his cell, the scientist in his laboratory . . . the poet under his tree " [37]—and to the sharing of these dialogues— the sharing of the insight and foresight of the scholar, the saint, the scientist and the poet. Action is the meeting

---

[36] David Nivison, "The Problem of 'Knowledge' and 'Action' in Chinese Thought Since Wang Yang-ming" in A. F. Wright, *Studies in Chinese Thought* (Chicago: University of Chicago Press, 1953), p. 112.

[37] G. N. Shuster in *Education in the Age of Science,* p. 26.

of minds and thought is action in that starkly personal vigil which scholar as well as master must keep over his own speciality. This is the proper ' action ' of the university. Lectures, tutorials and examinations are forms or modes of this action; they are *expressions* of the inner life, the inner action, of the university as a community of masters and scholars. But it is from *this inner life* that the university derives its power. This is the essential *being* of the university. . . . It is not a programme of studies, not a calendar or a corpus of syllabi; certainly, it is not an examination syndicate. These emphases all presuppose that the community is secondary to some other structure and to some other function. They presuppose that the master is a professional teacher whose excellence is in his skill in depositing knowledge as a definite quantity to the account of a pupil, and they presuppose the passive pupil who is to sit and wait for knowledge to be brought to him—a pupil who is a customer not an apprentice— who is a client of Cook's on a conducted tour, not a *viator indefessus,* a rugged pilgrim and an adventurous explorer.[38]

---

[38] This was a basic problem in Chinese education with a few notable exceptions of brief reforms and uncommon individuals. It has become an increasingly crucial problem in contemporary Western education. Certainly there is no justification for the dictated lecture today. Such lectures should be dictated to a stenographer not to a class. Dr. Purcell *op. cit.* and H. G. Creel, *Confucius and the Chinese Way* have collected some classical examples of the passive pupil in Chinese education. "Mo Tzu, born just after Confucius died, declared: "My words are an adequate guide. To abandon my words and think for oneself is like throwing away the harvest and merely picking up grains. Trying to refute my words with one's own words is like throwing eggs at a boulder. . ." From Hsun Tzu (Confucian scholar at the turn to the 3rd century B.C.): "Not to consider right the ways of one's teacher, but to prefer one's own ways, may be compared to using a blind man to distinguish colours, or a deaf man to distinguish sounds; there is no way to get rid of confusion and error." In contrast to these statements and similar ones to be found in Purcell, pp. 17-40, is Creel's description of Confucius as *The Teacher:* "His method of instruction

The *universitas scholarium* pattern failed at Salerno and elsewhere in southern Europe because it tended to become a collective bargaining syndicate, seeking to put the responsibility for a diploma upon the masters whom it regarded as its employees. It hired authorities to lecture—to read and expound the texts that would be the basis of the examination. The college of doctors at Bologna failed because it came to regard itself as a collective bargaining union providing expert coaching for examinations. It is the old issue between Socrates and some of the lesser Sophists—the old issue between Confucius and the professional tutors.[39] The university is a community of masters and scholars, a guild of masters and apprentices both committed to a craft, not a business with a management union and an employee's union. Too great an emphasis upon the recently devised British examination system can lead to a revival of the Salerno pattern and the neglect of the Paris pattern that made Oxford and Cambridge world renowned centers of learning justly proud of their masters *and their students*. Schools that put too great an emphasis upon syllabus, and the kind of examination based thereon, deserve the complaint of the pupils' union when something that may not come up in the examinations is inserted into lectures or tutorials: " But we don't have to know that. That isn't in the syllabus." Well, this just grievance will certainly keep

---

seems to have been completely informal. There is no mention of classes or set examinations. Instead, Confucius conversed with one or a few of his disciples at a time, sometimes talking himself and sometimes questioning them. Books, it would seem, they were expected to study for themselves, but the master suggested that they should study and he discussed particular passages with them . . . (This) closely resembles the tutorial method that is employed in some of the best colleges and universities." (p. 78). For a vivid description of the passive pupil in the West see J. L. Vives quoted in Ulich, *op. cit.*, p. 26.

[39] See Creel, *op. cit.*, pp. 75 ff.

the masters to the business of teaching. The idea of a university that lies behind it will keep the scholars to the business of preparing for exams. And it will validate the observation of G. M. Young that in the crucial years of the last decades of the nineteenth century, British education marched " through the gateway of the competitive examination out into the Waste Land of experts, each knowing so much about so little that he can neither be contradicted nor is worth contradicting." [40] As a result we have not only in middle school but in the university to face the horrible excesses of the little monsters with ' overstimulated memories ' and the bigger little monsters with their ' superficial omniscience.'

Wherever there is a university that is truly a community of masters and scholars, it will be a lively society. Certainly, it will not be dull. The impression one gets in the modern university is that of the appalling dullness of its prophylactic routine. Medieval university life was colourful and vivid. Throughout most of the thirteenth century, the scholars could not help but be infected by the virile life of the masters. It is a strange liberalism and a strange science that have reduced our students to bargain hunters and our professors to organization men. To a considerable degree the university has become the servant of the state and of industry and even of the church —accepting the practical standards and the expeditious demands they have pressed upon it. And in this the great price has not been so much a curtailment of freedom, nor the imposition of a point of view, but the acceptance of the horrible dullness that such service entails. All three tend to ignore the essential life of the university as

---

[40] *Victorian England: Portrait of an Age,* (London: Oxford University Press, 1936), p. 160. See Culler, *op. cit.,* pp. 192 f. for a perceptive comment. Professor Whitehead was more devastating. See his *Aims of Education* pp. 21, 25, 26.

197

a community fulfilling its own proper function. All three tend to evaluate it as a tool-producing industry that is to be encouraged and favoured in so far as its products are efficiently turned out to their specifications. In becoming an industry, the university ceases to be a community. It becomes a teaching institute. Such a service the university cannot accept. Like the guilds out of which it grew, the university must serve society in its own way. As a guild it is concerned to guide a scholar toward competence in a vocation but not for a post. Education, simply for the enjoyment of life or even for the art of living, whether secured in Peking or Athens or at Oxford, runs counter to the theology of the guild that life is vocation and that every calling, performed with candour and competence is a service to God so long as it is a service to man. The ideal of the university as a community and of its service as a training for vocation may create tensions that are real as well as apparent. These tensions press, however, towards a healthy realism in the estimate of all human institutions and hence of universities as well. Undergraduate education opens a door. It points out marks of bearing in the landscape that beckon the young traveller. It may provide a map of the ways that lead forth to the hills beyond. If it is a healthy community it will guide the student along the first stages of his journey, past the first blind alleys, to the first real branching of the ways. If as a working member of the guild the student has learned how to study, if he has gone far enough so that he can judge distances with fair accuracy and reckon his own strengths with prudence and his limitations with patience, he has received the better part of that which a university can give.[41] He is fit for vocation. So long as he is a member of the community, sharing its common

---

[41] See N. Fehl, "Religion in the University" pp. 4 ff.

tasks, his masters have a duty to demand that he be a serious and faithful apprentice—faithful to the craft of learning. And of his masters he has the right to ask that, beyond all else that they or others may deem important, the life of the community on all levels of its endeavour shall be vivid in its proper passion and in its peculiar reverence.

A Government official attempted to pull down the tree under which Confucius was teaching.

CHAPTER VII

TOWN AND GOWN—THE UNIVERSITY AND THE COMMUNITY

THE EARLY CONFLICTS OF TOWN AND GOWN

RELATIONS between town and gown have superficially improved over the past five hundred years, especially at Oxford and Cambridge. Since 1419, at least in the last few centuries, there is no record of the Mayor of Cambridge challenging the Chancellor of the University to a 'hand to hand' encounter to be fought out publicly in the church.[1] One reason may have been the prowess of the Cambridge chancellors. We hear from the middle years of the sixteenth century of one Cantab worthy, Dr. Crayforde, who was twice Vice-Chancellor and had won the respect of his colleagues for being as sound a pugilist as he was an administrator. He settled one dispute by cutting off the hand—and therewith the strongest argument —of one opponent, and in the university senate he was

---

[1] Coulton, *op. cit.,* p. 402.

200

able to secure consensus through the direct approach of throwing dissident parties out of the room ' by main force.' [2] The early history of relations between the community and the English university is the record of an increasing respect of the town for the gown, probably more on the score of action than of thought. High Street in Oxford enjoys the distinction of being one of the major battlefields of Europe. Rashdall was of the opinion that more blood ' per square yard ' had been spilled here than at the scene of several justly celebrated battles between the professional armies of warring kings.[3] In many of the skirmishes on High Street the masters and scholars acquitted themselves with greater honour than could be accorded to their studies. The Oxford Coroner's Register of 1314 describes in some detail an inter-mural contest on an otherwise dull Saturday afternoon when the Northern clerks (clergy) took on both the Southern and Western clerks. The young clerical gentlemen " came to St. John's Street and Grope Lane with swords, bucklers, bows, arrows and other arms, and there they fought together; and in that conflict Robert de Bridlington, Adam de Alderbeck, Richard de Louthy and Richard de Holwell stood together in a certain soler in Gutter Hall, situate in St. John's Street, shooting down through a window into Grope Lane: and there the said Robert de Bridlington, with a small arrow, smote the aforesaid Henry of Holy Isle and wounded him hard by the throat, on the left side in front; and the wound was of the breadth of one inch, and in depth even unto the heart; and thus he slew him. . . . And in the same conflict John de Benton came with a falchion into Grope Lane and gave David de Kirkby a blow on the back of the head, six inches in

---

[2] *Ibid*. 403.

[3] Rashdall, III p. 96.

length, and in depth even unto the brain. At which same time came Willian de la Hyde and smote the aforesaid David with a sword across his right knee and leg; and at the same time came Willian de Astley and smote the said David under the left arm with a misericorde, and thus slew him." The Northern ' nation ' at Oxford was also in the thirteenth century a lively bunch of lads who fought fiercely for their side against the Irish and the Welsh. During that century three major engagements were concluded with treaties and in one instance, among the survivors, with the ' kiss of peace.' [4]

The town at times chose to regard these incidents as the kind of behaviour to be expected of scholars. Attempts to discipline the young gentlemen by civil procedures were vigorously opposed by the university. Indeed more and more the university authorities either in their role as special servants of the Church or on the grounds of their status as college officials starkly restricted the powers of the town over masters and scholars and even took over many of the prerogatives of the government of the town. Early in the fourteenth century the Chancellor of Oxford won legal jurisdiction over the town prostitutes with the authority to imprison any whom he deemed to be of unsuitable character.[5] The most memorable of all incidents in the long history of the contest of town and gown has, since Wood's famous history of the University of Oxford, been known as ' The Great Slaughter.' It started with an incident in Swyndlestock's Tavern on the Feast of St. Scholastica the Virgin (February 10th) in the year 1355. Several of the clerical scholars had repaired there, no doubt to do honour to St. Benedict's worthy sister who ironically is best known as the saint to be

---

[4] H.E. Salter, *The Mediaeval Archives of the University of Oxford,* (Oxford Historical Society, 1917) I p. 28.

[5] Rashdall, III p. 91 fn. 5.

invoked against storms. They called for wine but when it was brought, 'disliking it, as it should seem,' they exchanged 'snappish words' with John de Croydon, the vintner. From snappish, the language degenerated to 'stubborn and saucy,' and in the heat of this lively disputation the young clerical gentlemen were led to throw the wine jug at the vintner's head. By one means or other the wine in question went to the heads of both townsmen and gownsmen. Thus inspired the vintner and his friends rang the alarm bell of the town church of St. Martin. Soon thereafter the chancellor ordered St. Mary's bell to be rung to call up the stout English archers in the defense of the masters and scholars. Blows and arrows were exchanged until sundown, and if we must blame de Croydon's wine for the start of the quarrel we must praise that of whoever refreshed the thirsty combatants who fought so valiantly that day without a mortal wound being suffered by either side. On the next day, however, eighty armed townsmen hid themselves in St. Giles's Church till after dinner (i.e. until about 11.00 A.M.) and then fell upon the students as they came out from halls for their daily exercise on Beaumont fields. This was the day of slaughter. Scholars were cut down by arrows on the fields and in the streets. Their hostels were invaded, pillaged and burned. Several halls were destroyed. Peasants from the countryside had joined with the townsmen in a furious mob that slew clergy clinging to the altars of the churches, tore off the tonsored scalps of chaplains, and even defaced precious books. The judicious Rashdall could not read the record of that day immune to its drama. He rises almost to the rhetoric of his source (the racy Wood) in his account of the aftermath : [6]

---

[6] From Anthony Wood, *Annals,* I pp. 456 ff.

"But now comes the day of vengeance. For more than a year the town lies under an interdict, which is proclaimed in all the churches with the accustomed paraphernalia of bells, curses, and extinguished tapers. . . . The mayor and bailiffs are sent to . . . prison . . . Both university and town surrender all their privileges and charters . . . into the King's hands . . . On every anniversary of St. Scholastica's day the mayor, bailiffs, and sixty burghers were to appear in St. Mary's Church at the celebration of Mass with deacon and subdeacon (at their own expense) for the souls of the slaughtered scholars, and at the offertory each one of them was to offer one penny at the high altar."

With two further official acts the incident fades into history: an Oxford statute announces severe punishment of any scholar who molests the townsmen in procession to St. Mary's for the penitential Mass on the Feast of St. Scholastica: five hundred years later (in the last century) the University of Oxford magnanimously allowed the townsmen to be dispensed from the penitential procession and the annual penny.

Behind these raucous struggles a kind of prescience was at work, an awareness that an issue more important than the incidents themselves was at stake—the growing certainty that the university was a new kind of community and that its special responsibility required a special license, a detachment from town and crown and mitre, a functional independence that would allow it to find its own way toward its true aims and their fulfilment. For good or ill the chancellor and proctors and masters were convinced that the university had to solve its problems itself, that it could not fulfill its function either as a ward of the town or as a separate yet similar organization on the level of a partner to the town.

There was another struggle which Oxford joined, not fully clear in its own mind as to the bearing of the surface issues but guided rather by an intuition abetted by several quite practical and personal motives. English education in the middle ages was almost exclusively the work of the Church. The schools were an organ of the Church and the laws regulating studies and the status of teachers and pupils were derived from canon law—the law of the Church. For the universities the first struggle was against the close supervision of the bishop. Oxford and Cambridge were determined to follow the Paris pattern of the *studium generale,* i.e. a school to which masters and students from all over the Church and the Empire could come and from which graduates could go with a diploma recognized throughout Christendom. These were the major distinctions between the cathedral school and the university. The cathedral schools were institutions of the diocese, created to serve the diocese in terms of its clerical needs. They were directly responsible to the bishop. The universities were not diocesan schools—they were schools of the whole Church and of the whole Empire. Both the pope and the English archbishop supported Oxford in its resistance to diocesan control. The king was prepared to protect the universities from papal interference and the pope from time to time responded to the masters' plea for a wider range of freedom for Oxford under the crown and the archbishop. The main struggle of the school with the Church arose from the exercise of the authority of the archbishop as visitor. The authority was constitutional and was never questioned on the theoretical level by the university, and so long as it was never exercised in conflict with the interests and integrity of the university, there was little concern over its theoretical implications. In 1277 Archbishop Kilwardby visited Oxford and condemned several doctrines which he found being taught by the Dominican masters. One of these was grammatical. Kilwardby forbade the assertion that *Ego currit* was good Latin. He pronounced also upon certain propositions in logic and philosophy. There is no record of any attempt on the part of the Oxford masters to reject or even to question the Primate's right to pronounce on these issues. There is, however, the record of the visit of his successor, the Franciscan Pecham, made seven years later when the same condemnations were pronounced. Apparently the Dominican masters received their Primate with due respect and between visitations persisted in the error that *Ego currit* was good Latin. One hundred years later during the Wycliffian controversy the issue came closer to a question of ecclesiastical authority over the conscience and convictions of the masters. Wycliffe's opinions were condemned by the Pope in 1377, but Oxford chose not to enforce the Bull owing to the sentiment of a number of its masters. Five years after the Bull had declared Wycliffe's teaching heretical a disciple, Nicholas Hereford, preached a bold sermon in support of the new doctrines at St. Frideswide's Church before the university on Ascension Day. The chancellor lent his support to the rebellion by appointing Philip Repingdon university preacher at the Feast of Corpus Christi less than a month after Hereford's bold defiance of the Bull. Repingdon, as expected, defended Wycliffe's views as true Christian doctrine against the Pope and the English Blackfriars. On his way from the Church he was joined by the chancellor who expressed himself as well pleased with the sermon, and so ' great joy came upon the Lollards ' at Oxford. Thirty-two years after the Bull, Oxford had still not capitulated but was now ordered to condemn Wycliffe itself by the Convocation of Canterbury. The faculties still demurred and no action was taken. Then two years later, in 1411, the archbishop

206

proposed to visit the university and condemn its heresies at the Church of St. Mary. It must have taken amazing courage for the chancellor and the proctors to organize a final stand against the authority of the Church and the Crown. They fortified St. Mary's and sent the scholars out into the streets to prevent the archbishop's entry into town. When the King demanded the resignation of the chancellor and proctors, the faculties re-elected them.[7] In the end the constitutional rights of crown and mitre were enforced, but the exercise of these rights was regarded as another matter. In a real sense Oxford had declared for, and substantially gained, the great privilege of academic freedom. It is hardly probable that the university as a whole had ever come close to an acceptance of Wycliffe's doctrines of the scriptures, the eucharist or the papacy, but it was deeply sensitive to the convictions of those masters who believed Wycliffe to be right, and it was of one mind on the just cause of defending such convictions against pope, prelate and king.

In long standing disputes of this kind where the issues lie deeper than the arguments, it would be unlikely that either side could exclude extraneous or mixed motives. There is a charge of lawlessness entered against the supporters of John Birch, the proctor who had stood so stalwartly with the chancellor. He was an Oriel man and in the aftermath of the long struggle there was an attempt to discredit him by the old technique of guilt by association with three Fellows of the college who are said to be ' habitual night-walkers, spending their days and nights in taverns, breaking into college at unreasonable hours, introducing armed men within its walls, knocking up the provost at ten o'clock at night, calling him a liar and challenging him to fight. . . .'[8]

---

[7] See Rashdall, III pp. 118-133.
[8] See Salter, *op. cit.*, pp. 196 ff.

The court fool warned Confucius against a misalliance with Power and Pelf in the State of Chu.

PRIVILEGE AND RESPONSIBILITY

Looking backward, after so many centuries, we are impressed by the violence of these struggles. On the basis of the bare records it is difficult to expose central issues or to see them clearly against the mixture of passion and pride and self interest that is ingredient in every human action. It is, perhaps, enough to say that in these transports of violence, the university came to understand its own proper purpose and to prize the independence essential to its task. Such understanding and judgment could come only after long years of working at its job and several centuries of reflection upon the deeper issues in its conflicts with town and crown and church. The Coroner's Register can tell us little of these matters nor do the treaties and the statutes disclose the inner side of the tensions and controversies affecting the lives of masters and scholars who from so many quarters had come to Oxford and Cambridge to realize the aims of higher learning in a new kind of community set within the context of the medieval town. The town had its own interest in the university as a market that should be

208

encouraged to respond to the various designs of the mayor and the citizens.[9] The medieval Church and the Crown, especially in the unsettled days at the close of the middle ages, were prepared to find in the university an organ to express their wills, or at least an ally in matters ecclesiastical and political. To be an ally of any other institution is precisely what the university cannot be and still be itself. Other institutions have the answers, or they are concerned about immediate answers. At least they are interested in answers to questions asked in such a way that the solution must take account mainly of practical implications and consequences.[10] This has not always been true of institutions that have sponsored and controlled universities. The medieval Church for the most part encouraged an amazing breadth of speculation and enquiry. Some modern states have been aware of the values of free dialogue pursued by competent and responsible scholars. Among the most gracious of the patrons of higher education were the early American Congregationalists, Presbyterians, and Baptists. For them freedom was a religious principle which they were prepared to defend in their colleges even to the point of the right of scholars to criticize and denounce their theological doctrines and ecclesiastical practices. The threat to the university comes from those who do not believe in that kind of freedom as a basic principle, or who do not believe that there are values beyond the service of practical ends either political

---

[9] Corpus Christi College, Cambridge, was founded in 1352 with funds collected by the townsmen who were members of craft or trade guilds for the non—academic purpose of providing for regular masses offered for the deceased members of the guilds.

[10] Dr. Flexner emphasizes this view in his somewhat radical observation that professors have 'no practical responsibility for the trouble (they) make.' It is their responsibility to get on with their thinking without taking any account of consequences. (*Universities, American, English, German*, p. 22.).

or material. Churches and churchmen are sometimes quite practical in this sense—so also is industry as well as the state. These practical people are seldom sensitive to the values of disputation and the variety of opinion. Industry is notorious for its appreciation of conformity and its singleness of purpose. What is good for General Motors might, in some instances, be good for the country, but it would not be good for the university. Stalin would have made an excellent chairman of the board of many corporations whose directors and investors would not have voted for him due to a superficial misunderstanding. It was Stalin who pointed up very clearly the basis of the threat to the university of alliance with other institutions. James B. Conant quotes him from a recent East German publication on higher education: " In front of us stands the citadel of learning. This citadel we must capture at any price." [11] It is this point of view whether it be found among the Nazis, the Communists, the Evangelical Churches, the John Birch Society, the Roman Church, industry or the government, that the university must resist to the death.

To be itself the university must make a clear distinction between itself and all other institutions. But this distinction cannot be made without some loss and limitation. It involves accepting an element of remoteness and detachment not only for the university as a whole but also for its masters and scholars as individuals. Within this context the sanctity of academic freedom compels our reverence. The university lays its just claim to a special freedom in that its function is academic, that it views, from a distance and with the luxury of the spectator, the sources, principles and implications of those matters with which industry and government, the home and the church,

---

[11] *The Citadel of Learning* (New Haven: Yale University Press, 1956), p. 2.

210

the acting associations of the ' men of affairs ' must deal
on a day to day basis, subject to the internal pressures
of their several special interests and of external pressures
which others may bring effectively to bear. Certainly, it
is not the case that the university should take no account
of these matters nor that its own special purposes should
have no bearing upon them. It bears the responsibility
for responsible criticism. But its criticism must be disinterested in the sense that it seeks no special pleading.
Neither the university nor its members, *qua* masters and
scholars, can enter the lists to persuade public opinion,
or to force practical action except in issues in which the
prerogatives of the guild itself are involved. On other
matters, masters and scholars have a right to speak but
not to act. The special freedom of the university to
speak is justified only in so far as it is disinterested, that
is, that its speaking is in the pursuit of its own purposes
and not the using of the university by its own members
or by others for purposes that are not its own. Because
of its claim to a special freedom of examination and
expression the university must demand of its members an
exacting loyalty—a loyalty to their own studies as sciences
and their loyalty to their school in terms of its exclusive
purposes and function.

Masters and scholars have a right to be liberals or
conservatives, to be contraceptionists or vivisectionists, but
they do not have a right to campaign for their individual
points of view as members of the university except in so
far as their convictions are disinterested in the best sense
of the word. They have no right to the special privilege
of the university if their first loyalty is to other institutions.
It is a real question to what extent university scientists
should be involved in government or industrial projects,
or that university laboratories should be, though heavily
subsidized by government or industry, organized to serve

211

the special purposes of these external demands. Governmental and industrial secrets involve a curtailment of freedom that poses a real problem for the university. Classified information has no place in a university on the academic level nor should the special needs of industry or government determine programmes of research. Great emergencies will of necessity qualify the principles of normal procedure, but the question of the place of government and industry in the university over any considerable time has become a serious and complex issue. The university has the responsibility to demand that its members' basic orientation is academic and not practical, that it is disinterested and not committed to the programmes of other organizations. Many good people, who are so deeply concerned about political and social issues that they have little energy left for their research and teaching, simply do not belong in the university. Too many brief cases are overnight bags filled with tooth brushes, a change of linen, and air schedules. The research of too many university people, who go about doing good, narrows down to Bradshaw and Baedecker.

The sanctity of academic freedom is inviolable only in so far as the university is a community of masters and scholars—in so far as it justifies its special and peculiar competence as an institution of disinterested research and responsible interpretation. Not even this limitation can be made without paying a price and without peril. The town has its own way of describing such detachment: ' ivy covered professors in ivy covered halls.' The peril is that of pedantry, of the life of empty leisure in a preoccupation with inert ideas, and this is the essential equipment of the university's do-it-yourself suicide kit. One sharp comment on such pedantry cuts close to the quick of many of us who have lived for sometime within a special field of research: " There have been humanists

212

whose enthusiasm for the aqueducts of ancient Rome had no bounds but for whom contemporary systems of water supply were undeserving of a cultivated man's interest." [12] Much that goes on in the university may seem to be a futile worrying over value judgments taken in the past about things that no longer matter, or it may be, to use a Chinese phrase, ' a plucking of the mystic cassia and a treading upon azure clouds.' [13]   I have known a few men in classics who pottered about with their ostraca and parchments quite happily for many years sustained in their more fervent moments by a vague hope that something might turn up that could shed some light on a detail of the wine trade between Athens and Delos, or that some obscure figure in antiquity might someday be identified with the author of a fragment from an obviously second rate scholiast.   Gilbert Highet has recalled, from E. F. Benson, a description of Walter Headlam, the Cambridge don, that deserves an honoured place in the gallery of university portraits.

" One morning . . . his water for shaving was not hot, so after breakfast he put a small kettle to boil over his spirit lamp, and as he waited for that, he sat down in the armchair where he worked and casually looked at a note he had made the evening before.   It was about a change of rhythm in a Greek chorus, or perhaps it was a word in his Herondas, which occurred in no dictionary, but which he knew he had seen before in some scholiast on Aristophanes.   But where was the particular book he wanted?   His room was lined with bookshelves, books that he was using paved the floor round his chair, and the table was piled high with them.   There it was underneath a heap of others on the table, and he pulled it out:

---

[12] *Education In the Age of Science*, p. 199.
[13] Purcell, *op. cit.*, p. 36.

those on the top of it tumbled to the ground. He put down his pipe on the edge of the table, and as he turned the leaves, he found not just that which he was looking for, but something else he had wanted yesterday. He made a note of this on a slip of paper and picked up his pipe which had gone out. There were no matches, so he folded up the paper on which he had made his note, thrust it into the flame of the spirit lamp and lit his pipe again. Then he found the passage he had originally started to hunt up. Awfully interesting: it was a slang word, not very polite, in use among the daughters of joy in Corinth during the fifth century B.C. These intelligent ladies seemed to have an argot of their own; there were several other words of the sort which he had come across. He became lost in this pursuit, his pipe had to be relit several times, and presently a smell of roasting metal brought him back for a brief moment to the surface of life. His shaving water had all boiled away, and so he put out the spirit lamp. Later in the morning his gyp came to see if he wanted any lunch ordered for him: bread and butter and cheese would do, with a tankard of beer. These were laid and left in the next room, and he wandered there after another hour or two deep in his investigation. The sight of food aroused no association of desire but he had a drink out of the tankard and carrying it back with him, put it in a nest of books on his table. Presently more books got piled up round the tankard; he absently laid a folio notebook on the top of it, and so it completely vanished. Then he wanted more books from his shelves, in one of these excursions he stepped on his pipe and broke the stem. It did not matter, for there were others about, but he forgot to look for them in the heat of this diverting chase. " I shall write a monograph on the slang current in Corinthian brothels," he said to himself.

214

" It began to grow dark on this early close of the autumn afternoon. There was no electric light in those days, and he fetched a couple of candles and put them on the edge of his table. He was hungry now, and he gobbled up his bread and cheese, wondering what time it was, for his watch had stopped. Beer too: he felt sure he had ordered some beer, but where the devil was it? It should have been on his table with the bread and cheese. He looked everywhere for it, even in his bedroom, but it was nowhere to be seen. Then his razor lying ready on his dressing-table reminded him that he had not yet shaved. It was true there was no hot water but cold water would do, and though it was rapidly getting dark, he had not yet found any matches to light his candles. But one ought to be able to shave in the dark, he thought, for an action often repeated, became, as Aristotle said, as instinctive process, and it would be interesting to see if he could not make quite a good job of it. He made a fair job of it, there were a few negligible cuts, and finding that he had a box of matches in his pocket all the time, he lit his candles and went back to the ladies of Corinth. Then his gyp came in to see if he would go into Hall for dinner, or dine in his room: he settled to have some cold meat here, but where was the beer he had ordered for lunch? The gyp felt sure he had brought it, but evidently he was mistaken for there was no sign of it. So he brought the cold meat and another tankard and with this comfortless refreshment Walter Headlam pursued the ladies of Corinth till the small hours of the morning. The missing tankard came to light the next day." [14]

---

[14] Gilbert Highet, *The Art of Teaching*, (New York: Vintage Books, 1955), pp. 76 ff.

In the case of Headlam's research an academic remoteness was, perhaps, advisable. Such an interest in the contemporary practitioners of the profession could by some, who had not Headlam's selflessness and breadth of interest ' nor his devotion to knowledge,' have been construed as extra-curricular. And more must be said for Headlam and his kind of university than this. There is something in principle better for the university's interests and purposes in his day of divertissement amongst his copies of ancient texts than for the procedures of the modern departments of sociology and economics. Somehow, it seems to me, Headlam's research belonged to the university and that Kinsey's does not. If Headlam had ever written his promised monograph it would have been a warm and sympathetic work filled with the healthy humour that gives perspective and appreciates anachronism. It would have been a humane work, not a tedious compilation of largely meaningless statistics garnered from tapes and questionnaires, quantitative in every sense but qualitative in none.

The Chancellor of Lu was so completely captivated by the gift of a Jam of Tarts that he ignored Confucius.

EXCURSIS FACETIOUS AND EARNEST

The Great Slaughter of Masters and scholars by the modern townsmen is far more efficiently and ruthlessly perpetrated. It is the invasion of the university and the subversion of its own purposes by Greeks bearing the gift of funds for institutes and conferences. To-day the townsmen are not content with the murder of a few scholars, the firing of a hall and the defacing or banning of a few books. They have moved into the university turning its laboratories into factories and its halls into shops. They have come with their tape recorders and computers, paying their penny before the slaughter. They have suppressed the language of learning and in its place have encouraged the barbarisms of the townsmen—the jargon of the shopkeepers and the hucksters. They speak of opinion polls and communications research, of inter-intra-and-sub-personal persuasion. They draw the scholars from their proper studies to be their market spies—to tell them what people will buy instead of what they want, if approached in the right way. They set the masters to invent methods for the detection of hidden agenda and

217

to discover the secrets of the management of committees. They ' cooperate ' with the universities in the establishment of meat institutes, management institutes, sales institutes, advertising institutes, market communication institutes. They patronize ' leading universities ' and ' outstanding scientists ' in nationwide dermatological tests of the effect of ' well known ' brands of electric shavers on the public's skins. They modestly announce, with the backing of the consensus of university scientists, the expected results. They finance mass circular migrations of scientists, sociologists, economists, and even anthropologists around the conference centers. Even the religious foundations are prepared to waste their substance in ' righteous ' giving if they can stimulate the merry-go-round of the conference circuit, and like all other foundations, they are never quite sure whether their role playing for the day should be in the character of the prodigal son or the elder brother. Of one thing they are sure: the jet plane is a new means of Grace. It is difficult to reject the doctrine that if a man has flown far enough and high enough and fast enough he has received the Holy Spirit, notwithstanding the external signs. Life in the Conference Age may well prove to be impossible for the university. To float a successful conference it is necessary to have an assortment of professionals, preferably in a variety of sizes, colours and shapes, capable of displacing both individually and collectively their weight in air. They must be also radio active and photogenic, and they must have the setting of a foundation sponsored institute against the background of the university's ivy covered walls. Even a ten megasonic conference can neutralize the academic and administrative potential of a fair sized university for some time. However, even though a huge cloud of correspondence, reports, pamphlets and other communication outlets is produced, the fallout is seldom dangerous. The only problem, after normal operations can safely be resumed, is the disposal of academic waste. There is of course the danger that those who are caught too often within the effective perimeter of these explosions will suffer from permanent intellectual sterility.

It was two years after Matthew Arnold, who was then Inspector of Schools under the Department of Education, had been outvoted in his contention that coal was not the real basis of England's national greatness, [15] that he published his satire on the ' new education.' He quotes Mr. Bottles who was educated at the Lycurgus House Academy under the mastership of Archimedes Silverpump, Ph.D. " We must be men of our age," he used to say. " Useful knowledge, living languages, and the forming of the mind through observation and practical experiment, these are the fundamental articles of my educational creed." Or as Mr. Bottles himself put it in his expansive moments after dinner: " Original man, Silverpump! fine mind! fine system! None of your antequated rubbish— all practical work—latest discoveries in science—mind constantly kept excited—lots of interesting experiments— lights of all colours—fizz! fizz! bang! bang! That's what I call forming a man." [16]

The real tragedy of the sociological and economic fizz! fizz! bang! bang! institute is that it is damnably dull and dulling, frantic work. It was Headlam and not Kinsey who found research exciting.

---

[15] See *Matthew Arnold, Poetry and Prose,* edited by J. Bryson, (London: Rupert Hart-Davis, 1954), pp. 489 ff.

[16] *Ibid.* pp. 526, 527.

Confucius willingly advised officials of the State of Tsi on the principles of Government and Welfare of the people.

THE UNIVERSITY IN THE COMMUNITY

The essential function of the university is not action but reflection. Its end is foresight. The great schools and the great educators have been of one mind in acclaiming politics as the supreme art, and they have been profoundly concerned with the basic issues and processes of industry—but on a different level than the professional politician or the shopkeeper. Confucius, Plato, and Aristotle, had a deep sense of vocation in relation to their times but they understood their responsible ministry as ' retrospective prophecy ' and foresight.[17] The Confucian scholar Fan Chung-yen (989-1052) reminded his students that it is the scholar who must worry ' over the problems of the time before anyone else begins to worry about them.' [18] In bearing this responsibility the university, like the prophet, stands between the past and the present. It is the articulate spokesman for the ' continuous human community '—for the living past that exposes the distorting pressures of the present. The ills of our age, the delin-

[17] See Creel, *op. cit.*, p. 142; Curtis, *op. cit.*, p. 35.
[18] MacNair, *op. cit.*, p. 228.

quency of our youth and the banality of our elders, ought as William Temple observed, to be faced not on the symptomatic level of morals but on the deeper level of the disintegration of culture.[19] The university must take its stand against the persistent threat of barbarism. Barbarism is essentially the loss of the past, the waste of experience. Science and commerce, especially in their applied studies, deal with change. They have the vigour and the realism of youth, the fierce objectivity that can so easily become harsh. They must ever bear the brunt of the temptation to become pre-occupied with force, almost brute force, in a cruel worship of technology as progress, and a valuation of efficiency above patience and of precision above tenderness. The greater learning, like religion, urges the tender care that nothing be lost, the infinite patience that much may be saved. The essential task of the university is the civilizing of intelligence, the enlarging of the capacity of its scholars to respond to intrinsic values.[20] It is *in* the town *but not of* the town. Its *raison d'etre* is not its service to the mayor or the shopkeepers, nor in the last resort can it be justified even by its theoretical research and discovery. Its ultimate obligation is no more narrow than a service to the whole human family through the minds it forms in the masters of this day and in the scholars whom it sends forth into the world of action to-morrow.

---

[19] See Moberly, *op. cit.*, p. 16.

[20] See Fehl, *Religion in the University,* p. 4.

Confucius exhorted his son to be a gentleman

CHAPTER VIII

THE UNIVERSITY AND THE INDIVIDUAL

AN ARISTOCRATIC COMMUNITY

THE community of masters and scholars is an aristocracy. Apart from technical training, education has everywhere and always been restricted to patricians. Plebeians have no place in the university either among the masters or the scholars.

The aristocrat is first of all the free man. He is not bound to the service of anyone. He is the man who is not under any bondage, economic or social. Only as a gentleman can he claim the privilege of the education of the free—a liberal education. Leisure and merit are the marks of the gentleman who can devote himself to the liberal arts, to literature, science and philosophy. The plebeian cannot. He must labour at his trade and serve his master. He is concerned with production, with earning, not with learning. The gentleman is not servile. Neither persons nor possessions can lay external claims upon him. He is not anyone's ' man.' He is not necessitous, and

222

hence he is not for hire. The market means little to him, for there is nothing of value that he needs either to buy or to sell. He does not sell nor can he be sold.

Since he does not work for a living he may devote his energy to the acquisition of liberal knowledge rather than to the practice of one trade or skill. His destiny is not to do something but to be something—to fulfill himself, and to exemplify the aristocratic ideal of true manhood. Being a gentleman means first of all to be a man—a person who stands before all in his own right and is known by his own name.[1] A menial is summoned not for himself but for his service. He is called as a hireling, not as a man. To his fellows and to his lord he is simply smith or cook or barber. The gentleman answers only to his own name, or he announces himself as his father's son. ' I am Glaucus,' he says. " Hippolochus begat me." As his son I stand before you, and I have no other obligation than " to strive always for the highest honour." [2] He need say no more; for that is enough to assure another that he has been met not by a menial but by a man.

The first aristocrats were men of strength and valour. They were mighty in battle. They rose above others by the healthy force of animal spirits. Men of breeding meant men of energy with a zest for life above the commoner. They were uncommon men for whom the ordinary ways were disdainful. Their zestful restlessness drove them toward heroic ventures and led them to prize the contest as much as the crown; for it is in the moment of heroic effort, in the high moment of the battle when the hero is most free. It is then he knows that nothing else than honour can mean aught to him. He is glorious and free in his exultant disdain of the possessions and

---

[1] See Emerson's essay on *Manners*.
[2] *Iliad* vi 208.

pleasures for which other men bind themselves in their mean service of mean ends. In that moment, Aristotle said, the noble man ' takes possession of the beautiful.' [3] Once he has known this, he has an insatiable thirst for honour and will gladly sacrifice everything, even life itself, for one hour of rapture. By this reverence for honour Plato is bound to Homer. For Socrates as for Odessyus nothing else matters in the life that is worth living than the race for the highest prize—for the greatest honour. Aristotle breathes with Achilles the air of aristocracy. The nobleman, he says, prizes the brief moment of heroic striving above the long quiet years of ordinary efforts, and he ' would choose one year of honour in place of many years of servile pursuits, one glorious exploit to many small triumphs.' [4] All that Socrates and Plato and Aristotle have to add to Homer is one word of earnest caution: *Only be sure that it is honour.* " Culture is simply the aristocratic ideal of a nation increasingly intellectualized." [5] The last word is not adequate. We can best understand what Aristotle meant by the resolve ' to take possession of the beautiful' from Plato's account of the trial of Socrates. For Greece and for the West the embodiment of *areté* is the Socrates of the *Apology*. When that old warrior of seventy years rose from the seat of the accused to make answer for his honour we hear something much more than an intellectualized perfection of Achilles' plaintive plea. You know, almost as well as I, that I cannot be anything other than what I am; and if you want to be rid of my offence then you shall have to do away with me; for let me tell you something about myself that you have not discovered for yourselves. " Men of Athens, I

---

[3] *Nicomachean Ethics* 1168b27. See *Jaeger, op. cit.,* I pp. 12 f.

[4] *Ibid.* 1169a18 f.

[5] *Paideia* I 4.

honour you and love you, but I shall obey God rather than you, and while I have life and strength, I shall never cease from the practice and teaching of philosophy, exhorting anyone whom I meet, and saying to him after my manner: You, my friend, a citizen of the great and mighty and wise city of Athens, are you not ashamed of heaping up the greatest wealth and honour and reputation, and caring so little about wisdom and truth and the improvement of the soul? " For know this: I speak at the command of God. And I believe that no greater good has ever happened to the state than my service to God. And I say to you: do what my accusers demand or do not do it. Either acquit me or not. But whichever you do, understand that " I shall never alter my ways, not even if I have to die many times." [6]

Deep down inside him his *areté* had told him that he had to die in order that he might more fully live and that others might have a fuller life. All his life, day by day, he had been making the same thrust and holding up the same vision. But he had been doing it the easy outward way—by conversing, teaching, laughing and crying, playing and drinking with his fellow citizens. In short, he had been pursuing his ends by living the common life. Now he knows that he has to do it the hard way, the inward way—by dying. He has now learned at this late and crucial moment of his life that human beings do not learn anything except by the hard way. In showing them that he had no care for what they meant by life he would have them see for the first time what he meant by life. To die was to enter into true life—to seize possession of the beautiful.[7]

---

[6] *Apology* 30.

[7] See N. Fehl, *A Guide To the Study of Plato's Republic* (Hong Kong: Chung Chi College, 1961), pp. 91-95. For this interpretation I am indebted to Dr. Preston Roberts of the University of Chicago.

Wherever you meet the aristocrat whether it be in Homer's tales of Ajax, Achilles and Odessyus, in the *Apology, Crito* and *Phaedo* of Plato, in *Raoul de Cambrai* and *Chanson de Roland*, in Tennyson or Sir Walter Scott, in Szema Ch'ien or in the *Gospels,* he will tell you what it means to ' take possession of the beautiful.' He will speak to you of honour and of worthy pride, of daring and of courage, of intemperate scorn for the petty calculations of little men, of a ' fortitude not to be wearied out,' of the glorious hour. He will tell you of the hilarity of the great hall, the good humour of brave knights in the afterglow of tournament and battle, of the love of sport and the merriment of heroism. And in this bright company you need not ask of duty or discipline. It was their duty to excel. It was their discipline to be ready for the great encounter. *Noblesse oblige*—the privilege of ultimate responsibility—flowed in their blood, and gave that posture to their bearing that men fain would call master. The heroic deed lives on. The hero is the immortal; for he wins the prize of imperishable honour.

Now of all ancient institutions, the university is the last in which the only lasting ideal of aristocracy lives on in the modern world. The academic freedom which it claims is the freedom of the hero and the gentleman intellectualized—the freedom of research and reflection that is not bound in liege to any lord to take account of its action in respect of another's interest. Master, scholar and gentleman are synonyms of the free and of the high born—the knights of knowledge. The university does not produce gentlemen. It is a community of gentlemen. When it ceases to be patrician—when it is invaded by plebeians who seek jobs within it, or to train for jobs outside it, it is degraded into an institute of commoners. The university is for learning not for earning. It is a community of heroes, not a school of child-rearing where boys are taught either the manners or the skills of the market place.

Shopkeepers who send their sons to the university so that they may ' get ahead in the world ' by making more money and improving their social position may be pardoned for their folly, but their sons, persisting in such error, deserve no pardon. The university is for all sorts and conditions of men so long as they be gentlemen. It searches for them in the byways and the hedges. It entreats them to come. Many are called. Few can be chosen, and, of these, some must be cast out. Of *Sacerdotum, Imperium* and *Studium* only the last is under no obligation to suffer fools gladly. The plebeian will find sufficient company where there is no discrimination in terms of commitment and ability. For the plebeian soul there must be property and the consolations of the flesh in rude plenty. For the merchant prince—adventurer and soldier of fortune—there must be the appropriate status symbols, the good, clear rewards of cleverness in subsidized risk-taking in which the man of affairs excels. For the government official there must be some recognition of the omnipotence and omniscience that radiate outward to all bureaus from sovereignty. For the prelates of the church, *la grand humilité* will be recognized by the world even though modestly concealed under vestments of misleading splendour.

The good university will also take account of honour. It will take care that its professorial and scholastic champions compete in the right way for the right honours. It must keep its old heroes in the battle and its young challengers at their proper games. It will encourage chivalrous competition, and it will keep alive the memory of great exploits. Presidents and Deans, above all else,

227

need this talent: to inspire quests and trystings, to maintain a lively round table, to incite to heroism and to keep bright the shield of gallantry. So much the Chancellor can do—but in the last resort, the university *is* its masters and its scholars—their heroism and their honour. Nothing else really matters, either if these be of the highest excellence or if they be not.

The good scholar knows by the thrill of the all-night vigil with a paper, storming some forbidding stronghold of text or theory, by the thrill of wrestling till the dawn with some worthy antagonist in the guise of a problem in maths, a poetic idea, a vexed issue of historical judgment, by the tournament in the laboratory with some adversary so cunning that in foiling his many devices time stands still—by all these he will know what it means to take possession of the beautiful. And the lecturer who well past middle age now and then skips a class because he is in the thrall of a higher pursuit and who now and then strives through the night to speak in a precise way on some complicated passage only in part for the sake of his class, by the joy of such adventures can tell what it has meant to him ' to take possession of the beautiful.' Universities are sanctified by such heroes. To have written one great essay, to have made one significant discovery, to have won distinction in the classroom—to have removed the cataracts of the mind from one or a few scholars of promise who because they came to you were made to see and because they saw, went on to conquer—these are the exploits of the academic aristocracy. The heroic hour is the significant unit of university time. Chronologies and necrologies will suffice for the readers of the calendar.

GENTLEMEN AND SCHOLARS

All this has been said many times from Plato to

Hutchins, with more restraint by Newman and with less by Arnold. And, before any of these, it was said by Confucius. What he sought in scholars was the quality of a man fit to rule. His ideal scholar was the true nobleman, the *chün tzu*君子, 'ruler's son.'[8] In reality he had found too many rulers who were not noblemen but only 'little men' (*hsiao ren* 小人), and for them and their plebeian sons he had little time. He expected of his disciples a knightly valour, the bearing of the aristocrat who has the capacity of spontaneous response without thought of personal ease or private gain. No one, he remarked, should count himself a knight (*shih*士) " who thinks only of the life of decent ease amidst the comforts of home." [9] His disciple, Tseng Shen, described the Confucian portrait of the aristocrat as the man who ' must be large of spirit and stout of heart, for he must reckon upon a heavy burden and a long crusade. The *shih* undertakes the quest of perfect virtue, and his pilgrimage ends only in death.' [10] At times Confucius described the expression (*li*禮) of the bearing of nobility as a gift, a charismatic endowment. At other times as a skill common to all men, but capable of cultivation and nurture. Of some men he observed that they had the form of *li* but not the power thereof.[11] Professor Creel defines *li* as ' good taste,' and as ' doing in every situation what is suitable.' [12] Certainly this essential quality of the gentleman is more than manners or courtly etiquette. Perhaps ' a sense of perspective ' is ingredient in this notion of ' good taste.' Perspective can be cultivated but only in

[8] Legge, *op. cit.*, IV *She King*, pp. 260 f. See Creel, *op. cit.*, p. 77.

[9] *Analects* xiv 3.

[10] *Ibid.* vii 7.

[11] *Ibid.* iii 26.

[12] *Op. cit.*, p. 84.

those who have an innate capacity and a ready appreciation. In one passage Confucius speaks of *li* as similar
to the aim of education. 'Righteousness is the substance
of character. To understand *li* is to know how to fulfill
all righteousness.' [13] Whether *li* be *charisma* or *askesis*
(grace or discipline), basic to the character of a gentleman
is the endowment of nature. The quality of a man's
nature determines the extent and kind of the education
he requires. When his training exceeds his capacity he is
a useless person—a misfit in the job he might have done,
and unfitted for any other. Throughout his university
career, and notwithstanding his success in examinations, he
will successfully defend his natural right to remain in a
state of ignorance. St. Augustin's Christian realism comes
to the same judgment: "Concerning all which is the
object of our intellectual activity, the master we consult
is not the person who speaks to us externally; the master
is within, the truth which dwells in the soul itself. The
words of the teacher can only stimulate us to consult the
inner master." [14]

The university is a community, and, in every meeting
of men, each receives more than he gives. Each participates in the wealth of that 'general bank and capital
of nations and of ages.' But the reserve of that bank in
any university at any time is not much in excess of the
contributions of the individual depositors. A university
is greater than the simple sum of the achievements of its
individual masters and scholars—but not much greater.
There is no magic in togetherness. When no miracle
occurs in the feasting of a thousand masters and scholars
on five loaves and two small fishes, and yet of the
fragments that remain twelve baskets are taken up, there

---

[13] *Analects* xv 17.
[14] *The Master.* See Curtis, *op. cit.* p. 81.

has been very little nourishment of anyone. Whitehead remarks that " the most striking phenomenon in the history of education is that schools of learning which at one epoch are alive with a ferment of genius, in a succeeding generation exhibit merely pedantry and routine." They have been ' overladen with inert ideas.' [15] Whitehead goes on to urge that the present is holy ground. But the rude truth is that the university which continues on with the dull pedantry and dreary routine of transferring inert ideas from the memory of masters to the memory of scholars is suffering from inert people. The halls and hostels are still in use, the library has in all probability grown, and in such times it may be taken for granted that much work has been done on syllabus and calendar. All that is lacking is the one thing essential—the people. The diagnosis can be carried one step further: dull masters were once dull students. The life of the university is its scholars. Eager youth rejuvenates weary age. At least alert students can disturb the ' dogmatic slumber ' of their elders. But to face the wretched mediocrity of maturating shopkeepers in their college blazer cocoons day after day is debilitating. The scribbling fingers of dull-eyed students ' whose minds know nothing, nothing care to know,' will send the lecturer not to the library but to the asylum. When they have served their menial sentence by one successful transference of their pothooks from their note books to their examination papers, the cycle of destruction is nearly complete. They have only to serve one more year in learning how to teach a subject of which they have little knowledge and less interest before they are sent forth to persecute learning with the government's blessing of a certificate in ' education.' These are not

---

[15] *The Aims of Education*, p. 13.

free men—they are slaves—tragically servile to the tyranny of secular success. Quality comes before quantity and quality begins at home—in the homes of the students, in the Home Office, in the hearts even more than in the minds of university people. The foundation of the university is something closer to conscience than to mind. No man can call learning 'lord' except by the spirit. The first universities were the venture of religious people. The great universities in their finest hours have been communities of 'godly learning.' [16] Secularism can produce technological schools of high merit. It has done so in Russia, in the United States and in Great Britain and throughout the Commonwealth. These are needed, and they serve a worthy purpose, but they are not universities. The university is an aristocracy, and, in the last resort, it is the aristocracy of heroes who worship no idols whether they be 'of the market, the tribe or the theatre,' and whose service is to no man but to God.

---

[16] See Moberly, *op. cit.*, pp. 34, 35.

"A river, like truth, will flow on for ever and have no end".

CHAPTER IX

THE UNIVERSITY EAST AND WEST

THE EASTERN UNIVERSITY

WITH few exceptions the Eastern university has its roots in twelfth century Europe as well as in the Asian past. It is thus the first all-inclusive *studium generale* in the history of higher education. In the European and American university, the meeting of East and West is still casual and theoretical—in a sense tangential rather than integral. Since the last war the Western arts student is likely to have some knowledge of Asian civilization, but in most instances it will have come to him as a kind of extra in an elective course or through collateral reading. In an increasing number of colleges in the States and in Canada there are departments of Oriental studies which attract students who are looking toward careers abroad or in a pioneer field at home. The importance of these departments is greater than their size—than the number of staff and students or the extent of the syllabus of courses offered. That an Orientalist

233

department is in the university, is significant. It will afford the professor in Western history or literature or science a colleague to whom he can go with questions about the other hemisphere of human culture. Little by little the university community as a whole may become aware of a new dimension of the human venture, of another way of looking at their studies than that of their own tradition. But these new departments are often foreign embassies within the university. To most professors and students they are foreign. They have the appeal of the exotic, but lack the significance of the substantial. The solid citizens wonder from time to time what those chaps over there are doing. Again, since the last war, there are in the small colleges, as well as in the huge universities, groups of Asian students. Most of these are in graduate divisions of the physical and social sciences, and they are so preoccupied with Western studies and with plans for a career in the West that they are seldom effective ambassadors of their own heritage.[1]

In the Eastern university the meeting of East and West is an existential encounter. Both Eastern and Western studies are essential elements of the syllabus of every student. In most Asian universities the faculties are international. A goodly number are foreigners and of the Asian members most have had many years of study in America or Europe. East and West meet in the perspectives and the problems of individual masters and scholars, in the day to day life of the university, in the routine deliberations of the academic board, in the departmental syllabus. For the student the meeting may often be more of a collision than a casual and pleasant contact with the exotic.

---

[1] See the opening paragraphs in Pearl S. Buck's "Chinese Literature in Today's World" in MacNair, *op. cit.*, pp. 397 ff.

THE LANGUAGE PROBLEM

In the better Eastern universities the language problem is the first shock that is felt in the collision of Asian and Western studies. I use the word *shock* here in its medical sense. The learning and daily use of Western language is a veritable shaking of the foundations of the student's psychic and cultural existence. Few Western students have ever been subjected to anything like this traumatic disruption of the elemental processes of thought and learning. Secondary education in all cultures chiefly concentrates upon precision in the use of language: the structure of sentences—the complex sentence as the expression of finer shades of discriminative description and connotation—the precise word for the accurate communication of knowledge in specific disciplines—history, geography, biology, the poetic word as the bearer of the richness of concrete experiences of goodness and beauty. Middle school sharpens the basic tool of language to the point that it can be used effectively and with ease in the conquest of university studies. The great compensation for the rigorous and, in the specialized-syllabus type of college, for the highly concentrated university curriculum is the discovery by the student that language has suddenly transformed itself from an enemy into an ally. A brief passage in the *Confessions* of St. Augustin speaks for all students in their crossing of this threshold. " Why," he asks himself, " did I so much hate the Greek which I studied as a boy? I do not yet fully know. For the Latin I loved; not what my first teachers, but what the (later masters) taught me. For these first lessons, reading, writing and arithmetic, I used to find no less burdensome and tasklike than all my Greek . . . (but) in the other I was (privileged) to accompany the wanderings of some

235

Aeneas or other, and (released from my own anxieties), to weep for dead Dido when she killed herself for love. . . ." [2] Greek was never anything more than a lower school subject for Augustin. He never got beyond the study of it to the use of it. Latin, his first language, he regarded as the enemy throughout the period of his pupilage. Then suddenly it became a warm and responsive companion in the pursuit of high adventure. Without the joy and consolation of language, university study is drudgery. The Eastern student has never been as fortunate as the Western in his conquest of language. Purcell remarks, as one of the most significant aspects of Asian education, the fact that ' the student was well advanced in life before he was able to regard his own language as a servant and not as a master.' His best years were given to obtaining command over the medium of expression alone. [3]

Most Eastern languages are far more difficult to master to the extent that they can be easily used on the level of university study. For the Western reader who has no knowledge of Eastern languages a few simple facts in respect of the Chinese language point up its complexity. In contrast to English the Peking dialect has only four hundred sounds. Most Chinese words are monosyllabic, or more precisely, they are vocalized by the use of one of the four hundred sounds. Variation is achieved by means of tones of which there are four in Mandarin and nine in Cantonese. [4] In English there are a number of words which have the same phonetic value in speech, for example, the word ' fast.' Including colloquial use, the word has five meanings. In Chinese, one sound in the same tone may have as many as forty different meanings. Purcell

---

[2] *Confessions* i 13.
[3] See Purcell, *op. cit.*, p. 102.
[4] *Ibid.*, p. 12.

cites the sound *li* for which there are one hundred thirteen distinct characters. "Even when these are divided up amongst the four tones with diacritical marks to distinguish them, there will still be about twenty-eight guesses at the identity of *li* in each of the four tones.[5] The written language developed as did the Egyptian and Sumerian from pictographs. The basic scholarly vocabulary, with the exception of many recently coined scientific words, numbers well beyond twenty thousand characters whose origins have been traced to about six hundred pictographs. Only the advanced scholar can, however, detect the pictograph that lies behind more than a few modern characters. In reading a script in which many characters have exactly the same sound and tone there are obvious difficulties. Most were built up over the centuries by adding to one character a simplified form of another to supply in the written language both the clue to the sound and the clue to the meaning. A classical instance is the spoken word *kung* written as 工 and meaning work. But the sound in the spoken language may mean also *red, carrying-pole, merit, discord* and *river.* The character for work 工 became the hint for the sound of the word and other characters became the hint as to the meaning of the word. Red (紅) then came to be written as 工 (indicating sound) with the character for silk 綢. Pole (杠) became 工 and 木 wood; merit (功) 工 with strength 力. discord (訌) 工 with words 言; and river (江) 工 with water 氵. It is estimated that nine tenths of the characters in the modern Chinese language are thus composed of two or parts of two characters—one giving the clue to the meaning of the word (the radical) and one to the sound (the phonetic).[6] In these instances the reference is in respect

[5] *Ibid.*, p. 109. See Karlgren, Bernhard, *The Chinese Language.*

[6] Karlgren, *op. cit.* and Purcell p. 10.

of each word to a specific and concrete thing. But these things may also have connotative meanings. The colour 'red' is rich in associative nuances. Concepts are expressed by characters on the basis of their associative meanings. The richness of the language in its suggestion of a wide range of allusions and nuances can render the attempt at precision and accuracy fairly difficult.[7] Yet Chinese is a vivid language, its words more lively and with closer association to the concrete experiences out of which they first arose, than those of the European languages, which separated from their origins by the development of the alphabet, have become 'a gallery of faded metaphors.'[8] There is great joy in the Chinese language—the joy associated with warm humour in the infinite possibility of puns, and the joy associated with intimate understanding by the possibility of allusion to shared experience in conversation concerning ordinary things. And there is great consolation in this language—the consolation of perfect form, and the consolation of poetic imagery. As in all languages poetry is music—the aesthetically pleasing ordering of sounds. In Chinese poetry, the musical potential is at its highest; for it depends upon the skillful arrangement of tones as well as sounds. The finest compliment the Chinese teacher can pay to the foreign student is to say to him on some rare occasion: 'Ah, that was good to hear.' It is a language that invites the quiet mood of savouring the

---

[7] See the comments of Dr. W. W. Yen in Purcell, p. 158. See also the articles by I. A. Richards "Toward a Theory of Translating," Achilles Fang "Some Reflections on the Difficulty of Translation", and Arthur F. Wright "The Chinese Language and Foreign Ideas" in Wright, *Studies in Chinese Thought*, (Chicago: University of Chicago Press, 1953).

[8] Florence Ayscough, *A Chinese Mirror*, (London, 1925), p. 17, and Purcell, *The Spirit of Chinese Poetry*, (Shanghai, 1929). Cf. J. J. L. Duyvendak, "A Literary Renaissance in China" in *Acta Orientalia*, 1922-24.

flavour of sound in the ear as fine tea is savoured for some moments after the drinking of it. These are discrete moments—moments that should not be disturbed by other sounds or other tastes. The good life is possible only with grand leisure—with appropriate pauses between discrete delights, and with unhurried pace to allow a ruminative contemplation of past joy and future pleasure. The language encourages a sense of the infinite variety of moments and hence of the mystery of experience. It invites the joy and wonder of viewing, as much as you will, one by one, the numberless stars of heaven, and it asks you in simple sincerity: Can you number them? Why should you? Can you explain them? Why should you want to?

The greatest achievement of Chinese culture is its language. Here is its genius and its joy, its humanity and its humour, its individualism and its almost perfect sense of relationship. The mastery of such language is the labour of a lifetime of love. For the Chinese, to be bi-lingual is to lose so much more than for the Westerner. The Western student gains in his appreciation of his own language by a knowledge of Latin, and of the languages— sisters to his own—that are her children. But for the Chinese student, Western language study is a breaking of the magic circle that encloses a culture. To study another language is to impair his excellence in his own. And yet he must; for the excellence of his language in expressing his culture is by so much its limited excellence in expressing the analytical and the abstract, the precise and the universal. The language of science is the language of the West. And the life of the new Asia is now, no less than that of America and Europe, a new life born of the scientific revolution of the seventeenth century in the West. Science, by its altering of the world's economy, has also altered society. It has thrust its wedge between the past and the present changing the character of importance of all human knowledge. Both literature and history must make their claims on new grounds.

Just now at this point of radical transition, the practical issues are for the student even more determinative than the theoretical. The Eastern student who desires a distinguished career in his chosen field has little hope for success apart from graduate study abroad. Even the student who looks toward success in the expanding commerce of the Eastern city has only a limited chance without English. To paraphrase Heine one may ask was it fortunate that the West did not have to learn Chinese so that it had time to devote to science and to the building of empire? [9]

There is no easy solution to the problem of language, and the deeper aspect of the bi-lingual university—the undermining of the emotional and aesthetic supports of culture—cannot be ignored. For the Chinese university, language is the key to the past and the oracle who alone can give answer to the question ' What is Chinese? '

There are a few people who can enjoy literature in several languages, but they are very few. Good writers have for the most part cultivated one language intensively. During the reign of the classics at Oxford, some scholars came to have a real feeling for the turn of a Latin phrase; but it was the case that after Oxford days their joy and consolation was in just those few Latin and Greek passages they had pursued intensively, and in no others. Few ever read anything else that had been written even by those few authors. There was an emotional as well as literary resistance to any change in the classics syllabus. " We

---

[9] See Curtis, *op. cit.*, p. 444.

did not construe that book of the Iliad in Oxford in my day." Yet the problem for Oxford was not nearly so great as it is for Chung Chi. The ancient 'Greats' required only those languages which were the ancestors of English. Yet even for the Oxonian, Continental literature is known to him for the most part only in translation. He reads Dostoyevsky and Goethe in English, and while he knows he is missing something, it is less than he is willing to gain at the labour of reading them in a cognative form of the common Indo-Germanic language family. A fact worth noting is that very few linguists are serious readers. A flair for language seems often to have proved a handicap to real breadth and certainly to depth. Multi-linguists seldom read either as widely or as deeply as those who have to all practical purposes a single language. This is a serious problem in the Eastern university. For the Hong Kong student both Chinese and English are awkward tools. His grandfather would have had at least fifteen years of uninterrupted concentration upon a dozen fairly short but fundamental Chinese texts by the time he was of university age. His recreational use of poetic forms and allusions would have re-enforced his formal study; and his daily use of the polite language of relationship, dramatized by ritual, guarded the integrity of the mood and matter of his education.

Now the university student in Hong Kong has from early primary school struggled with a foreign language. He has had to sacrifice literary Chinese for a more efficient and simplified means of communication in order to get in the many new subjects that are basic pre-requisites for the university. And these new subjects—Western mathematics, physical science, Western history and literature—do not re-inforce or complement his Chinese studies. The two sides of his adolescent education are at many points mutually destructive. The student who has gone to English primary and secondary schools in preparation for the English or American university has bartered away a huge portion of his birthright. He has lost his past and in no real sense has he possessed another inheritance. The student who has gone to Chinese lower schools will have gained a little better grasp of his own language and its literature; but he would be judged a barbarian compared to the learning of his grandfather at the age of twenty. Few Chinese middle school students have been able to get that kind of competence in English that is equal to reading and conversation without strain in the area of their university major. The English and American student has nothing like the strain that the Eastern student must bear. Intellectually that strain is great, but emotionally it is no less crucial. The Western student has learned his own language by the time he reaches the university, and his studies, for the most part, are in his own language. The Eastern student has still a long way to go in the mastery of his own language and has yet the burden of a foreign language in a large portion of his reading, of lectures and of his examinations. Yet the ' Eastern University ' that permits or encourages the barter of birthright for status in civil service or in careers abroad has much for which it must someday give answer, not only to its alumni in their maturity, but also to their people with its destiny under God. The bilingual or trilingual university with all its tensions and handicaps is probably the more realistic as well as the better pattern for the present. There is a simple honesty in this: the university cannot ignore the past nor can it ignore present realities. But such stretching in language reduces the joy and consolation of the university and that sacrifice is justified only in terms of a greater good. Professor Needham in his history of Chinese science observes that a basic influence of the West upon the East, due to the superiority of the former's applied science, was that of language: ' . . . while the progress of the world has forced Chinese scientists and technologists to be bilingual, the converse has proved so little true. . . .' [10] Levenson comments: " The metaphor of language is suggested irresistibly: what the West has probably done to China is to change the latter's language." [11] But this change has been on the positive side superficial and on the negative side profound. The new language is not one of thought and feeling. It is only a fragment of a language—the Western language of applied science and commerce—not the language of poetry and philosophy.

EASTERN STUDIES AND WESTERN STUDIES

The new language was welcomed at first because it was not a language but a code. It was to serve only a limited function and the use of two languages could then sharply differentiate culture from commerce and politics. This distinction was clearly expressed in the slogan of Chang Chih-Tung (1837-1909) in his *Exhortation to Learn* which was published in 1898 with the official backing of the Emperor. " Chinese learning," Chang proposed, " should be the substance " of the new China while " Western Learning should serve as the instrument " for efficiency in politics, military operations, industry and commerce. [12]

---

[10] Needham, *op. cit.,* I p. 4.

[11] Joseph R. Levenson, *Confucian China and Its Modern Fate* (Berkeley: University of California Press, 1958), p. 157.

[12] See de Bary, *op. cit.,* p. 744.

The terms (t'i 體 'substance' and yung 用 'function') may be translated in several ways: as essence and efficiency, the moral and the practical, the personal and cultural over against the political, military and commercial, the doctrine and the method.[13] Chan Wing-tsit has traced their pedigree to the terms of the Sung metaphysicians where they were used to differentiate the ontological and functional aspects of reality. *Tao* and *Ch'i*—the principle and the instrument or the Chinese way (the moral ground) and the Western instrument (science and politics)—have been used in paraphrase of Chang's slogan.[14] But in both instances the sense of the Sung philosophers is destroyed. They had in view aspects of one reality: the substance and function of the *Tao*. In Chang's slogan substance and function have no intrinsic relation to each other. In a real sense, however, the formula is the summary of a long chapter in the history of Chinese thought. It is symbolized in the stories of the dialogue between Lao-tze and Confucius as the eternal tension between thought and action. Nivison's brilliant essay on "Knowledge and Action in Chinese Thought" finds this tension to be the basic dualism in Neo-Confucian tradition since the Sung Dynasty with roots that go as deep as the Chinese mind itself. He cites Han Yü's essay *Yüan Tao* on the two classes of illustrious men of creative thought and men of action. But this classification is in turn based upon the fundamental categories of *te* 德 (virtue: innate goodness and foresight) and *wei* 威 (authority, or more properly, power—i.e. the power to make ideas visible in action.[15]

---

[13] *Ibid*. p. 748. Cf. Purcell, *Problems of Chinese Education,* pp. 63, 77., and Nivison, "The Problem of Knowledge and Action In Chinese Thought Since Wang Yang-ming" in Wright, *op. cit.,* pp. 112 ff.

[14] de Bary, *op. cit.,* p. 744.

[15] Nivison in Wright, *op. cit.,* p. 114.

The writer and the doer, the man of words and the man of deeds, mean different things in the several strains of ancient tradition. The man of words may be the man of ' mere words,' or he may be the man of poetic and aesthetic genius whose work is valued above empty abstraction as form was preferred to content. The man of deeds may be the superior man, for he has spoken more clearly by his actions than he could by ' empty words ' (general statements) [16] or he may be the common man who can be, in Confucius' words, ' made to follow the way even though he cannot be brought to understand it.' [17] Again he may be in Plato's language the man of courage—the spirited man—who is inferior to the man of wisdom—the philosopher king. There is a formal parallel to this in the opposites of *wen* 文 men of culture and wu 武 men of action.[18]

For Plato the auxiliaries and the philosopher-king are not opposites: they are closely related in a hierarchy of essential qualities and appropriate functions.[19] This distinction is vital in seeing the significant difference in the treatment accorded to thought and action in East and West. Generally speaking the West has emphasized the direct and dependent relation of the practical to the theoretical. This relation is a function of both the Hebrew and Greek traditions where the concern for the ultimate—though differently defined—was the determinative motif. Western philosophy may be to a large degree appropriately described as a preoccupation with the problem of the relation of the ultimate to the

---

[16] Ssu-ma Ch'ien, *Shih Chi.*

[17] Legge, *op. cit.,* I p. 211.

[18] Nivison in Wright, *op. cit.,* p. 141.

[19] See Fehl, *A Guide to the Study of Plato's Republic* (Hong Kong: Chung Chi College, 1961), pp. 41 ff.

concrete. It was in the working out of that problem that the important concepts of *Arche, Logos,* Idea, form, substance, nature, reason, spirit, will, revelation and mediation had their origin. Philosophy has throughout the ages dealt with God under two aspects: God as He is in Himself—ultimate and absolute, and God as related— as the dynamic of the world, as power working either in or upon nature, history and human experience. Greek thought in general (as also Hindu and Buddhist) attempts to derive God as related from God as Absolute, God as the dynamic of the world from God as order (fate— *moira*); and has done so after the analogy of mind—the fecundity of the Absolute Mind overflowing into the potencies of thoughts or as a kind of field of force surrounding the pure actuality of Aristotle. It was the insight and the organizing principle of Christianity that God as related is not secondary to God as absolute—that God is the Living God and that he is One in Himself and in His relationship of creation and redemption to the world. There is One Divine Power of Being.[20] This identification of ultimacy with the Living God who is subject as well as object pressed upon philosophy the problem of the relation of faith to knowledge and of experience to reason. In China, however, the ultimate is the Remote and the impersonal whether it be symbolized in *Shang-Ti*, the lord in the heights, or in *Tao* the impersonal way of all things. But *Shang-Ti* does not speak, and *Tao* does not become incarnate. The ultimate is ' Power and Will in the Background,' [21] and hence there is little demand for metaphysics or theology; for meta-

---

[20] Fehl, *A Preface to Theology,* (Hong Kong, 1961), p. 28.

[21] See G. van der Leeuw, *Religion in Essence and Manifestation* (New York: Macmillan Company, 1938), pp. 597 ff.

physics would be only pure speculation, and if God does not speak there can be no theology.

Language also had its part in the special treatment which China has accorded to the problem of knowledge and action. Nivison points out the different direction taken here in the development of language. In the West the powerful word became the meaningful symbol—the essential tool for the highest task of reason—the definition of the character and basis of the correspondence of thought to reality.[22] In China, the powerful word became the perfect form—the bearer of beauty rather than of meaning or truth. Where there were sacred words—the ancient words of relationship and authority, such as the names of office and kinship—they remained powerful. Real life should be made to correspond to the powerful word. Otherwise there was a violation of power—a violation of tabu, and hence the Chinese language became the bearer of beauty rather than meaning, the medium of form rather than thought. Here is perhaps another basis for the long standing distrust of the articulation of abstract thought in words. Literature may lead to contemplation, or meditation may lead to literary expression, but here there is no contradiction, for discursive thought is not involved. Such contemplation leads to a feeling of communion or, when it is most articulate, to an intuition of relatedness which is best expressed in poetry or painting. Calligraphy can be prized not for what is written, but for the revelation in form and strength of strokes of the contemplative moment. It will speak more clearly than words of the calmness, the peace and harmony of the artist's mind. Poetry and painting, but above all, music, will give the highest and truest expression of the spirit. Wang could say

---

[22] In Wright, *op. cit.*, p. 115.

Tao is simply events.[23] Events are *Tao* and hence the Classics are really history—records in sublime form not of doctrine but of the aesthetic contemplation of the remote ultimate.

The science and politics of which Chang Chih-Tung speaks could not, of course, be in any sense the instrument of which aesthetic contemplation was the substance, except in this: the function of military power and efficient political organization is to provide peace and comfort. These can be understood as power and beauty reduced to materialistic values. The actual effect of Chang's programme was to lead, among the new men, to an exclusive concern for action—the action of science in technological warfare and in providing a higher material standard of living.

Chang's one-sided notion of science as the Western learning can, as we have tried to show, be in part explained in terms of the long history of Chinese reflection upon the polarities of knowledge and action. In part it was a misunderstanding of Western science. Few of his generation or of the next realized that mechanical techniques had been derived from a precise study of materials and the principles of machines, that these in turn had been gained from specific theories which had been derived from general laws, and that all these inductive and deductive processes of scientific research had been made possible by a system of thought involving not only a radical criticism of traditional beliefs and mores but also a religious devotion to seminal concerns of Hebrew, Greek and Christian culture. The same misunderstanding of Western learning is apparent in Chang's notion of the adaption of American and European political structures to the service of Chinese culture. Neither in Chang nor

---

[23] *Ibid.*, p. 121.

in Sun Yat Sen was there an adequate grasp of Western
political theory with its roots in Plato and Augustin or
of the long history of the science of administration.

Within a generation of the publication of Chang's
Exhortation to Learn (1898) the function had devoured
the substance. His *via media* had been rejected in favour
of a thorough-going scientific materialism. The vote had
already been cast when on 14 February, 1923 Dr. Chang
Chün-mai (Carsun Chang) delivered his famous lecture at
Tsinghua College.[24] Professor Chang was well aware of
what had happened to the mind of the new Chinese
university, especially to the University of Peking. He was
himself a new man, but he had grave misgivings of the
harsh materialism as well as of the cruel indifference
of the ' New Culture ' movement to the past. He was
led by his judgment of the new age, both in China and
in Europe, and by the appeal of Bergson's thought to
propose, as an antidote to the materialism of the science
faculty, a parallel emphasis upon a ' philosophy of life '
that would preserve the values of a humane individualism.
Within two months Chang's lecture was answered in a
fiery article published by Ting Wen-chiang, the professor
of geology at the University of Peking. " Chang is my
friend," he wrote, " but metaphysics is the enemy of
science." [25] His whole article could have been written by
Auguste Comte at least seventy-five years before. He is
convinced that the frontiers of religion and philosophy
should and must retreat before the triumphant advance of
positive knowledge. Many others joined with V. K. Ting
in the ' Great Debate.' Hu Shih countered Chang's plea
with the proposal for a ' Scientific Philosophy of Life '

---

[24] See de Bary, *op. cit.,* p. 834.
[25] *Ibid.,* p. 838.

which reads now like a fifth form essay with its nineteenth century sociologist's knowledge of the eighteenth century layman's understanding of the physical sciences.[26] Perhaps the most striking fact in this ' war of words ' (which in the end numbered over two hundred fifty thousand) is how close together were the opponents in their basic viewpoints. Chang Chün-mai was, in good Bergsonian fashion, a thorough-going anti-intellectualist. He had accepted the Kantian divorce of science and moral value—of ontological presuppositions and scientific theory. To the degree that his emphasis upon subjective value judgment, personalism and individualism could be considered metaphysical, he was in full disagreement with the materialists; but on the fundamental issue of a philosophy of nature and its relation to a philosophy of history he was no more than they an exponent of metaphysics.

The second impression one gets from the more outstanding contributions to this controversy is that they present a final rehearsal of the old arguments in the debate over the meaning and relation of knowledge and action from Confucius to Chang Chih-Tung. To all intents and purposes, the issue had been decided before the philosophy of life debate was joined. The laurels were duly given to the supporters of science, but the real champion was the mood of the times—the failure of nerve throughout the culture. There were two live options and no other: the choice between a materialistic individualism and a materialistic collectivism. Chinese culture in respect of its classical pattern had ground down to a grumbling stop. In part the latter choice was forced upon China by Western commerce and government. In the end these were the decisive forces in the tragic meeting in those years

---

[26] *Ibid.*, p. 841.

of East and West. The missionaries could contribute to predisposing factors but the determinative, precipitating incidents were under the strategic commercial and political programmes of government and trade. Even beyond the nineteenth century these powers spoke almost exclusively for just those 'functions' that were neatly reducible to materialistic terms. They did not speak for the culture of the West—for Plato, Augustin, Anselm or Abelard, nor for Jefferson or Lincoln, nor for Pitt or Arnold. The one forceful ideological impact upon China was Communism, not Christianity. Government and industry would have felt it wrong to speak for Christian perspectives. Opium was something about which a gentleman should have the right to have his way, but he would be trespassing upon the rights of man to exhibit any convictions in the area of religious opinion. Levenson is quite definite in his judgment that China was not, at the turn to this century, the immovable defender against all cultural change. 'Communist ideas came to China from a Western world which unmistakably had impinged socially on China, and the old saw about China's absorbing everything should be buried once and for all. Modern China, with industrialism pressing from without and planted within, seems frankly implausible in the role of unmoved mover. . . . The Confucian tradition, transformed and abandoned, has led directly to the communist version of Chinese change of mind, not by preserving itself immanent in communist doctrine, but by failing in self-preservation, leaving its heirs bereft and potentially strange in their own land, and thus commending that latest doctrine as an answer to a need." [27]

---

[27] Levenson, *op. cit.,* pp. 161, 163.

The final cultural collapse was perhaps inevitable for in the crucial years the intellectual leadership in the West was at a low point. The social sciences were still under the doctrinaire positivism of Comte and his disciples. The university scientists were almost as materialistic and irresponsible as Hu Shih's unintentional caricature of a ' scientific philosophy of life.' The arts syllabus left quite open the choice of Cephalus or Socrates, Protagoras or Plato. In general, liberalism in the first half of the twentieth century felt that it must have Merlin and not Anselm, Fugger and not Luther, Hume and not Kant, Durkheim and Nietzsche and Dewey but not Kierkegaard, Royce or Oman, Russell but not Whitehead.

A NEW STUDIUM GENERALE

Now after the mid-century what is abundantly evident is that neither in the East nor in the West is the humanistic or liberal ideal of the university a continuing live option.[28] The neo-humanism of the recent Western past was frivolous and naive. Confucius reborn in the fashion of the French *savant* or as exemplified in the young Hu Shih was an aborted renascence. Renaissance, like religion, cannot be invented.[29]

These are now years of exile for Chinese culture. As the Israelites of the sixth century B.C. had, after humiliating political and military defeat, fled to Egypt or lived as captives in Babylon, so Chinese culture today survives in exile. One Hebrew prophet was convinced, during the last days of Jerusalem, that cultural and spiritual bank-

---

[28] See Moberly, *op. cit.*, p. 50.
[29] See the article, "Dark Age and Renaissance in the Twentieth Century" by Dr. William G. Pollard in *The Christian Idea of Education*, ed. by E. Fuller, (New Haven: Yale University Press, 1957), pp. 3 ff.

ruptcy was the real tragedy of that time and of the years before. But then Israel found in exile the opportunity to review its history and to weigh its values—to reconsider the character of importance in respect of defeat and destiny. In fulfilling that task of ' retrospective prophecy,' it found the courage to go on. There are significant disparities in all historical parallels, and there are many in this comparison of the Chinese Diaspora in the mid-twentieth century and the exile of Israel twenty-five hundred years ago. And yet the task of retrospective prophecy by the waters of this fragrant stream (Hong Kong 香港) offers the elements of realism and heroism that are lacking in the alternatives. The department of Western sinology, whether it be a foreign embassy on the American campus or a cultural attache's office set down in an English university in Asia, has its proper function. The Eastern university, however, has the right to demand something more: a greater realism and heroism than could be asked of the sinophile or the sinologue. Neither the worship nor the ' doubting of antiquity ' seems very relevant in these great commercial cities of the East—not much more, I suspect, than it did by the waters of ancient Babylon. Nineteenth century historical and literary criticism with its naive scientific objectivity did not save the humanities in the West, nor did it, except where it was an instrument of retrospective prophecy—of existential concern—light the torch of useful learning. By the waters of Babylon a community that remembered Moses and suffered deeply from conscience concerning its destiny did light a torch that was handed on from generation to generation of refugees and rebuilders. Chinese studies are the rightful heritage of those who care—not just for porcelains and calligraphy—but for China, for a people, and not in a sentimental way, or in the sad sweet sorrow that mourns a mistress of rare delight, but for the moments of greatness that God has vouchsafed to his people—for those moments that are eternal amidst the perpetual perishing of past and present. To discover those moments and what it was once and is now, even in exile, that constitutes their greatness is the task of retrospective prophecy. This is the only justification of a department of Chinese studies or of any other ' humanities ' department. Of science and language you need only ask when you dwell in Babylon: Is it required? What certificate will it command? Of humanities you must ask: Is it great?

With all due respect to hard-working secularists whether they be Western, and therefore disdainful of Christ, or they be Eastern, and therefore disdainful of Christianity, the question must be raised: Where among the secularists of East and West, with so few exceptions, is the hero who is passionate for retrospective prophecy? It will be difficult enough to find him among the ' Christians.' And yet if there is one impression that persists in this city of various poses, it is that among those who remember Christ are to be found those who remember Confucius. Chauvinism is not Confucianism, nor is it Christianity. Levenson remarks that " if Christianity is singled out (as the Western analogue of Confucianism) then Chinese history need not suffer in comparison with Western; when Christianity alone is Confucianism's opposite number, then a surrender of Confucianism to industrialism need not seem a surrender of China to the West." [30] So in

---

[30] Levenson, *op. cit.*, pp. 120 ff.

the Chinese Diaspora there is one other privileged shelter. It is that of the malingering Confucianist who claims a compensation for the distress of the age on the basis of ' how different things would be if they were not as they are.'

There has been for a long time in both East and West the need of a re-organization of the arts as basic as the comparatively recent recognition in the English university that there were modern ' Greats.' That re-organization must take account not only of literature but also of the theoretical thrust of the social and physical sciences. There is in our time, as in any other, the need of the wholesome man. In the past, men went from Oxford into Government as graduates who had a grasp of human values and therefore could be expected to cope in a principled way with the affairs of state. In some ways such a modern gentleman with humane foresight might be a worthy colleague to Snow's ' new men ' with the gift of divining our technological future.

The Eastern university with its internal strains, and particularly the university in exile, may be especially fitted to undertake the re-organization of the arts curriculum. The Eastern university lives in a leanness that makes it keen, a tenderness that makes it perceptive, and a realism that forces the alternative of conscience or comfort. It can look with an equal eye at Western civilization and Eastern secularism, and it can listen with ' the strength made perfect in weakness ' to the powers that be today. But above all, the strength made perfect in weakness is the power of retrospective prophecy in respect of history both of the East and the West. If the Eastern university can rise to this vocation it will be a new force as well as the first genuine *studium generale* in the modern world.

CONTRIBUTIONS CONFUCIAN AND CHRISTIAN

Retrospective Prophecy

Retrospective prophecy is the first demand of an adequate philosophy of life in the contemporary Eastern university. Two positive conclusions of the quarter century of turmoil between Chang Chih-Tung and Chang Chün-mai affirm its importance: 1. the conviction that the meeting of East and West was not only inevitable but desirable, and that neither learning was evil or useless, and 2. the conviction that some basis of unity should be sought—some principle of integration of the new and old learning had to be found. Now in the aftermath of all the violence of those years, the Eastern university can undertake, with better perspective, a realistic appraisal of the seminal ideas of a vital culture that spanned the longest tract of continuous national expression in human history; [31] and it can look with an objective, and yet not hostile interest, over the same span of years in the history of the West—from Jeremiah and Heraclitus to Whitehead. The West, no less than the East, needs now a retrospective prophetic study of history, especially of the history of science. Here in the Eastern university that has a Christian commitment there can be a tenderly perceptive concern for history. It was Christian historiography that first developed the concept of world history; for it saw all history as a unity because God is one. All history is thus sacred history, and the sanctity of its record consists in the faithfulness, sensitivity and insight with which the historian deals with the problems of evidence and interpretation. There is no *Christian History* in the

---

[31] Such a programme was proposed by Chang Hsueh-ch'eng and Y'ang Leang-li.

256

sense that only certain passages of the human venture are meaningful and the rest empty, or that only certain peoples were important and others not, or that the significant aspects of the historical process are illumined only by isolated events separable from the wider context. The Christian perspective urges that " God hath nowhere left Himself without a witness." Nor is there a Christian history in the sense that there is a special heuristics or methodics or even hermeneutics proceeding by its own canons which are not subject to criticism. An historical theory or the elucidation of an historical event amenable to religion is of no use to the theologian if it be the product of careless assumption rather than careful inquiry, or of dogmatism rather than retrospective prophecy. There is, of course, no presuppositionless history; and it is a concern of a Christian university in East and West that presuppositions that are obviously biased shall not dominate the curriculum by the power of privilege.[32]

Rejection of Idols

We have now come to a second major concern for a philosophy of life and it is also the concern of a Christian university: the rejection of the worship of idols. These may be, to use, with some re-defining, Francis Bacon's famous classification: the idols of the market place, the idols of the theatre, the idols of the tribe, or the idols of the cave.[33] We have already spoken of the idols of the market and the theatre. We have now to speak of tribal idolatries as they threaten the life of the university. Some of these idolatries may be quite subtle. No one who believed that Christianity had been on the whole a

---

[32] Fehl, *Religion in the University,* p. 6.
[33] From the Preface to his *Novum Organum.*

divisive and stultifying force in Western civilization over against the seminal, though secular, ideas of art and science that were the contribution of Greece and the ideas of law and organization that were the contribution of Rome, would feel that the roots of Christianity need be a required course for history majors. There has been a half century tradition in certain Western universities of a one-root theory of Western culture.[34] This tradition is translated into the history curriculum in terms of required courses or papers in Greek and Roman history, a course in the Renaissance, and several courses in the seventeenth, eighteenth and nineteenth centuries in Europe and America. The rise of Christianity is thus linked with the decline of the glory that was Greece and the grandeur that was Rome. The dominance of Christianity in Europe is linked with the ' Dark Ages,' its failing grasp of temporal power with the importation of new ideas from Islamic civilization in the crusades. The rebirth of European culture is then associated with the decay of the Church in the Renaissance, and the ' long withdrawing, melancholy roar ' of Christendom with the rise of secular society and democracy and the emergence of the new physical and social sciences.

Of course it would be quite impossible to find a competent historian who would accept the defence of this thesis, certainly none who was an authority in Hellenistic culture, the middle ages, or the seventeenth and eighteenth centuries. Yet this bias determines the teaching of history in many Western schools and has become the pattern for the curriculum in Western history throughout the East. A most crucial implication of this bias is the total neglect of two of the most exciting and constructive passages in the whole of world history: the history of the Israelites

---

[34] See Pollard in Fuller, *op. cit.,* pp. 4, 5.

from 1500 B.C. to A.D. 70, and the history of the synthesis of Graeco-Roman and Hebrew perspectives in the period from Alexander the Great to St. Augustin.[35]

A second idol of the tribe sometimes rears its head in the form of a national type of university with pretensions of sanctity. America and England are now the two nations sponsoring, on any broad scale, university education in the East. Science as the important faculty of the modern university makes the Eastern University, to a large extent, dependent upon the graduate schools, particularly in America, both for the preparation of its masters and advanced research opportunities for its promising students. America's concern for public education and her success as the major producer in the new technological civilization, together with her wealth and the responsibility for education in the area of international relations, has given to the American university pattern a new importance in the East. The United Kingdom with its transformation of Empire into Commonwealth and its creation of the Association of British Commonwealth Universities has made the English type of university the standard in many areas.

These programmes of American and British support of higher education in Asia are essential, and they contribute, for the most part, one of the finest chapters in the history of these sister nations. Both have approached their opportunity sincerely desiring to serve with grace and humility. And yet the very limitation of this effort of the West to two nations has obvious evils. It is narrower as a base for international higher education than it should be. It focuses too much attention upon the pretensions of one culture. It invites the caricature of

---

[35] See Fehl, *op. cit.,* p. 6.

the American millionaire and the British aristocrat—or more precisely upon technological success and cultural pretension. American support has, in most instances, allowed greater autonomy in the expression of aims and their implementation in terms of curriculum and examination. But this larger freedom may be simply an extension of the autonomous pattern of American higher education at home, or it may reflect a grievous lack of concern for standards and a failure to recognize the value of uniformity in curriculum that would in the long run be of advantage both to masters and scholars. British programmes tend, like the American, to follow their own procedures at home, and because colonial governments desire only the best for their subjects, it is devoutly desired that the Eastern university should conform to the syllabus, papers and machinery of the Redbrick universities at home. There may be some middle ground between these two policies and it might be that a people who have endured the blessings and enjoyed the imperfections of the examination type of higher education from the Former Han (165 B.C.) to the last of the Ching (A.D. 1906) could contribute some retrospective prophecy on the sacred history of syllabus, papers and examiners which were instituted at Oxford in the eighteenth century for masters and in the nineteenth century for bachelors. It will be a very great temptation to the masters and scholars of the Eastern university, set as it is, in the midst of the commercial city to settle for that kind of education which is immediately translated into jobs with comfortable pay. But if we do this in Tokyo or Manila, in Seoul or Taipei, in Singapore or especially in Hong Kong, the Eastern university will then be a training center for the menial scientific skills and the Western university will be the school for the masters in the sense that one is basically practical and the other basically theoretical. But then the governments or the foundations will have failed in their trust of those whom they serve if they shall be pleased to regard the Eastern university as a lower school or a second son. For in the Eastern university with its honesty in respect of languages and its sincerity in respect of cultures is the real meeting of East and West. Nor may either government or the foundations in good conscience say ' Here is tu'ppence—Let us hear you sing the Lord's song in a strange land.'

Another idol who is particularly desirous of university status is the semi-divinity who presides over sentiment. In a Christian university moral perspective is related to a larger whole—to a sense of the ultimate.[36] A concern for the ultimate is the university's proper business. The university must have its minimal regulation in terms of what is fitting in the public deportment of all its members. But this has not so much to do with morals as with the practical requirements of community life. It is an idol who insists that students ought to be taught what to do. But you do not begin with morals—at least not in a Christian university. You begin with facts and theories, and you go on to encourage judgment and the importance of ultimate commitment. All this is the proper business of the university. The home will have taught taste, and the community, form. The religious tradition will have inculcated a sense of the holy and of tabu. The university is a community of people with different tastes, forms and tabus. What it can do—perhaps the most important task of all—is to foster a community of wide concern for the concept of the ultimate whence all morality derives. The parochial school or the denominational college which

---

[36] See P. Tillich, *Systematic Theology* I p. 211. See also his *Theology of Culture.*

emphasizes 'character building' as the tradition of the school without relating its moral nurture to its regular studies, or to the ultimate perspective of all studies, is not Christian. It is an institution of pious secularism. What the university can do and must do is to make abundantly clear that its course in ethics is not extra-curricular—that ethics is related to the arts and to social science and physical science and philosophy, and that theological ethics is an application of value judgments which can be made only after listening to the whole word of God: His speaking in nature, in history and in individual experience.

The most demonic of all idols is he who demands the sacrifice of first fruits, who regards as sacred the separate fruits of each department of each faculty. The Christian university is committed to the quest of ontological truth, to a goal of all studies, or in Bacon's words, to a 'science of sciences.' The meeting of East and West must be at the point of their spiritual ultimates and the Christian valuation of science must press toward the worth of theoretical science and its implications for our under-standing of God's working in nature. At the deeper level, at the nethermost piers of university structure, the concern for ontological truth and the concern for competence in a field are not sources of strain. They are mutually supporting. Criticism in the arts or research in the sciences without a sense of the ultimate is demonic. Discrimination and judgment involve devotion but devotion to something less than the unity of the God whose speaking in nature, in history and in individual experience, it is the duty of the university to interpret, is idolatry. Perhaps the greatest service that Christianity can render to the university, as a daughter who is flesh of its own flesh and bone of its bone, is the protection against idolatry.

Idolatry means enslavement, it means loss of academic freedom, or what is worse, loss of the only concern that justifies academic freedom. It is historically and essentially a truism that a non-Christian university is a contradiction in terms. Certainly this does not mean that there are not and should not be many institutes of catechetical training or of advanced research whose proper purpose is limited to a training in, or a contribution to, descriptive knowledge in a specialized field. Nor does it mean that an aggregation of such institutes at a particular location is a dangerous or evil thing. It simply means that we are under some obligation to deal fairly with the history and essence of the idea of a university, and that not even a magnificent conformity to quantitative procedures will do in lieu of a *community* of masters and scholars.

CREDO UT INTELLIGAM

The peculiar freedom of a university is, in the last resort, a spiritual freedom. The deepest foundation of the idea of a university is the Platonic faith in the unity of truth. It found expression in Augustin and in Anselm, and it was the resource of Abelard's courage and Aquinas' vision: *Credo ut intelligam*—I believe in order that I may know. St. Augustin had first put it in terms that bespoke better the temper of his age and of ours. The only thing I cannot doubt is that I doubt. But if I doubt it must be because I have implanted within me a concern for truth. Were it not for this I could not doubt. My doubting then is a very act of faith—faith in the goodness and the beauty of truth, in the reality and unity of truth. The university has its ground in such faith—the faith that God speaks in nature, in history and in human

263

experience. The university is the community of the faithful, of those who *believe* nature, history and human experience are all the speaking of God in order that they may *know* them in their fullness and unity.[37]   And it is by such faith that the Eastern university alone can live— the faith by which each generation can face the present and the future in the knowledge that the physical shape of the past is not important.   The past cannot survive unless it can transform itself into a new being.   The past and the present will always perish.   But death—horrible death—means the impossibility of the past to be relevant to the present.   When a civilization dies it is because it can no longer relate itself to the present.   It cannot transform itself so that it becomes a present reality.   But when that transformation is accomplished you cannot recognize the past.   It has become the present.

President Yung Chi-tung, with his early training in Chinese language and literature and his later graduate study and university career in science, has held up to us all this vision of the Eastern university.   I am privileged to quote two passages from two recent addresses.   The first from his Address to the Graduating Class of 1961, and the second from The Fifth Presidents' Conference of Christian Universities in Asia.

> " The crucial religious encounter for the college student is in his studies.   We want our science students to appreciate the presuppositions of their studies as well as the functions of them, and we want our arts students to be able to live in this age not as strangers but as responsible citizens. . . .   We want to build on this campus a college that brings China's great heritage to bear upon the present and to shape the future. . . .   We shall cherish the good from whatever

---

[37] See Fehl, *A Preface to Theology* p. 1.

source it has come to us; and from our several sources—Chinese, American and British—much has come. And we shall need the humility and the courage to be constantly aware that for our Chinese past and our American past and our British past there is but one place of meeting and that is the present . . . (the Eastern university) set within the great world of opportunity and responsibility which is Asia.[38]

I would suggest that Christian witness in the Asian college will be made in the future at the deepest level in the patient and humble contribution toward a new kind of university. This is the great frontier of the Asian college. The Western university is concerned with the problem of the relation of arts and sciences to the commercial culture of the modern world. But the Asian college faces an even broader and more challenging frontier: the integration on a curriculum level not only of arts and sciences but also of the values of two cultures. The Asian university must be a new kind of university. It cannot be either Eastern or Western only. It must be ' a new creation.' Living on this wild frontier, the life of the Asian college involves adventure. But adventure is something more than daring. In education, adventure demands sensitivity, patience and faith.

An important part of the Christian witness in higher education in the next decade in Asia will be beneath the surface. It will be an unobtrusive working on the underside of the tapestry. . . . Now we see only through a glass darkly. Now it does not yet appear what the new Asian university will be. The Christian witness is ultimately a willingness ' to endeavour to do the right as God gives us to see the right,' not only to plan, but to be patient, not only to legislate, but also to listen. . . . This is the huge task which our several heritages

---

[38] *Chung Chi College Bulletin* (Hong Kong, 1961), No. 28, p. 27.

have laid upon us. We may expect that it shall not prove a light or simple responsibility, nor that we shall find answers to its problems without much searching and some stumbling. But this endeavour is of the essence both of religion and of learning. It is a translation into the many-sided tasks of college administration and of the class room and laboratory of what it means ' to walk by faith in the living God and to pray without ceasing.' " [39]

All that has been said in these chapters of duty and reverence illumines the concept of the university as an organism. There are many members in one body and all members have not the same office. The glory of a university is the diversity of its talents and its tasks. The glory of an organism is the differentiation of its several members, each developed for a specific function. Cells and tissues differ in terms of their adaption to the special needs and functions of the several organs; but the life of all depends upon the life of the whole. The life of an organism is a unity. This is a paraphase of St. Paul, and it is not stretching Paul. The idea of society as an organism *in motion* is Pauline. This unity in diversity, the presence of the spiritual in the spatial, derives from the uniquely and crucially Christian belief in the Incarnation, the Word made flesh. The tragic limitation of Greek thought was its nearly spatial differentiation of truth and existence. Christianity focused its sensitive perception upon the differentiation of time, and thus emphasized life and event as the concurrence of existence and meaning. It beheld the glory of the eternal in time, and lived by faith in a new age that was to come. Its crucial categories

---

[39] *Fifth Presidents' Conference of Christian Universities related to The United Board for Christian Higher Education in Asia: The Christian Colleges of Asia and their Spiritual Task.* (Seoul: Yonsei University, 1961), pp. G. 5, 6.

are the *no longer* and the *not yet*. For no other city than Hong Kong, and for no other college than Chung Chi, could these categories carry such a weight of poignant memory of precious hope.

The members, old and young, of this college, which is itself now poised so critically on the narrow line between the no longer and the not yet, have witnessed the passing of a whole way of life in a few short years. Old China is no more—either here or on the mainland, or even in Taiwan. Whatever the future holds, the old days are gone. Indeed, none of us can go home again, not to the same home. And we dwell in a city that lives from day to day. In this, Hong Kong may be the dramatic symbol for the whole world. Here the sense of change is perhaps more poignant, the memory of yesterday etched in deeper purple. Yet these broken waters, swelling outward from the great storms of world revolution, political and scientific, though they break with dramatic violence upon the shores of this colony, swirl and sweep with no less force against all coasts of the world. All sound learning is living in the narrow time between the *no longer* and the *not yet*. It is a thrusting into that horrible vacuum. It is a facing up to the ' horrible simplifiers ' who live in anxious ease between the past and the future, forgetful of the past and well insured against the future. Even universities—even new universities—may sleep in ' the enchanted garden that lies between dawn and sunrise.' But all sound learning lives in the tension of an insistent present that punctuates the no longer and the not yet. Its leisure is the calm of crisis between the violence of the past and the violence of the future, that calm that lies at the center of the storm.

One way of exposing the difference in pedigree between the academy of secular knowledge and the university is to suggest the difference between the refugee and the pilgrim. Both are travellers. Neither is a settler. The refugee is in flight away from something. The pilgrim is on the way in quest of something. The refugee mourns a lost security. The pilgrim seeks something beyond security—perhaps the meaning of the journey itself. Yet for the pilgrim the present can be holy ground. He is sensitive to the incidents of the journey. He feels the earth in travail. He hears the cry of the insistent present, the thrill of its great ventures, the exaltation of its visions, the immensity of its problems, the tragedy of its strictures upon the tender working, amidst its passions and violence, of the Spirit of God.[40] In this moment, between the no longer and the not yet, in which the Eastern university as the new *studium generale* stands with so short a past, and by the grace of God, so long a future, pray God, let it be a university of pilgrims, not an academy of refugees.[41]

I should like to leave the two last words of this book to two men from whom I have learned much. First, because he came first into my life, Alfred North Whitehead who died on December 30th, 1947.

> The early Benedictine monks rejoiced in their labours because they conceived themselves as thereby made fellow-workers with Christ. . . . If, in the troubled times which may be before us, you wish appreciably to increase the chance of some savage upheaval, introduce wide-spread technical education and ignore the Benedictine ideal. Society will then get what it deserves.[42]

---

[40] See Bernard E. Meland, *Seeds of Redemption,* (New York: The Macmillan Company, 1947), pp. 95 ff.

[41] See Fehl, *Religion in the University,* p. 7.

[42] *The Aims of Education,* pp. 53, 54.

And then from Confucius who died in 479 B.C., nine years before Socrates was born:

> Last of all, the Master asked Tsang Hsi, 'Tien, what are your wishes?' Tien, pausing as he was playing on his lute, while it was yet twanging, laid the instrument aside, and rose. 'My wishes,' he said, 'are different from the cherished purposes of these three gentlemen.' 'What harm is there in that?' said the Master; 'do you also, as well as they, speak out your wishes.' Tien then said, 'In this, the last month of spring, with the dress of the season all complete, along with five or six young men who have assumed the cap, and six or seven boys, I would wash in the river, enjoy the breeze among the rain altars, and return home singing.' The Master heaved a sigh and said, 'I give my approval to Tien.' [43]

[43] *Analects* X (Heang Tang) xxv 7.

FINIS

"Why have you come so late?" Confucius impatiently demanded.

A UNIVERSITY READER

PART ONE: READINGS IN LITERATURE

FROM *THE BOOK OF RITES* (禮記) C. 400 B.C.? —

A Fairly Free Translation!

Confucius observed: " When one enters a country he can easily discern what is the emphasis of its education. Gentleness, affection and loyalty reveal the teaching of the *Book of Odes*.   Scholarship, wisdom and a full knowledge of the past reveal the teaching of the *Book of History*.   Broad sympathies and a spontaneous good will reflect the teaching of the *Book of Music*.   Clarity, purity, refinement and carefulness reveal the teaching of the *Book of Changes*.   Humility, naturalness, poise and graciousness reveal the teaching of the *Book of Rites*.   The precise use of terms and an impartial judgment of facts disclose the teaching of the *Spring and Autumn*.

Where the *Book of Odes* is not taught there is the meanness of stupidity.   Where the *Book of History* is neglected there is falsehood.   Where the *Book of Music* is ignored there is *hybris*.   Without attention to the *Book of Changes* there will be carelessness.   Where there is no knowledge of the *Book of Rites* there will be discord. Where the *Spring and Autumn* classic is not taught there is chaos.

When a man is gentle, affectionate and loyal and yet is not ignorant of the ways of the world then he has the wisdom of the *Book of Odes*.   When he is learned and understanding and, though he pursues with all zeal a knowledge of the remote past, is yet faithful both to the past and to the present, he has that wisdom which the *Book of History* can give.   When a man has broad sympathies, is readily kind and forgiving, yet is himself a disciplined and integritous person, he possesses that

273

excellence which the *Book of Music* can bestow. When
a man combines clarity of thought, precision of expression
and refinement of manner with a conscientious regard
for justice, he has fulfilled all that is purposed in the
Book of Changes.

When a man exhibits unaffected humility, respect and
propriety and yet is at peace in the inner thoughts of
his heart, he possesses the greater treasure of the *Book
of Rites.* When a man has a feeling for language and
a concern for the unprejudiced evaluation of facts and
yet is not vague or disorganized in his thought, he has
understood the deeper wisdom of the *Spring and Autumn.*

FROM "THE GREAT PREFACE" 大序 TO THE *SHE KING* 詩經 .

A Free Translation!

Poetry is the expression of a compelling urge. In the
heart it is passion; released through words it is poetry.
Passion surging up from the depths is given form in words.
But when passion cannot be harnessed by thought it leaps
out in sighs and shouts. When these cannot satisfy it
finds release in the sustained sound of song, or, if this
fails, in the movement of hands and feet in gesture and
in the dance.

Thus the feelings seek expression in sound; and when
these sounds are artfully arranged there is music. The
mood of music in well ordered times ranges from tranquillity to joy, for the government is then harmonious.
But in a disordered time the mood ranges from the
expression of resentment to that of anger, for the government is then discordant. Of a state in decline the style
of music is mournful, lamenting lost glories, for then
there is distress amongst the people.

Thus for the true insight into the soundness or the disease of the commonwealth or to move Heaven and Earth—to persuade the gods to act—there is no more effectual means than poetry. It served the ancient kings in their concern to regulate the respective duties of husband and wife, to increase filial obedience and strengthen reverence, to set in order and maintain all the interior relations of the nation, to grace the work of instruction, and to elevate manners and the customs of the realm.

"LITERATURE OF KNOWLEDGE AND LITERATURE OF POWER"

From *The Poetry of Pope,* 1848, *by* THOMAS DE QUINCEY

What is it that we mean by literature? Popularly, and amongst the thoughtless, it is held to include everything that is printed in a book. Little logic is required to disturb that definition. The most thoughtless person is easily made aware that in the idea of literature one essential element is—some relation to a general and common interest of man, so that what applies only to a local or professional or merely personal interest, even though presenting itself in the shape of a book, will not belong to literature. So far the definition is easily narrowed; and it is as easily expanded. For not only is much that takes a station in books not literature, but, inversely, much that really is literature never reaches a station in books. The weekly sermons of Christendom, that vast pulpit literature which acts so extensively upon the popular mind—to warn, to uphold, to renew, to comfort, to alarm—does not attain the sanctuary of libraries in the ten-thousandth part of its extent. The drama, again, as for instance the finest of Shakespeare's plays in England and all leading Athenian

275

plays in the noontide of the Attic stage, operated as a literature on the public mind, and were (according to the strictest letter of that term) published through the audiences that witnessed their representation, some time before they were published as things to be read; and they were published in this scenical mode of publication with much more effect than they could have had as books during ages of costly copying or of costly printing.

Books, therefore, do not suggest an idea co-extensive and interchangeable with the idea of literature, since much literature, scenic, forensic, or didactic (as from lectures and public orators), may never come into books, and much that does come into books may connect itself with no literary interest. But a far more important correction, applicable to the common vague idea of literature, is to be sought, not so much in a better definition of literature, as in a sharper distinction of the two functions which it fulfills. In that great social organ which, collectively, we call literature, there may be distinguished two separate offices, that may blend and often do so, but capable, severally, of a severe insulation, and naturally fitted for reciprocal repulsion. There is, first, the literature of knowledge, and, secondly, the literature of power. The function of the first is to teach; the second an oar or a sail. The first speaks to the mere discursive under-standing; the second speaks ultimately, it may happen, to the higher understanding, or reason, but always through affections of pleasure and sympathy. Remotely it may travel towards an object seated in what Lord Bacon calls dry light; but proximately it does and must operate—else it ceases to be a literature of power—on and through that humid light which clothes itself in the mists and glittering iris of human passions, desires, and genial emotions. Men have so little reflected on the higher functions of literature as to find it a paradox if one should describe it as a mean or subordinate purpose of books to give information. But this is a paradox only in the sense which makes it honourable to be paradoxical. Whenever we talk in ordinary language of seeking information or gaining knowledge, we understand the words as connected with something of absolute novelty. But it is the grandeur of all truth which can occupy a very high place in human interests that it is never absolutely novel to the meanest of minds: it exists eternally, by way of germ or latent principle, in the lowest as in the highest, needing to be developed but never to be planted. To be capable of transplantation is the immediate criterion of a truth that ranges on a lower scale. Besides which, there is a rarer thing than truth, namely, power, or deep sympathy with truth. What is the effect, for instance, upon society, of children? By the pity, by the tenderness, and by the peculiar modes of admiration, which connect themselves with the helplessness, with the innocence, and with the simplicity of children, not only are the primal affections strengthened and continually renewed, but the qualities which are dearest in the sight of heaven—the frailty, for instance, which appeals to forbearance, the innocence which symbolizes the heavenly, and the simplicity which is most alien from the worldly—are kept up in perpetual remembrance, and their ideals are continually refreshed. A purpose of the same nature is answered by the higher literature, viz., the literature of power. What do you learn from Paradise Lost? Nothing at all. What do you learn from a cookery-book? Something new, something that you did not know before, in every paragraph. But would you therefore put the wretched cookery-book on a higher level of estimation than the divine poem? What you owe to Milton is not any knowledge, of which a million separate items are still but a million of advancing steps on the same earthly level; what you owe is power, that is exercise, and expansion to your own latent capacity of sympathy with the infinite, where every pulse and each separate influx is a step upwards, a step ascending as upon a Jacob's ladder from earth to mysterious altitudes above the earth. All the steps of knowledge, from first to last, carry you further on the same plane, but could never raise you one foot above your ancient level of earth; whereas the very first step in power is a flight, is an ascending movement into another element where earth is forgotten.

Were it not that human sensibilities are ventilated and continually called out into exercise by the great phenomena of infancy or of real life as it moves through chance and change, or of literature as it recombines these elements in the mimicries of poetry, romance, etc., it is certain that, like any animal power or muscular energy falling into disuse, all such sensibilities would gradually droop and dwindle. It is in relation to these great moral capacities of man that the literature of power, as contra-distinguished from that of knowledge, lives and has its field of action. It is concerned with what is highest in man; for the Scriptures themselves never condescended to deal by suggestion or co-operation with the mere discursive understanding: when speaking of man in his intellectual capacity, the Scriptures speak, not of the understanding, but of " the understanding heart," making the heart—that is, the great intuitive (or non-discursive) organ, to be the interchangeable formula for man in his highest state of capacity for the infinite. Tragedy, romance, fairy tale, or epopee, all alike restore to man's mind the ideals of justice, of hope, of truth, of mercy, of retribution, which else (left to the support of daily life in its realities) would languish for want of sufficient illustration. What is meant, for instance, by poetic justice? It does not mean a justice that differs by its object from the ordinary justice of human jurisprudence, for then it must be confessedly a very bad kind of justice; but it means a justice that differs from common forensic justice by the degree in which it attains its object, a justice that is more omnipotent over its own ends, as dealing, not with the refractory elements of earthly life, but with elements of its own creation and with materials flexible to its own purest preconceptions. It is certain that, were it not for the literature of power, these ideals would often remain amongst us as mere notional forms; whereas, by the creative forces of man put forth in literature, they gain a vernal life of restoration and germinate into vital activities. The commonest novel, by moving in alliance with human fears and hopes, with human instincts of wrong and right, sustains and quickens those affections. Calling them into action, it rescues them from torpor. And hence the pre-eminency, over all authors that merely teach, of the meanest that moves, or that teaches, if at all, indirectly by moving. The very highest work that has ever existed in the literature of knowledge is but a provisional work, a book upon trial and sufferance, and *quamdiu bene se gesserit*. Let its teaching be even partially revised, let it be but placed in a better order and instantly it is superseded. Whereas the feeblest works in the literature of power, surviving at all, survive as finished and unalterable among men. For instance, the *Principia* of Sir Isaac Newton was a book militant on earth from the first. In all stages of its progress it would have to fight for its existence: first, as regards absolute truth; secondly, when that combat was over, as regards its form, or mode of presenting the truth. And as soon as a La Place, or anybody else, builds higher upon the foundations laid by this book, effectually he throws it out of the sunshine into decay and darkness; by weapons won from this book he superannuates and destroys this book, so that soon the man of Newton remains a mere *nominis umbra*, but his book, as a living power, has transmigrated into other forms. Now, on the contrary, the *Iliad*, the *Prometheus* of Aeschylus, the *Othello* or *King Lear*, the *Hamlet* or *Macbeth*, and the *Paradise Lost* are not militant but triumphant forever, as long as the languages exist in which they speak or can be taught to speak. They never can transmigrate into new incarnations. To reproduce these in new forms or variations, even if in some things they should be improved, would be to plagiarize. A good steam-engine is properly superseded by a better. But one lovely pastoral valley is not superseded by another, nor a statue of Praxiteles by a statue by Michael Angelo. These things are separated, not by imparity, but by disparity. They are not thought of as unequal under the same standard, but as different in kind, and, if otherwise unequal, under a different standard. Human works of immortal beauty and works of nature in one respect stand on the same footing: they never approach so near as not to differ; and they differ not as better and worse, or simply by more and less; they differ by undecipherable and incommunicable differences, that cannot be caught by mimicries, that cannot be reflected in the mirror of copies, that cannot become ponderable in the scales of vulgar comparison.

FROM *SESAME AND LILIES*, 1864, *by* JOHN RUSKIN

The good book of the hour, then,—I do not speak of the bad ones,—is simply the useful or pleasant talk of some person whom you cannot otherwise converse with, printed for you. Very useful often, telling you what you need to know; very pleasant often, as a sensible friend's present talk would be. These bright accounts of travels; good-humored and witty discussions of question; lively or pathetic story-telling in the form of novel; firm fact-telling, by the real agents concerned in the events of passing history;—all these books of the hour, multiplying among us as education becomes more general, are a peculiar possession of the present age: we ought to be entirely thankful for them, and entirely ashamed of ourselves if we make no good use of them. But we make the worst possible use if we allow them to usurp the place of true books: for, strictly speaking, they are not books at all, but merely letters or newspapers in good print. Our friend's letter may be delightful, or necessary, to-day: whether worth keeping or not, is to be considered. The newspaper may be entirely proper at breakfast time, but assuredly it is not reading for all day. So, though bound up in a volume, the long letter which gives you so pleasant an account of the inns, and roads, and weather, last year at such a place, or which tells you that amusing story, or gives you the real circumstances of such and such events, however valuable for occasional reference, may not be, in the real sense, of the work, a " book " at all, nor, in the real sense, to be " read." A book is essentially not a talking thing, but a written thing; and written, not with a view of mere communication, but of permanence. The book of talk is printed only because its author cannot speak to thousands of people at once; if he could, he would—the volume is mere multiplication of his voice. You cannot talk to your friend in India; if you could, you would; you write instead: that is mere conveyance of voice. But a book is written, not to multiply the voice merely, not to carry it merely, but to perpetuate it. The author has something to say which he perceives to be true and useful, or helpfully beautiful. So far as he knows, no one had yet said it; so far as he knows, no one else can say it. He is bound to say it, clearly and melodiously if he may; clearly at all events. In the sum of his life he finds this to be the thing, or group of things, manifest to him;—this, the piece of true knowledge, or sight, which his share of sunshine and earth has permitted him to seize. He would fain set it down forever; engrave it on rock, if he could; saying, " This is the best of me; for the rest, I ate, and drank, and slept, loved, and hated, like another; my life was as the vapor, and is not; but this I saw and knew: this, if anything of mine, is worth your memory." That is his " writing; " it is, in his small human way, and with whatever degree of true inspiration is in him, his inscription, or scripture. That is a " Book."

Perhaps you think no books were ever so written?

But, again, I ask you, do you at all believe in honesty, or at all in kindness, or do you think there is never any honesty or benevolence in wise people? None of us, I hope, are so unhappy as to think that. Well, whatever bit of a wise man's work is honestly and benevolently done, that bit is his book or his piece of art. It is mixed always with evil fragments—ill-done, redundant, affected work. But if you read rightly, you will easily discover the true bits, and those are the books.

Now books of this kind have been written in all ages by their greatest men:—by great readers, great statesmen, and great thinkers. These are all at your choice; and Life is short. You have heard as much before—yet have you measured and mapped out this short life and its possibilities? Do you know, if you read this, that you cannot read that—that what you lose to-day you cannot gain to-morrow? Will you go and gossip with your housemaid, or your stableboy, when you may talk with queens and kings; or flatter yourself that it is with any worthy consciousness of your own claims to respect, that you jostle with the hungry and common crowd for entree here, and audience there, when all the while this eternal court is open to you, with its society, wide as the world, multitudinous as its days, the chosen, and the mighty, of every place and time? Into that you may enter always; in that you may take fellowship and rank according to your wish; from that, once entered into it, you can never be outcast but by your own fault; by your aristocracy of companionship there, your own inherent aristocracy will be assuredly tested, and the motives with which you strive to take high place in the society of the living, measured, as to all the truth and sincerity that are in them, by the place you desire to take in this company of the Dead.

" The place you desire," and the place you fit yourself for, I must also say; because, observe, this court of the past differs from all living aristocracy in this : —it is open to labor and to merit, but to nothing else. No wealth will bribe, no name overawe, no artifice deceive, the guardian of those Elysian gates. In the deep sense, no vile or vulgar person ever enters there. At the portieres of that silent Faubourg St. Germain, there is but brief question : —" Do you deserve to enter? Pass. Do you ask to be the companion of nobles? Make yourself noble, and you shall be. Do you long for the conversation of the wise? Learn to understand it, and you shall hear it. But on other terms?—no. If you will not rise to us, we cannot stoop to you. The living lord may assume courtesy, the living philosopher explain his thought to you with considerate pain; but here we neither feign nor interpret; you must rise to the level of our thoughts if you would be gladdened by them, and share our feelings, if you would recognize our presence."

This, then, is what you have to do, and I admit that it is much. You must, in a word, love these people, if you are to be among them. No ambition is of any use.

283

They scorn your ambition. You must love them, and show your love in these two following ways.

(1) First, by a true desire to be taught by them, and to enter into their thoughts. To enter into theirs, observe; not to find your own expressed by them. If the person who wrote the book is not wiser than you, you need not read it; if he be, he will think differently from you in many respects.

(2) Very ready we are to say of a book, " How good this is—that's exactly what I think! " But the right feeling is, " How strange that is! I never thought of that before, and yet I see it is true; or if I do not now, I hope I shall, some day." But whether thus submissively or not, at least be sure that you go to the author to get at his meaning, not to find yours. Judge it afterwards if you think yourself qualified to do so; but ascertain it first. And be sure, also, if the author is worth anything, that you will not get at his meaning all at once;—nay, that at his whole meaning you will not for a long time arrive in any wise. Not that he does not say what he means, and in strong words too; but he cannot say it all; and what is more strange, will not, but in a hidden way and in parables, in order that he may be sure you want it. I cannot quite see the reason of this, nor analyze that cruel reticence in the breasts of wise men which makes them always hide their deeper thought. They do not give it you by way of help, but of reward; and will make themselves sure that you deserve it before they allow you to reach it. But it is the same with the physical type of wisdom, gold. There seems, to you and me, no reason why the electric forces of the earth should not carry whatever there is of gold within it at once to the mountain tops, so that kings and people might know that all the gold they could get was there; and without any trouble of digging, or anxiety, or chance, or waste of

time, cut it away, and coin as much as they needed. But Nature does not manage it so. She puts it in little fissures in the earth, nobody knows where: you may dig long and find none; you must dig painfully to find any.

And it is just the same with men's best wisdom. When you come to a good book, you must ask yourself, "Am I inclined to work as an Australian miner would? Are my pickaxes and shovels in good order, and am I in good trim myself, my sleeves well up to the elbow, and my breath good, and my temper?" And, keeping the figure a little longer, even at cost of tiresomeness, for it is a thoroughly useful one, the metal you are in search of being the author's mind or meaning, his words are as the rock which you have to crush and smelt in order to get at it. And your pickaxes are your own care, wit, and learning; your smelting furnace is your own thoughtful soul. Do not hope to get at any good author's meaning without those tools and that fire; often you will need sharpest, finest chiseling, and patientest fusing, before you can gather one grain of the metal.

And, therefore, first of all, I tell you earnestly and authoritatively (I know I am right in this), you must get into the habit of looking intensely at words, and assuring yourself of their meaning, syllable by syllable—nay, letter by letter. For though it is only by reason of the opposition of letters in the function of signs, to sounds in the function of signs, that the study of books is called " literature," and that a man versed in it is called, by the consent of nations, a man of letters instead of a man of books, or of words, you may yet connect with that accidental nomenclature this real fact:—that you might read all the books in the British Museum (if you could live long enough), and remain an utterly " illiterate," uneducated person; but that is to say, with real accuracy,—you are for evermore in some measure an educated person. The

285

entire difference between education and non-education (as regards the merely intellectual part of it), consists in this accuracy. A well-educated gentleman may not know many languages,—may not be able to speak any but his own,—may have read very few books. But whatever language he knows, he knows precisely; whatever word he pronounces, he pronounces rightly; above all, he is learned in the peerage of words; knows the words of true descent and ancient blood, at a glance, from words of modern canaille; remembers all their ancestry, their inter-marriages, distant relationships, and the extent to which they were admitted, and offices they held, among the national noblesse of words at any time, and in any country. But an uneducated person may know, by memory, many languages, and talk them all, and yet truly know not a word of any,—not a word even of his own. An ordinarily clever and sensible seaman will be able to make his way ashore at most ports; yet he has only to speak a sentence of any language to be known for an illiterate person: so also the accent, or turn of expression of a single sentence, will at once mark a scholar. And this is so strongly felt, so conclusively admitted, by educated persons, that a false accent or a mistaken syllable is enough, in the parliament of any civilized nation, to assign to a man a certain degree of inferior standing forever.

PARAGRAPHS FROM *THE POET*, 1850,

by RALPH WALDO EMERSON

Those who are esteemed umpires of taste, are often persons who have acquired some knowledge of admired pictures of sculptures, and have an inclination for whatever is elegant; but if you inquire whether they are beautiful souls, and whether their own acts are like fair pictures,

you learn that they are selfish and sensual. Their cultivation is local, as if you should rub a log of dry wood
in one spot to produce fire, all the rest remaining cold.
Their knowledge of the five arts is some study of rules
and particulars, or some limited judgment of colour or
form, which is exercised for amusement or for show. It
is a proof of the shallowness of the doctrine of beauty,
as it lies in the minds of our amateurs, that men seem
to have lost the perception of the instant dependence of
form upon soul. There is no doctrine of forms in our
philosophy. We were put into our bodies, as fire is put
into a pan, to be carried about.

But we are not pans and barrows, nor even porters
of the fire and torch-bearers, but children of the fire,
made of it, and only the same divinity transmuted, and
at two or three removes, when we know least about it.
And this hidden truth, that the fountains whence all this
river of Time, and its creatures, floweth are intrinsically
ideal and beautiful, draws us to the consideration of the
nature and functions of the Poet or the man of Beauty,
to the means and materials he uses, and to the general
aspect of art in the present time.

The breadth of the problem is great, for the poet is
representative. He stands among partial men for the
complete man, and apprises us not of his wealth, but of
the commonwealth. The young man reveres men of
genius, because, to speak truly, they are more himself
than he is. They receive of the soul as he also receives,
but they more. Nature enhances her beauty to the eye
of loving men, from their belief that the poet is beholding
her shows at the same time. He is isolated among his
contemporaries, by truth and by his art, but with this
consolation in his pursuits, that they will draw all men
sooner or later. For all men live by truth, and stand in

need of expression. In love, in art, in avarice, in politics, in labour, in game, we study to utter our painful secret. The man is only half himself, the other half is his expression.

Too feeble fall the impressions of nature on us to make us artists. Every touch should thrill. Every man should be so much an artist, that he could report in conversation what had befallen him. Yet, in our experience, the rays or appulses have sufficient force to arrive at the senses, but not enough to reach the quick, and compel the reproduction of themselves in speech. The poet is the person in whom these powers are in balance, the man without impediment, who sees and handles that which others dream of, traverses the whole scale of experience, and is representative of man, in virtue of being the largest power to receive and to impart.

For the Universe has three children, born at one time, which reappear, under different names, in every system of thought, whether they be called cause, operation, and effect; or, more poetically, Jove, Pluto, Neptune; or, theologically, the Father, the Spirit, and the Son; but which we will call here, the Knower, the Doer, and the Sayer. These stand respectively for the love of truth, for the love of good, and for the love of beauty. These three are equal. Each is that which he is essentially, so that he cannot be surmounted or analysed, and each of these three had the power of the others latent in him, and his own patent.

The poet is the sayer, the namer, and represents beauty. He is a sovereign, and stands on the centre. For the world is not painted, or adorned, but is from the beginning beautiful; and God has not made some beautiful things, but Beauty is the creator of the universe. Therefore the poet is not any permissive potentate, but is emperor in his own right. Criticism is infested with a cant of materialism, which assumes that manual skill and activity is the first merit of all men, and disparages such as say and do not, overlooking the fact, that some men, namely, poets, are natural sayers, sent into the world to the end of expression, and confounds them with those whose province is action, but who quit it to imitate the sayers. But Homer's words are as costly and admirable to Homer, as Agamemnon's victories are to Agamemnon. The poet does not wait for the hero or the sage, but, as they act and think primarily, so he writes primarily what will and must be spoken, reckoning the others, though primaries also, yet, in respect to him, secondaries and servants; as sitters or models in the studio of a painter, or as assistants who bring building materials to an architect.

For poetry was all written before time was, and whenever we are so finely organised that we can penetrate into that region where the air is music, we hear those primal warblings, and attempt to write them down, but we lose ever and anon a word, or a verse, and substitute something of our own, and thus miswrite the poem. The men of more delicate ear write down these cadences more faithfully, and these transcripts, though imperfect, become the songs of the nations. For nature is as truly beautiful as it is good, or as it is reasonable, and must as such appear, as it must be done, or be known. Words and deeds are quite indifferent modes of the divine energy. Words are also actions, and actions are a kind of words.

The sign and credentials of the poet are, that he announces that which no man foretold. He is the true and only doctor; he knows and tells; he is the only teller of news, for he was present and privy to the appearance which he describes. He is a beholder of ideas, and an utterer of the necessary and causal. For we do not speak now of men of poetical talents, or of industry and skill in metre, but of the true poet.

For it is not metres, but a metre-making argument, that makes a poem—a thought so passionate and alive, that like the spirit of a plant or an animal, it has an architecture of its own, and adorns nature with a new thing. The thought and the form are equal in the order of time, but in the order of genesis the thought is prior to the form. The poet has a new thought: he has a whole new experience to unfold; he will tell us how it was with him, and all men will be the richer in his fortune. For the experience of each new age requires a new confession, and the world seems always waiting for its poet. I remember, when I was young, how much I was moved one morning by tidings that genius had appeared in a youth who sat near me at table. He had left his work, and gone rambling none knew whither, and had written hundreds of lines, but could not tell whether that which was in him was therein told: he could tell nothing but that all was changed—man, beast, heaven, earth, and sea. How gladly we listened! how credulous! Society seemed to be compromised. We sat in the aurora of a sunrise which was to put out all the stars. Boston seemed to be at twice the distance it had the night before, or was much farther than that. . . . It is much to know that poetry has been written this very day, under this very roof, by your side. What! that wonderful spirit has not expired! These stony moments are still sparkling and animated!

Nature offers all her creatures to him as a picture language. Being used as a type, a second wonderful value appears in the object, far better than its old value, as the carpenter's stretched cord, if you hold your ear close enough, is musical in the breeze. " Things more excellent than every image," says Jambilicus, " are expressed through images." Things admit of being used as symbols, because nature is a symbol, in the whole, and in every part. Every line we can draw in the sand has expression; and there is no body without its spirit or genius. All form is an effect of character; all condition, of the quality of the life; all harmony, of health; (and, for this reason, a perception of beauty should be sympathetic, or proper only to the good). The beautiful rests on the foundations of the necessary.

As it is dislocation and detachment from the life of God that makes things ugly, the poet, who re-attaches things to nature and the Whole—re-attaching even artificial things disposes very easily of the most disagreeable facts. Readers of poetry see the factory-village and the railway, and fancy that the poetry of the landscape is broken up by these; for these works of art are not yet consecrated in their reading; but the poet sees them fall within the great Order not less than the bee-hive, or the spider's geometrical web. Nature adopts them very fast into her vital circles.

The chief value of the new fact, is to enhance the great and constant fact of Life, which can dwarf any and every circumstance, and to which the belt of wampum, and the commerce of America, are alike.

The world being thus put under the mind for verb and noun, the poet is he who can articulate it. For, though life is great, and fascinates, and absorbs—and though all men are intelligent of the symbols, through which it is named—yet they cannot originally use them. We are symbols, and inhabit symbols; workmen, work, and tools, words and things, birth and death, all are emblems; but we sympathize with the symbols, and being infatuated with the economical uses of things, we do not know that they are thoughts. The poet, by an ulterior intellectual perception, gives them a power which makes their old use forgotten, and puts eyes, and a tongue, into every dumb and inanimate object.

He uses forms according to the life, and not according to the form. This is true science. The poet alone knows astronomy, chemistry, vegetation, and animation, for he does not stop at these facts, but employs them as signs. He knows why the plain or meadow of space was strown with these flowers we call suns, and moons, and stars; why the great deep is adorned with animals, with men, and gods; for, in every word he speaks he rides on them as the horses of thought.

By virtue of his science the poet is the Namer, or Language-maker, naming things sometimes after their appearance, sometimes after their essence, and giving to every one its own name and not another's, thereby rejoicing the intellect, which delights in detachment or boundary. The poets made all the words, and therefore language is the archives of history, and, if we must say it, a sort of tomb of the muses. For, though the origin of most of our words is forgotten, each word was at first a stroke of genius, and obtained currency, because for the moment it symbolized the world to the first speaker and to the hearer. The etymologist finds the deadest word to have been once a brilliant picture. Language is fossil poetry.

This insight, which expresses itself by what is called Imagination, is a very high sort of seeing, which does not come by study, but by the intellect being where and what it sees, by sharing the path or circuit of things through forms, and so making them translucid to others. The path of things is silent. Will they suffer a speaker to go with them? A spy they will not suffer; a love, a poet, is the transcendency of their own nature—him they will suffer.

Poets are liberating gods. Men have really got a new sense, and found within their world, another world, or nest of worlds . . . I will not now consider how much this makes the charm of algebra and the mathematics, which also have their tropes, but it is felt in every definition; as, when Aristotle defines space to be an immovable vessel, in which things are contained;—or, when Plato defines a line to be a flowing point; or *figure* to be a bound of solid. The poets are liberating gods. The ancient British bards had for the title of their order, " Those who are free throughout the world." They are free, and they make free. An imaginative book renders us much more service at first, by stimulating as through its tropes, than afterward, when we arrive at the precise sense of the author. If a man is inflamed and carried away by his thought, to that degree that he forgets the authors and the public, and heeds only this one dream, which holds him like an insanity, let me read his paper, and you may have all the arguments and histories and criticism.

We do not, with sufficient plainness, or sufficient profoundness, address ourselves to life, nor dare we chant our own times and social circumstance. If we filled the day with bravery, we should not shrink from celebrating it. Time and nature yield us many gifts, but not yet the timely man, the new religion, the reconciler, whom all things await. Dante's praise is, that he dared to write his autobiography in colossal cipher, or into universality. We have yet had no genius in America, with tyrannous eye, which knew the value of our incomparable materials, and saw, in the barbarism and materialism of the times, another carnival of the same gods whose picture he so much admires in Homer; then in the middle age; then in Calvinism. Banks and tariffs, the newspaper and caucus, methodism and unitarianism, are flat and dull to dull people, but rest on the same foundations of wonder as the town of Troy, and the temple of Delphos, and are as swiftly passing away. Our log-rolling, our stumps and their politics, our fisheries, our Negroes, and Indians, our boats, and our repudiations, the wrath of rogues, and the pusillanimity of honest men, the northern trade, the southern planting, the western clearing, Oregon, and Texas, are yet unsung. Yet America is a poem in our eyes; its ample geography dazzles the imagination, and it will not wait long for metres. . . . But when we adhere to the ideal of the poet, we have our difficulties even with Milton and Homer. Milton is too literary, and Homer too literal and historical.

Art is the path of the creator to his work. . . . Doubt not, O poet, but persist. Say, ' It is in me, and shall out.' Stand there, balked and dumb, stuttering and stammering, hissed and hotted, stand and strive, until, at last, rage draw out of thee that dream power which every night shows thee is thine own; a power transcending all limit and privacy, and by virtue of which a man is the conductor of the whole river of electricity. . . . Wherever snow falls, or water flows, or birds fly, wherever day and night meet in twilight, wherever the blue heaven is hung by clouds, or sown with stars, wherever are forms with transparent boundaries, wherever are outlets into celestial space, wherever is danger, and awe, and love, there is Beauty, plenteous as rain, shed for thee, and though thou shouldst walk the world over, thou shalt not be able to find a condition inopportune or ignoble.

"A READING OF KING LEAR "

by NOAH EDWARD FEHL

In the first decade of the Seventeenth Century the two corner stones of the English Language and its literature were laid. This was the decade of the flowering of

Shakespeare's genius and the revision of the English Bible ordered by King James. The latter had been projected at the Hampton Court Conference of 1604. This was the year of the first full quarto printing of *Hamlet*. On September 26th of that year *Measure for Measure* was acted at Court. In 1605 a play by an unknown author was published under the title: *The True Chronicle History of King Leir and His Three Daughters*. While preparations were under way for implementing the revision of the Scriptures ordered by James, Shakespeare, undoubtedly in possession of the anonymous play, must have been devising his own treatment of its plot for the repertoire of the royal players at the Globe. It would appear that he had turned to the writing of *Lear* soon after the first production of *Macbeth* in the early spring of 1606. His stage script was completed within that year and a special performance was given before " the Kings Majestie at Whitehall upon S. Stephans night in the Christmas Hollidayes." During that year three centers had been readied for the six companies of biblical scholars appointed under the King's commission. One was at Westminster, the other two at the universities of Oxford and Cambridge. The players' copy of *Lear* had been revised for publication by late November in 1607, and the printed play was offered for sale by Nathaniel Butter at his shop in "Paul's Churchyard at the signe of the Pide Bull neere St. Austin's Gate, 1608." Within a few months the work of the several companies of revisors had been, in the main, completed. Shortly thereafter a final editing of the revision in the interests of literary and theological unity was undertaken by representatives from the three centers, and in 1611 the Authorized Version went to press. It bore in its *Epistle Dedicatory*, addressed to the King, a eulogy of the late Elizabeth, and noted the evidences, in joyful confidence, that peace and godliness did not sleep with her but now did flourish the more under James. It is possible that the opening paragraph of this epistle had its model in the speech of Cranmer with which Shakespeare had brought to its close his *King Henry VIII*, probably produced in the summer of 1604, just six months after the Hampton Court Conference in January.

Thus the two great monuments of the English Language and its literature are historically linked together. The parallel goes further. Both brought to a sublime expression the thought and emotions of Englishmen; for there is a curious similarity between the English and the ancient Hebrew minds. Together they provided the chief documents for literary scholarship in the English-speaking world.

I know enough of a portion of that vast literature of comment and criticism of Scripture and Shakespeare to know that if I knew a little more, I should not venture to discuss either and certainly not both at once. Quite candidly, it is my intention in this casual essay to ignore as many of these tongues of men and of angels as charity to my own purposes shall require.

Certainly these tongues have spoken much that would enlighten and enrich. Some have discussed with erudition upon the debt of Shakespeare to the English Bible, and others with inspiration upon the debt of the English Bible to Shakespeare. The themes of Shakespeare have been studied in their relation to biblical perspectives. The drama of English life to which Shakespeare held up his bright mirror has been remarked to be itself very like the drama of Hebrew life. Attempts have been made to reconstruct the " religion of Shakespeare," to find in him either the defender of the " old learning " or the champion of the " new." Some have considered it worthwhile to delineate his views on the sacraments, predestination, original sin, miracles, and ecclesiastical polity.

Most of these studies deal with a side, an aspect, a facet, of Shakespeare. They deal with his thought, or with one aspect of his thought, apart from his art—the content or a fragment of the content apart from the form of his drama. However inadequate or simply irrelevant Aristotle's notion of form and matter and their integral relation may now be for the physicist or the metaphysician, his application of these principles to poetics is still the foundation of literary criticism. The poet, in so far as he is an artist, is a whole man. His work is not divisible into parts: thought and expression, content and form, meaning and art, what is said and the way of saying it. If this be true, we should find in the literary structure itself a clue to meaning. The way in which something is said tells us something about what is said. To get at the theology of Shakespeare, the appropriate question would be: What theological presuppositions are implied in the literary structure of the Shakespearean drama?

A careful reading of the *Poetics*, particularly as its principles are illustrated (as Aristotle believed they were most fully) in Sophocles' *Oedipus Rex*, presses one to the conclusion that the perfect drama as here described in terms of story, plot, character and theme is the most precise and appropriate expression of the Greek view of the human and the divine, of the actual and the possible in life, of man's nobility and his tragic flaw, of experience and meaning. In explaining the art of Sophocles, Aristotle laid down the canons of a literary structure best capable of expressing Greek classical theology.

297

No one has yet written a *Christian Poetics.** The question raised in this essay is whether *King Lear* could serve this task as Sophocles' *Oedipus Rex* served Aristotle's criticism? Does Shakespeare treat in *Lear* of the same theme in the dramatic form that the Authorized Version treats in an epic form? Is Lear the Christian counterpart of Oedipus?

One answer would be: No. Two basic Christian objections could be raised:

1. The Christian story is an epic, not a drama. The drama deals with the purely tragic, with an event in the past that makes the present moment inevitably tragic. In the epic, the deep wound of life finds healing. The epic faces the future. The tragic drama faces the past. The epic deals with redemption, the tragic drama with judgment. Tragedy is essentially a Greek idea, and where there is dramatic tragedy it is rooted in a pagan, albeit a noble pagan, view of human destiny.

2. If there were a Christian tragic drama, there could be only one. It would be the story told in the Gospels of the passion and death of Jesus Christ. No other setting could be appropriate than that which constituted the fullness of time in which God sent His Son. No other versions of the story, no other development of its plot, no other treatment of theme and character, would be possible. This was Divine Act. Human imitation could

---

* Professor Preston Roberts of the University of Chicago has at least supplied a prolegomena to such a work. His doctoral dissertation and an article "Christian Tragedy" published in the *Journal of Religion* (Chicago) several years ago raise the questions to which a *Christian Poetics* must respond. I am in large measure indebted to Dr. Roberts for much of this essay from the many conversations on literature by which he instructed me while we were both students at the University. Other views of which I have made use in this essay are those of F.L. Lucas, *Tragedy*, Butcher's commentary on the *Poetics,* and Kitto's *Greek Tragedy*. M. Nilsson's *Greek Religion* and W. Jaeger's *Paideia* are also in the background.

298

be only travesty. Any other setting, any other telling, would violate the heart of the matter, the uniqueness of the Christ and the once-for-allness of the Christ-event. This is the deeper reason than the simply moral or ascetic for the Puritan rejection of drama. It is a basically theological argument in a class with Plato's denunciation of all imitation of life.

The first objection could be answered from the position of a refusal to be bound to that concept of tragedy which is Sophocles' theology canonized in Aristotle's delineation of plot (the necessary nature of the beginning, middle, and end of a play, the necessary nature of the scenes of recognition and reversal) and of character (the nature of human imperfection or even of action itself as it should unfold between characters and within characters). The implication is that only the inevitably and irredeemably tragic is dramatic. It should be asked whether this notion arises as a presupposition of drama or a presupposition of Greek theology.

I would answer the second argument by suggesting that the passion, death, and resurrection of the Christ is the *ground* of Christian drama. The Christian play, in so far as it tells the story of human experience in a Christian way must be the story not of the Christ but of everyman, even as the Greek drama in telling the story of man's life in a Greek way was the story of Oedipus as everyman. Lear need not be (as he cannot be) the Christ to be the Christian counterpart of the Greek Oedipus.

There are several other arguments against the reading of *Lear* as a Christian tragedy. It is not clearly Christian. It is indeed the most Greek of all Shakespeare's greater tragedies. There are some grounds for the notion that *Lear* represents the effort of Shakespeare to write a tragedy

299

based in part upon Oedipus. The time is that of the pre-Christian era. The action centers in the familial relations of a king. Gloster is strikingly reminiscent of Oedipus. There is a recurrent theme of nature as *Moira* (fate). There is no clear distinction between nature and (the) god(s). The double plot intensifies the feeling of necessity, of the inevitable in the cycle of the generations. Lear's tragic flaw is best understood as the author's attempt to portray the Greek notion of *hybris*. Lear is at last shielded from a fate he cannot face by recourse to a piteous madness even as Oedipus sought to shut out the world in blindness.

In part these objections are a matter of the reading of the play. They can be met only by raising the question of whether they are the most adequate, the most illuminating interpretation, that is, whether through these insights the play achieves its highest dramatic effect, its most powerful impact. In part they must be answered in the comparison and contrast of the literary structure of the play as a whole with that of *Oedipus Rex*, and in this the ideological implications are significant.

We have a right to assume that other answers to the problem of plot and character can be proposed than those laid down in the *Poetics* on the basis of the Greek story of man's life as told by Sophocles in the *Oedipus Rex* or even by Plato in the *Apology*. Professor Roberts has devised a schema for the three basic stories in Western literature: the Greek, the Christian and the modern skeptical. With respect to the tragic idea, the Greek is here seen to be a concern for what is simply and purely tragic in existence; the Christian for what is more than tragic, the redemptive; and the modern for what is less than tragic, the pathetic. The Greek tragic plot revolves around the conjunction of finiteness and fate; the Christian around the redemptive relations of sin, judgment, and grace; the modern sceptical around the pathetic connections between despair and meaninglessness. In the Greek play the protagonist is nobler than we, in the Christian he is like us, in the sceptical he is less noble than we. His flaw in Sophocles is intellectual ignorance or finiteness, the failure to take the widest possible view; in the Bible man's flaw is moral pretention and religious idolatry, or quite simply, sin; in the modern play it is emotional insecurity, debilitating anxiety, disease. Sophocles creates in the reversal scene the recognition that what was most loved has been destroyed in the very effort to preserve it; in the Christian drama, man is led to recognize himself as a sinner and yet at the same time as loved; the movement is from a vanity and a pretention to a judgment that is deserved yet bearing a mercy that was not sought. In the modern sceptical drama (e.g. *Death of A Salesman* or *Streetcar Named Desire*) the tragic hero comes to the recognition of his dream world for what it is. He comes to see himself as hopelessly sick and insane. The reversal is from pretention to hopelessness, from bad to worse. Aristotle saw the purpose of the Sophoclean drama as the cathartic uses of pity and fear. The sceptical play induces in us a heightened sense of poignancy and despair. The Christian play heightens our perception of judgment and grace.

In the Greek story of man's life, Oedipus appears before us as the gracious sovereign, just and wise, the ideal man whose sympathy for the plight of his subjects presages the courage he will have in his own. His nobility as well as his failure, though the wisest of mortals, to take the widest possible view leads us to dread the unfolding of his destiny. Little by little the tragic idea becomes clear: he was doomed before his birth, doomed

301

indeed by the very fact of his being begotten. The genuineness of his piety in the opening scene does not put us off. He is and will be noble despite his destiny, the torturous unravelling of the mystery of his origin cannot change the man himself, it cannot rob him of his grandeur. Nothing will happen within him; but what is there conjoined with outward circumstance must spell his doom.

How different is the beginning of *Lear*. We are treated immediately to the robust character of Elizabethan language. The lusty tale of Gloster's sport in the making of a bastard tells us at least that, whatever moral the author has in store for us, we need not fear that its telling will be in tedious platitudes. The beginning is essentially open, as open as life itself, with its earthy vitalities and spiritual subtleties. We know immediately the flaw of Lear: " he hath ever but slenderly known himself," and there is a vanity in his sovereignty: " his power to flattery bows." He is not merely ignorant, nor suffering from the sickness of senility. He is a sinner. But Cordelia is not pure whiteness to his blackness. Her integrity is as mixed with inflexible selfhood as is Lear's love with vanity. Shakespeare's protagonists are sculptured in the round. They are not mere symbols of pride (Aeschylus' Agamemnon) or of one defect in an otherwise nearly perfect wisdom (Oedipus). They mirror rather the biblical picture of man who is both created in God's image (intelligent, sentient, with at least the freedom to affirm and to deny) and a sinner (in some sense an idolater, worshipping either self or some aspect of the self in the place of God). Shakespeare thus fathoms the demonic dimension of life as Sophocles did not. Aeschylus' Agamemnon lacks the element of goodness necessary to the demonic.

302

Sophocles' story is one simply of fate. Arbitrarily Apollo has spoken. There is nothing intrinsically good in the injunction he has placed upon Laius. The story of Shakespeare deals with a basic fact of human existence: the occasion for brokenness between the generations as the children press toward the independence of maturity and parents seek to hold on to the possession of an idealized image of themselves. Such is the well-nigh inevitable occasion for sin: the sinful domination of parents and the sinful rebellion of children. It is an occasion that must be faced not only in one family (Lear's) but in most (Gloster's as well). The double plot of brokenness between Lear and Cordelia and between Gloster and Edgar recalls the dark oracle of the prophet Malachi: the judgment of God upon mankind that must come upon this divisiveness at the very heart of human society unless there be a healing of the generations, a reconciliation of the hearts of fathers and sons. Shakespeare makes us feel the malignant spirit that rises like a miasma from the swamps of parental distrust and vanity, poisoning the springs of pity, blinding the eyes to all humanity, turning brother against brother and sister against sister. Whence come these powers of evil? Both Kent and Gloster see them as a dark fate that operates above the heads of men. They accuse the gods.

> (Gloster) These late eclipses in the sun and moon portend no good . . . nature finds itself scourged.
> (Kent) It is the stars, the stars above us, govern our condition.

Edmund denies a fate above but finds it in the sublunar realm. He accuses human nature.

> This is the excellent foppery of the world, that when we are sick in fortune, often the surfeit of our own

303

behaviour, we make guilty of our disaster the sun, the moon, and the stars: as if we were villains by necessity, fools by heavenly compulsion . . . and all that we are evil in by a divine thrusting on: an admirable evasion of whoremaster man, to lay his goatish disposition to the charge of a star . . . I should have been that I am, had the maidenliest star in the firmament twinkled on my bastardizing.

In the Greek story of man's life, the present (the middle of the play) is simply an aspect of the past. We know what is to happen could not be otherwise as we learn what has happened in the past. Fate makes a foil even of the audience as each bit of the knowledge of the past seems to point away from what is felt must happen until the last least fact locks into place the doom of Oedipus which was sensed but now is known. The beginning of the play has supplied the intuition of tragedy. The art of the middle skilfully leads on to recognition and reversal by a logic of the pattern of the past which seems up to the last may prove the intuition false. The end comes swiftly on with the knowledge of the last fact, showing that what we had dreaded by intuition must be by necessity. Throughout the middle of the play, Oedipus is an " effect facing the past."

In the Christian play the middle must present the reality of the present. This is its witness to a living God. In *Lear* as the screw tightens by the eldest daughter's turning, other forces are also at work. Lear faces not only the consequences of the past. What is open to him is something more than simply the working out of his own past action. His present possibility is related to something more than just his former self. It is related to his daughter's action and to the impact upon him of

304

his fool and of Kent and Edgar and Gloster. Each new situation presents new alternatives. By the very action that forces Lear to reconsider his judgment of his daughters, the fool, Kent and Edgar are given opportunity both to extend and deepen for him the issue he faces. Goneril's action presses him toward a recognition of his failure to see beyond pretention in others. Kent and the fool press him toward a recognition of pretention in himself.

Lear's response is to accuse an aspect of himself. He sees himself in part responsible for his plight. He has made an error in judgment. He has allowed himself to be deceived by Goneril. " Where are his eyes? . . . O Lear, Lear, Lear! Beat at this gate (striking his head) and let thy folly in. . ."

The screw presses him again as it is turned by Regan. Lear's response is vengeance and defiance. He prays the boon of " noble anger " that, without a tear, he shall wreck such vengeance on his daughters as the world has yet not seen. But this action of defiance that sends him out onto the storm-besieged heath also brings him into a more intimate encounter both with nature and his fellowmen. Nature's larger rage can to some degree purify his own. In part he is persuaded that vengeance belongs to the gods, that he must trust his vindication as a " man more sinned against than sinning " to their powers.

Up to this point Lear has pictured his flaw as blindness. He has accused his eyes and he has threatened his eyes. His eyes have betrayed him as he looked upon his daughters in judgment, and they may betray him by their tears if he gives place to pity for himself or swerves, in old affection, from the cause of vengeance. From this point on, the state of Lear turns upon the meaning of madness. Was Lear sane when his vanity served as his interpreter of life? Is he insane when his vanity is smitten, and, as a humbled man, childlike and sometimes childish, his follies are of the head rather than the heart? The question is crucial to the play both with respect to its structure and to its theme. It is in the same speech where he says " my wits begin to turn " that he is able for the first time to look outside himself to others : " Come on, my boy: art cold? . . . Poor fool and knave, I have one part in my heart that's sorry yet for thee." It is now that Lear comes first to insights also of himself, to see that both all-consuming vengeance and self-pity are madness. Now Lear can pray. He is perhaps beside himself, but he has also been able to get outside the wall of self, to feel for others. He can accuse his former self of neglect of the poor, of a failure to put himself in their place.

In the action between himself and Edgar, disguised as Old Tom, Lear is at times sane, in the sense of his former self, at times, in witless speech, he probes beneath the differences of rank and raiment to the unadorned soul of common humanity. The action that has brought Kent, Edgar and Gloster together with Lear has also made something else possible. Edgar can be taught by Lear how great is the loss a father feels in the defection of his child, how human is a father's vanity and how weak his blindness. In coming to know Lear's pain and his folly, Edgar is being prepared better to understand his own father. In the hovel on the heath he is readied for the service to be rendered on the cliff at Dover.

The theme from this point on is reconciliation. We are led to feel that " the deep wound of tragedy will be no longer deep " if Gloster, now blind but for the first time seeing, can accept Edgar's forgiveness, and if Lear can receive the forgiveness of Cordelia. Gently Gloster is led to forgive himself, to tolerate his life, to live with the knowledge of his own sin against Edgar. Edgar supplies the clue: " Ripeness is all." Is this the counsel of Sophocles: the *arete* and *sophrosyne* of Greek piety? In some ways this answer satisfies. Gloster learns to endure his going hence even as did Oedipus. Both were blind men who had first to lose their eyes before they could see. Neither finally succumbed to the temptation that betrayed Jocasta's inner weakness. Is there another meaning? To be ready, to be willing, to be reconciled—to forgive oneself, to accept the forgiveness of another—that is all that matters. There is then nothing in life that can prevent man from realizing the meaning of his existence. When that happens a man is fulfilled. He is able to die. *Telos* has come before *finis*. Ripeness is all.

Lear has one last refuge in his flight from what he has cherished most, the love of Cordelia. "A sovereign shame so elbows him . . . burning shame detains him from Cordelia." Such is the last refuge of man's pride under judgment. But Lear does win through to love, to see that power and place and all else in the world are vanity save love. Ripeness is all, and thus the prospect of prison becomes a promise of paradise.

> No, no, no, no! Come, let's away to prison:
> We two alone will sing like birds i' the cage:
> When thou dost ask me blessing I'll kneel down
> And ask of thee forgiveness: so we'll live, and pray, and sing. . . .

Finally, though she dies and he wavers between choking sorrow and groundless hope, his last moment is one of ecstasy.

> Do you see this? Look on her—look—her lips,
> Look there, look there.

There are other readings of this final movement. It has been argued that an ironic doom pursues Lear to the end. His vanity leads him to insanity. It is a witless old man that is led as a child to prison. It is a pathetic old man, bending over the corpse of Cordelia, that is slowly tortured to death by alternate hope and despair. "As flies to wanton boys are we to the gods; they kill us for their sport." But that would be poor drama, and one would be led to say that the flies had in this case the better of the wanton boys.

More persuasive would be the reading that a " gentle weariness and madness transport Lear beyond tragic facts no mortal can suffer and endure." One could accept this reading more easily, however, were *Lear* a modern, rather than a Shakespearean, drama. Even then it would be a dangerous thing, from the purely dramatic point of view, to treat of the sickness of forgiveness.

Equally unsatisfactory for good drama as well as life would be the notion that the final movement points to fulfilment in another world—in a life beyond or after death.

There *is* reconciliation. The heart of Lear *is* turned to Cordelia. Lear has perceived her goodness and her love for him. His last word of ecstasy may be based on the illusion that she lives, and so by illusion his final moment is joyous. This would be true to life where high faith sometimes embraces grand illusions. The basic fact is that Lear's illusion was an expression of a real experience of reconciliation. He has known Cordelia's love and he has loved Cordelia. To be 'a prisoner of hope' is in some sense to be free.

PART TWO: THE PHYSICAL SCIENCES

A. *PHYSICS AND ASTRONOMY*

" THE METHODS OF ACQUIRING KNOWLEDGE "
by ROGER BACON (1214-1294)

There are two methods in which we acquire knowledge : argument and experiment. Argument allows us to draw conclusions, and may cause us to admit the conclusion; but it gives no proof, nor does it remove doubt, and cause the mind to rest in the conscious possession of truth, unless the truth is discovered by way of experience, e.g. if any man who had never seen fire were to prove by satisfactory argument that fire burns and destroys things, the hearer's mind would not rest satisfied, nor would he avoid fire; until by putting his hand or some combustible thing into it, he proved by actual experiment what the argument laid down; but after the experiment has been made, his mind receives certainty and rests in the possession of truth which could not be given by argument but only by experience. And this is the case even in mathematics, where there is the strongest demonstration. For let anyone have the clearest demonstration about an equilateral triangle without experience of it, his mind will never lay hold of the problem until he has actually before him the intersecting circles and the lines drawn from the point of section to the extremities of a straight line.

FROM *CONCERNING THE REVOLUTIONS OF THE HEAVENLY BODIES*
by NICHOLAS COPERNICUS (1473-1543)

That the universe is spherical

First of all we assert that the universe is spherical; partly because this form, being a complete whole, needing no joints, is the most perfect of all; partly because it constitutes the most spacious form, which is thus best suited to contain and retain all things; or also because all discrete parts of the world, I mean the sun, the moon and the planets, appear as spheres; or because all things tend to assume the spherical shape, a fact which appears in a drop of water and in other fluid bodies when they seek of their own accord to limit themselves. Therefore no one will doubt that this form is natural for the heavenly bodies.

That the earth is likewise spherical

That the earth is likewise spherical is beyond doubt, because it presses from all sides to its center. Although a perfect sphere is not immediately recognized because of the great height of the mountains and the depression of the valleys, yet this in no wise invalidates the general spherical form of the earth. This becomes clear in the following manner: To people who travel from any place to the North, the north pole of the daily revolution rises gradually, while the south pole sinks a like amount. Most of the stars in the neighborhood of the Great Bear appear not to set, and in the South some stars appear no longer to rise. Thus Italy does not see Canopus, which is visible to the Egyptians. And Italy sees the outermost star of the River, which is unknown to us of a colder zone. On the other hand, to people who travel toward the South, these stars rise higher in the heavens, while those stars which are higher to us become lower. Therefore, it is plain that the earth is included between the poles and is spherical. Let us add that the inhabitants of the East do not see the solar and lunar eclipses that occur in the evening, and people who live in the West do not see eclipses that occur in the morning, while those living in between see the former later, and the latter earlier.

That even the water has the same shape is observed on ships, in that the land which can not be seen from the ship can be spied from the tip of the mast. And, conversely, when a light is put on the tip of the mast, it appears to observers on land gradually to drop as the ship recedes until the light disappears, seeming to sink in the water. It is clear that the water, too, in accordance with its fluid nature, is drawn downwards, just as is the earth, and its level at the shore is no higher than its convexity allows. The land therefore projects everywhere only as far above the ocean as the land accidentally happens to be higher. . . .

Whether the earth has a circular motion, and concerning the location of the earth

Since it has already been proved that the earth has the shape of a sphere, I insist that we must investigate whether from its form can be deduced a motion, and what place the earth occupies in the universe. Without this knowledge no certain computation can be made for the phenomena occurring in the heavens. To be sure, the great majority of writers agree that the earth is at rest in the center of the universe, so that they consider it unbelievable and even ridiculous to suppose the contrary. Yet, when one weights the matter carefully, he will see that this question is not yet disposed of, and for that reason is by no means to be considered unimportant. Every change of position which is observed is due either to the motion of the observed object or of the observer, or to motions, naturally in different directions, of both; for when the observed object and the observer move in the same manner and in the same direction, then no motion is observed. Now the earth is the place from which we observe the revolution of the heavens and where it is displayed to our eyes. Therefore, if the earth should

311

possess any motion, the latter would be noticeable in everything that is situated outside of it, but in the opposite direction, just as if everything were traveling past the earth. And of this nature is, above all, the daily revolution. For this motion seems to embrace the whole world, in fact, everything that is outside of the earth, with the single exception of the earth itself. But if one should admit that the heavens possess none of this motion, but that the earth rotates from west to east; and if one should consider this seriously with respect to the seeming rising and setting of the sun, of the moon and the stars; then one would find that it is actually true. Since the heavens which contain and retain all things are the common home of all things, it is not at once comprehensible why a motion is not rather ascribed to the thing contained than to the containing, to the located rather than to the locating. This opinion was actually held by the Pythagoreans Heraklid and Ekphantus and the Syracusean Nicetas (as told by Cicero), in that they assumed the earth to be rotating in the center of the universe. They were indeed of the opinion that the stars set due to the intervening of the earth, and rose due to its receding. . . .

Refutation of the arguments, and their insufficiency

It is claimed that the earth is at rest in the center of the universe and that this is undoubtedly true. But one who believes that the earth rotates will also certainly be of the opinion that this motion is natural and not violent. Whatever is in accordance with nature produces effects which are the opposite of what happens through violence. Things upon which violence or an external force is exerted must become annihilated and cannot long exist. But whatever happens in the course of nature remains in good condition and in its best arrangement. Without cause, therefore, Ptolemy feared that the earth and all earthly

312

things if set in rotation would be dissolved by the action of nature, for the functioning of nature is something entirely different from artifice, or from that which could be contrived by the human mind. But why did he not fear the same, and indeed in much higher degree, for the universe, whose motion would have to be as much more rapid as the heavens are larger than the earth? Or have the heavens become infinite just because they have been removed from the center by the inexpressible force of the motion; while otherwise, if they were at rest, they would collapse? Certainly if this argument were true the extent of the heavens would become infinite. For the more they were driven aloft by the outward impulse of the motion, the more rapid would the motion become because of the ever increasing circle which it would have to describe in the space of 24 hours; and, conversely, if the motion increased, the immensity of the heavens would also increase. Thus velocity would augment size into infinity, and size, velocity. But according to the physical law that the infinite can neither be traversed, nor can it for any reason have motion, the heavens would, however, of necessity be at rest.

But it is said that outside of the heavens there is no body, nor place, nor empty space, in fact, that nothing at all exists, and that, therefore there is no space in which the heavens could expand; then it is really strange that something could be enclosed by nothing. If, however, the heavens were infinite and were bounded only by their inner concavity, then we have, perhaps, even better confirmation that there is nothing outside of the heavens, because everything, whatever its size, is within them; but then the heavens would remain motionless. The most important argument, on which depends the proof of the finiteness of the universe, is motion. Now, whether the world is finite or infinite, we will leave to the quarrels of the natural philosophers; for us remains the certainty that the earth, contained between poles, is bounded by a spherical surface. Why should we hesitate to grant it a motion, natural and corresponding to its form; rather than assume that the whole world, whose boundary is not known and cannot be known, moves? And why are we not willing to acknowledge that the appearance of a daily revolution belongs to the heavens, its actuality to the earth? The relation is similar to that of which Virgil's Æneas says: " We sail out of the harbor, and the countries and cities recede." For when a ship is sailing along quietly, everything which is outside of it will appear to those on board to have a motion corresponding to the movement of the ship, and the voyagers are of the erroneous opinion that they with all that they have with them are at rest. This can without doubt also apply to the motion of the earth, and it may appear as if the whole universe were revolving. . . .

Concerning the center of the universe

Since nothing stands in the way of the movability of the earth, I believe we must now investigate whether it also has several motions, so that it can be considered one of the planets. That it is not the center of all the revolutions is proved by the irregular motions of the planets, and their varying distances from the earth, which cannot be explained as concentric circles with the earth at the center. Therefore, since there are several central points, no one will without cause be uncertain whether the center of the universe is the center of gravity of the earth or some other central point. I, at least, am of the opinion that gravity is nothing else than a natural force planted by the divine providence of the Master of the World into its parts, by means of which they, assuming

314

a spherical shape, form a unity and a whole. And it is to be assumed that the impulse is also inherent in the sun and the moon and the other planets, and that by the operation of this force they remain in the spherical shape in which they appear; while they, nevertheless, complete their revolutions in diverse ways. If then the earth, too, possesses other motions besides that around its center, then they must be of such a character as to become apparent in many ways and in appropriate manners; and among such possible effects we recognize the yearly revolution.

FROM *THE HEAVENLY MESSENGER*

by GALILEO (1610)

About ten months ago a report reached my ears that a Dutchman had constructed a telescope, by the aid of which visible objects, although at a great distance from the eye of the observer, were seen distinctly as if near; and some proofs of its most wonderful performances were reported, which some gave credence to, but others contradicted. A few days after, I received confirmation of the report in a letter written from Paris by a noble Frenchman, Jaques Badovere, which finally determined me to give myself up first to inquire into the principle of the telescope, and then to consider the means by which I might compass the invention of a similar instrument, which after a little while I succeeded in doing, through deep study of the theory of Refraction; and I prepared a tube, at first of lead, in the ends of which I fitted two glass lenses, both plane on one side, but on the other side one spherically convex, and the other concave. Then bringing my eye to the concave lens I saw objects satisfactorily large and near, for they appeared one-third of

315

the distance off and nine times larger than when they are seen with the natural eye alone. I shortly afterwards constructed another telescope with more nicety, which magnified objects more than sixty times. At length, by sparing neither labour nor expense, I succeeded in constructing for myself an instrument so superior that objects seen through it appear magnified nearly a thousand times, and more than thirty times nearer than if viewed by the natural powers of sight alone.

First telescopic observations

It would be altogether a waste of time to enumerate the number and importance of the benefits which this instrument may be expected to confer, when used by land or sea. But without paying attention to its use for terrestrial objects, I betook myself to observations of the heavenly bodies; and first of all, I viewed the Moon as near as if it was scarcely two semidiameters of the Earth distant. After the Moon, I frequently observed other heavenly bodies, both fixed stars and planets, with incredible delight. . . .

Discovery of Jupiter's satellites

There remains the matter, which seems to me to deserve to be considered the most important in this work, namely, that I should disclose and publish to the world the occasion of discovering and observing four planets, never seen from the very beginning of the world up to our own times, their positions, and the observations made during the last two months about their movements and their changes of magnitude. . . .

On the 7th day of January in the present year, 1610, in the first hour of the following night, when I was viewing the constellations of the heavens through a telescope, the planet Jupiter presented itself to my view,

316

and as I had prepared for myself a very excellent instrument, I noticed a circumstance which I had never been able to notice before, owing to want of power in my other telescope, namely, that three little stars, small but very bright, were near the planet; and although I believed them to belong to the number of the fixed stars, yet they made me somewhat wonder, because they seemed to be arranged exactly in a straight line, parallel to the ecliptic, and to be brighter than the rest of the stars, equal to them in magnitude. The position of them with reference to one another and to Jupiter was as follows:

Ori.   *   *   0   *   Occ.

On the east side there were two stars, and a single one towards the west. The star which was furthest towards the east, and the western star, appeared rather larger than the third.

I scarcely troubled at all about the distance between them and Jupiter, for, as I have already said, at first I believed them to be fixed stars; but when on January 8th, led by some fatality, I turned again to look at the same part of the heavens, I found a very different state of things, for there were three little stars all west of Jupiter, and nearer together than on the previous night, and they were separated from one another by equal intervals, as the accompanying figure shows.

Ori.   0   *   *   *   Occ.

At this point, although I had not turned my thoughts at all upon the approximation of the stars to one another, yet my surprise began to be excited, how Jupiter could one day be found to the east of all the aforesaid fixed stars when the day before it had been west of two of them; and forthwith I became afraid lest the planet might have moved differently from the calculation of astronomers, and so had passed those stars by its own proper motion. I, therefore, waited for the next night with the most intense longing, but I was disappointed of my hope, for the sky was covered with clouds in every direction.

But on January 10th the stars appeared in the following position with regard to Jupiter, the third, as I thought, being

Ori.   *   *   0   Occ.

hidden by the planet. They were situated just as before, exactly in the same straight line with Jupiter, and along the Zodiac.

When I had seen these phenomena, as I knew that corresponding changes of position could not by any means belong to Jupiter, and as, moreover, I perceived that the stars which I saw had always been the same, for there were no others either in front or behind, within a great distance, along the Zodiac—at length, changing from doubt into surprise, I discovered that the interchange of position which I saw belonged not to Jupiter, but to the stars to which my attention had been drawn, and I thought therefore that they ought to be observed henceforward with more attention and precision.

Accordingly, on January 11th I saw an arrangement of the following kind:

Ori.   *   *   0   Occ.

namely, only two stars to the east of Jupiter, the nearer of which was distant from Jupiter three times as far as from the star further to the east; and the star furthest to the east was nearly twice as large as the other one; whereas on the previous night they had appeared nearly of equal magnitude. I, therefore, concluded, and decided unhesitatingly, that there are three stars in the heavens moving about Jupiter, as Venus and Mercury round the Sun; which at length was established as clear as daylight by numerous other subsequent observations. These observations also established that there are not only three, but four, erratic sidereal bodies performing their revolutions round Jupiter. . . .

These are my observations upon the four Medicean planets, recently discovered for the first time by me; and although it is not yet permitted me to deduce by calculation from these observations the orbits of these bodies, yet I may be allowed to make some statements, based upon them, well worthy of attention.

Orbits and periods of Jupiter's satellites

And, in the first place, since they are sometimes behind, sometimes before Jupiter, at like distances, and withdraw from this planet towards the east and towards the west only within very narrow limits of divergence, and since they accompany this planet alike when its motion is retrograde and direct, it can be a matter of doubt to no one that they perform their revolutions about this planet while at the same time they all accomplish together orbits of twelve years' length about the centre of the world. Moreover, they revolve in unequal circles, which is evidently the conclusion to be drawn from the fact that I have never been permitted to see two satellites in conjunction when their distance from Jupiter was great, whereas near Jupiter two, three, and sometimes all four, have been found closely packed together. Moreover, it may be detected that the revolutions of the satellites which describe the smallest circles round Jupiter are the most rapid, for the satellites nearest to Jupiter are often to be seen in the east, when the day before they have appeared

319

in the west, and contrariwise. Also, the satellite moving in the greatest orbit seems to me, after carefully weighing the occasions of its returning to positions previously noticed, to have a periodic time of half a month. Besides, we have a notable and splendid argument to remove the scruples of those who can tolerate the revolution of the planets round the Sun in the Copernican system, yet are so disturbed by the motion of one Moon about the Earth, while both accomplish an orbit of a year's length about the Sun, that they consider that this theory of the universe must be upset as impossible; for now we have not one planet only revolving about another, while both traverse a vast orbit about the Sun, but our sense of sight presents to us four satellites circling about Jupiter, like the Moon about the Earth, while the whole system travels over a mighty orbit about the Sun in the space of twelve years.

"CONCERNING THE LAW OF GRAVITATION"

From SIR ISAAC NEWTON'S *Principia,* edition of 1726

Hitherto we have explained the phaenomena of the heavens and of our sea by the power of gravity, but have not yet assigned the cause of this power. This is certain, that it must proceed from a cause that penetrates to the very centres of the sun and planets, without suffering the least diminution of its force; that operates not according to the quantity of the surfaces of the particles upon which it acts (as mechanical causes used to do), but according to the quantity of the solid matter which they contain, and propagates its virtue on all sides to immense distances, decreasing always in the duplicate proportions of the distances. Gravitation towards the sun is made up out of the gravitations towards the several particles of which the body of the sun is composed; and in receding from the sun decreases accurately in the duplicate proportion of the distances as far as the orb of Saturn, as evidently appears from the quiescence of the aphelions of the planets; nay, and even to the remotest aphelions of the comets, if these aphelions are also quiescent. But hitherto I have not been able to discover the cause of those properties of gravity from phaenomena, and I frame no hypotheses; for whatever is not deduced from the phaenomena is to be called an hypothesis; and hypotheses, whether metaphysical or physical, whether of occult qualities or mechanical, have no place in experimental philosophy. In this philosophy particular propositions are inferred from the phaenomena, and afterwards rendered general by induction. Thus it was that the impenetrability, the mobility, and the impulsive force of bodies, and the laws of motion and gravitation were discovered. And to us it is enough that gravity does really exist, and act according to the laws which we have explained, and abundantly serves to account for all the motions of the celestial bodies, and of our sea.

NEWTONIANA

" I do not know what I may appear to the world, but to myself I seem to have been only like a boy playing on the seashore, and diverting myself in now and then finding a smoother pebble and a prettier shell than ordinary, whilst the great ocean of truth lay all undiscovered before me."—Sir Isaac Newton.

" If I have seen farther than Descartes, it is by standing on the shoulders of giants."—Sir Isaac Newton.

" There may have been minds as happily constituted as his for the cultivation of pure mathematical science;

there may have been minds as happily constituted for the cultivation of science purely experimental; but in no other mind have the demonstrative faculty and the inductive faculty co-existed in such supreme excellence and perfect harmony."—Lord Macaulay.

" Taking mathematics from the beginning of the world to the time when Newton lived, what he had done was much the better half."—Leibnitz.

" The law of gravitation is indisputably and incomparably the greatest scientific discovery ever made, whether we look at the advance which it involved, the extent of truth disclosed, or the fundamental and satisfactory nature of this truth."—William Whewell.

" On the day of Cromwell's death, when Newton was sixteen, a great storm raged all over England. He used to say, in his old age, that on that day he made his first purely scientific experiment. To ascertain the force of the wind, he first jumped with the wind and then against it, and by comparing these distances with the extent of his own jump on a calm day, he was enabled to compute the force of the storm. When the wind blew thereafter, he used to say it was so many feet strong.—James Parton.

" His carriage was very meek, sedate and humble, never seemingly angry, of profound thought, his countenance mild, pleasant and comely. I cannot say I ever saw him laugh but once, which put me in mind of the Ephesian philosopher, who laughed only once in his lifetime, to see an ass eating thistles when plenty of grass was by. He always kept close to his studies, very rarely went visiting and had few visitors. I never knew him to take any recreation or pastime either in riding out to take the air, walking, bowling, or any other exercise whatever, thinking all hours lost that were not spent in his studies, to which he kept so close that he seldom left his chamber except at term time, when he read in the

322

schools as Lucasianus Professor, where so few went to
hear him, and fewer that understood him, that oft-times
he did in a manner, for want of hearers, read to the walls.
Foreigners he received with a great deal of freedom,
candour, and respect. When invited to a treat, which
was very seldom, he used to return it very handsomely,
and with much satisfaction to himself. So intent, so
serious upon his studies, that he ate very sparingly, nay,
oft-times he had forgot to eat at all, so that, going into
his chamber, I have found his mess untouched, of which,
when I have reminded him, he would reply—" Have I? "
and then making to the table would eat a bite or two
standing, for I cannot say I ever saw him sit at table
by himself. He very rarely went to bed till two or three
of the clock, sometimes not until five or six, lying about
four or five hours, especially at spring and fall of the
year, at which times he used to employ about six weeks
in his laboratory, the fires scarcely going out either night
or day; he sitting up one night and I another till he had
finished his chemical experiments, in the performance of
which he was the most accurate, strict, exact. What his
aim might be I was not able to penetrate into, but his
pains, his diligence at these set times made me think he
aimed at something beyond the reach of human art and
industry. I cannot say I ever saw him drink either wine,
ale or beer, excepting at meals and then but very sparingly.
He very rarely went to dine in the hall, except on some
public days, and then if he had not been minded, would
go very carelessly, with shoes down at heels, stockings
untied, surplice on, and his head scarcely combed.

His laboratory was well furnished with chemical
materials, as bodies, receivers, heads, crucibles, etc. which
was made very little use of, the crucibles excepted, in
which he fused his metals; he would sometimes, tho' very
seldom, look into an old mouldy book which lay in his

laboratory, I think it was titled *Agricola de Metallis*, the transmuting of metals being his chief design, for which purpose antimony was a great ingredient. He has sometimes taken a turn or two, has made a sudden stand, turn'd himself about, run up the stairs like another Archimedes, with an Eureka fall to write on his desk standing without giving himself the leisure to draw a chair to sit down on. He would with great acuteness answer a question, but would very seldom start one. Dr. Boerhave, in some of his writings, speaking of Sir Isaac: " That man " says he, " comprehends as much as all mankind besides."—Humphrey Newton.

FROM A LETTER TO PETER COLLINSON, 1752,

by BENJAMIN FRANKLIN

The Kite

As frequent mention is made in public papers from Europe of the success of the Philadelphia experiment for drawing the electric fire from clouds by means of pointed rods of iron erected on high buildings, and, it may be agreeable to the curious to be informed, that the same experiment has succeeded in Philadelphia, though made in a different and more easy manner, which is as follows:

Make a small cross of two light strips of cedar, the arms so long as to reach to the four corners of a large thin silk handkerchief when extended; tie the corners of the handkerchief to the extremities of the cross, so you have the body of a kite; which being properly accommodated with a tail, loop, and string, will rise in the air, like those made of paper; but this being of silk, is fitter to bear the wet and wind of a thunder-gust without tearing. To the top of the upright stick of the cross is to be fixed a very sharp pointed wire, rising a foot or more above the wood. To the end of the twine, next the hand, is to be tied a silk ribbon, and where the silk and twine join, a key may be fastened. This kite is to be raised when a thunder-gust appears to be coming on, and the person who holds the string must stand within a door or window or under some cover, so that the silk ribbon may not be wet; and care must be taken that the twine does not touch the frame of the door or window. As soon as any of the thunder-clouds come over the kite, the pointed wire will draw the electric fire from them, and the kite, with all the twine, will be electrified, and the loose filaments of the twine will stand out every way, and be attracted by an approaching finger. And when the rain has wet the kite and twine, so that it can conduct the electric fire freely, you will find it stream out plentifully from the key on the approach of your knuckle. At this key the phial may be charged; and from electric fire thus obtained, spirits may be kindled, and all the other electric experiments be performed, which are usually done by the help of a rubbed glass globe or tube, and thereby the sameness of the electric matter with that of lightning completely demonstrated.

FROM *STARS AND ATOMS*

by SIR ARTHUR EDDINGTON

In ancient days two aviators procured to themselves wings. Daedalus flew safely through the middle air and was duly honored on his landing. Icarus soared upwards to the sun till the wax melted which bound his wings and his flight ended in fiasco. In weighing their achievements, there is something to be said for Icarus. The classical authorities tell us that he was only " doing a stunt," but

I prefer to think of him as the man who brought to light a serious constructional defect in the flying machines of his day. So, too, in science, cautious Daedalus will apply his theories where he feels confident they will safely go; but by his excesses of caution their hidden weaknesses remain undiscovered. Icarus will strain his theories to the breaking point till the weak points gape. For the more adventure? Perhaps partly; that is human nature. But if he is destined not yet to reach the sun and solve finally the riddle of its constitution we may hope at least to learn from his journey some hints to build a better machine.

"ADDRESS BEFORE THE STUDENT BODY OF THE CALIFORNIA INSTITUTE OF TECHNOLOGY"

by ALBERT EINSTEIN

My dear young friends:

I am glad to see you before me, a flourishing band of young people who have chosen applied science as a profession.

I could sing a hymn of praise with the refrain of the splendid progress in applied science that we have already made, and the enormous further progress that you bring about. We are indeed in the era and also in the native land of applied science.

But it lies far from my thought to speak in this way. Much more, I am reminded in this connection of the young man who had married a not very attractive wife and was asked whether or not he was happy. He answered thus: " If I wished to speak the truth, then I would have to lie."

So it is with me. Just consider a quite uncivilized man whether his experience is less rich and happy than that of the average civilized man. I hardly think so. There lies a deep meaning in the fact that the children of all civilized countries are so fond of playing " Indians."

Why does this magnificent applied science, which saves work and makes life easier, bring us so little happiness? The simple answer runs—because we have not yet learned to make a sensible use of it.

In war, it serves that we may poison and mutilate each other. In peace it has made our lives hurried and uncertain. Instead of freeing us in great measure from spiritually exhausting labor, it has made men into slaves of machinery, who for the most part complete their monotonous, long day's work with disgust, and must continually tremble for their poor rations.

You will be thinking that the old man sings an ugly song. I do it, however, with a good purpose, in order to point out a consequence.

It is not enough that you should understand about applied science in order that your work may increase man's blessings. Concern for man himself and his fate must always form the chief interest of all technical endeavors, concern for the great unsolved problems of the organization of labor and the distribution of goods— in order that the creations of our mind shall be a blessing and not a curse to mankind. Never forget this in the midst of your diagrams and equations.

B. *BIOLOGY*

" DARWINISMS "

" I think that I am superior to the common run of men in noticing things which easily escape attention, and in observing them carefully. My industry has been nearly as great as it could have been in the observation and collection of facts."

"Accuracy is the soul of Natural History. It is hard to become accurate; he who modifies a hair's breadth will never be accurate. . . . Absolute accuracy is the hardest merit to attain, and the highest merit."

" I have steadily endeavored to keep my mind free so as to give up any hypothesis, however much beloved (and I cannot resist forming one on every subject), as soon as the facts are shown to be opposed to it."

" I had, also, during many years followed a golden rule, namely, that whenever a published fact, a new observation or thought came across me, which was opposed to my general results, to make a memorandum of it without fail and at once; for I had found by experience that such facts and thoughts were far more apt to escape from the memory than favorable ones."

" I have been speculating last night what makes a man a discoverer of undiscovered things; and a most perplexing problem it is. Many men who are very clever —much cleverer than the discoverers—never originate anything. As far as I can conjecture, the art consists in habitually searching for the causes and meaning of everything which occurs."

" I look at it as absolutely certain that very much in the *Origin* will be proved rubbish; but I expect and hope that the framework will stand."

" It is a horrid bore to feel as I constantly do, that I am a withered leaf for every subject except Science. It sometimes makes me hate Science, though God knows I ought to be thankful for such a perennial interest, which makes me forget for some hours every day my accursed stomach."

" I do not believe any man in England naturally writes so vile a style as I do."

328

"Now for many years I cannot endure to read a line of poetry: I have tried lately to read Shakespeare, and found it so intolerably dull that it nauseated me."

*　　*　　*

"It is doubtful if any single book, except the "Principia," ever worked so great and so rapid a revolution in science, or made so deep an impression on the general mind."

T. H. Huxley.

"TURTLE EGGS FOR AGASSIZ"

by DALLAS LORE SHARP, 1910.

It is one of the wonders of the world that so few books are written. With every human being a possible book, and with many a human being capable of becoming more books than the world could contain, is it not amazing that the books of men are so few?　And so stupid!

I took down, recently, from the shelves of a great public library, the four volumes of Agassiz's *Contributions to the Natural History of the United States.* I doubt if anybody but the charwoman, with her duster, had touched those volumes for twenty-five years. They are an excessively learned, a monumental, an epoch-making work, the fruit of vast and heroic labors, with colored plates, showing the turtles of the United States and their embryology. The work was published more than half a century ago (by subscription); but it looked old beyond its years—massive, heavy, weathered, as if dug from the rocks. It was difficult to feel that Agassiz could have written it—could have built it, grown it, for the laminated pile had required for its growth the patience and painstaking care of a process of nature, as if it were a kind of printed coral reef. Agassiz do this?　The big, human, magnetic man at work upon these pages of capital letters, Roman figures, brackets, and parentheses in explanation of the pages of diagrams and plates! I turned away with a sigh from the weary learning, to read the preface.

When a great man writes a great book he usually flings a preface after it, and thereby saves it, sometimes, from oblivion. Whether so or not, the best things in most books are their prefaces. It was not, however, the quality of the preface to these great volumes that interested me, but rather the wicked waste of durable book material that went to its making. Reading down through the catalogue of human names and of thanks for help received, I came to a sentence beginning:—

"In New England I have myself collected largely; but I have also received valuable contributions from the late Rev. Zadoc Thompson of Burlington . . . from Mr. D. Henry Thoreau of Concord . . . and from Mr. J. W. P. Jenks of Middleboro." And then it hastens on with the thanks in order to get to the turtles, as if turtles were the one and only thing of real importance in all the world.

Turtles no doubt are important, extremely important, embryologically, as part of our genealogical tree; but they are away down among the roots of the tree as compared with the late Rev. Zadoc Thompson of Burlington. I happen to know nothing about the Rev. Zadoc, but to me he looks very interesting. Indeed any reverend gentleman of his name and day who would catch turtles for Agassiz must have been interesting. And as for Henry Thoreau, we know he was interesting. The rarest wood turtle in the United States was not so rare a specimen as this gentleman of Walden Woods and Concord. We are glad even for this line in the preface about him; glad to know that he tried, in this untranscendental way, to serve his day and generation. If Agassiz had only put a chapter in his turtle book about it! But this is the material he wasted, this and more of the same human sort, for the Mr. " Jenks of Middleboro " (at the end of the quotation) was, years later, an old college professor of mine, who told me some of the particulars of his turtle contributions, particulars which Agassiz should have found a place for in his big book. The preface says merely that this gentleman sent turtles to Cambridge by the thousands—brief and scanty recognition. For that is not the only thing this gentleman did. On one occasion he sent, not turtles, but turtle eggs to Cambridge—brought them, I should say; and all there is to show for it, so far as I could discover, is a sectional drawing of a bit of the mesoblastic layer of one of the eggs!

Of course, Agassiz wanted to make that mesoblastic drawing, or some other equally important drawing, and had to have the fresh turtle egg to draw it from. He had to have it, and he got it. A great man, when he wants a certain turtle egg, at a certain time, always gets it, for he gets someone else to get it. I am glad he got it. But what makes me sad and impatient is that he did not think it worth while to tell about the getting of it, and so made merely a learned turtle book of what might have been an exceedingly interesting human book.

It would seem, naturally, that there could be nothing unusual or interesting about the getting of turtle eggs when you want them. Nothing at all, if you should chance to want the eggs as you chance to find them. So with anything else—good copper stock, for instance, if you should chance to want it, and should chance to be along when they chance to be giving it away. But if you want copper stocks, say of C & H quality, when you want it, and are bound to have it, then you must command more than a college professor's salary. And likewise, precisely, when it is turtle eggs that you are bound to have.

Agassiz wanted those turtle eggs when he wanted them—not a minute over three hours from the minute they were laid. Yet even that does not seem exacting, hardly more difficult than the getting of hen eggs only three hours old. Just so, provided the professor could have had his private turtle coop in Harvard Yard; and provided he could have made his turtles lay. But turtles will not respond, like hens, to meat scraps and the warm mash. The professor's problem was not to get from a mud turtle's nest in the back yard to the table in the laboratory; but to get from the laboratory in Cambridge to some pond when the turtles were laying, and back to the laboratory within the limited time. And this, in the days of Darius Green, might have called for nice and discriminating work—as it did.

Agassiz had been engaged for a long time upon his *Contributions*. He had brought the great work nearly to a finish. It was, indeed, finished but for one small yet very important bit of observation: he had carried the turtle egg through every stage of its development with the single exception of one—the very earliest—that stage of first cleavages, when the cell begins to segment, immediately upon its being laid. That beginning stage had brought the *Contributions* to a halt. To get eggs that were fresh enough to show the incubation at this period had been impossible.

There were several ways that Agassiz might have proceeded: he might have got a leave of absence for the spring term, taken his laboratory to some pond inhabited by turtles, and there camped until he should catch the reptile digging out her nest. But there were difficulties in all of that—as those who are college professors and naturalists know. As this was quite out of the question, he did the easiest thing—asked Mr. "Jenks of Middleboro" to get him the eggs. Mr. Jenks got them. Agassiz knew all about his getting of them; and I say the strange and irritating thing is that Agassiz did not think it worth while to tell us about it, at least in the preface to his monumental work.

It was many years later that Mr. Jenks, then a gray-haired college professor, told me how he got those eggs to Agassiz.

" I was principal of an academy, during my younger years," he began, " and was busy one day with my classes, when a large man suddenly filled the doorway of the room, smiled to the four corners of the room, and called out with a big, quick voice that he was Professor Agassiz.

" Of course he was. I knew it, even before he had had time to shout it to me across the room.

" Would I get him some turtle eggs? he called. Yes, I would. And would I get them to Cambridge within three hours from the time they were laid? Yes, I would. And I did. And it was worth the doing. But I did it only once.

" When I promised Agassiz those eggs I knew where I was going to get them. I had got turtle eggs there before—at a particular patch of sandy shore along a pond, a few miles distant from the academy.

" Three hours was the limit. From the railroad station to Boston was thirty-five miles; from the pond to the station was perhaps three or four miles; from Boston to Cambridge we called about three miles. Forty miles in round numbers! We figured it all out before he returned, and got the trip down to two hours—record time: driving from the pond to the station; from the station by express train to Boston; from Boston by cab to Cambridge. This left an easy hour for accidents and delays.

" Cab and car and carriage we reckoned into our time-table; but what we didn't figure on was the turtle." And he paused abruptly.

" Young man," he went on, his shaggy brows and spectacles hardly hiding the twinkle in the eyes that were bent severely upon me, " young man, when you go after turtle eggs, take into account the turtle. No! no! That's bad advice. Youth never reckons on the turtle—and youth seldom ought to. Only old age does that; and old age would never have got those turtle eggs to Agassiz.

" It was in the early spring that Agassiz came to the academy, long before there was any likelihood of the turtles laying. But I was eager for the quest, and so fearful of failure that I started out to watch at the pond fully two weeks ahead of the time that the turtles might be expected to lay. I remember the date clearly: it was May 14.

"A little before dawn—along near three o'clock—I would drive over to the pond, hitch my horse near by, settle myself quietly among some thick cedars close to the sandy shore, and there I would wait, my kettle of sand ready, my eye covering the whole sleeping pond. Here among the cedars I would eat my breakfast, and then get back in good season to open the academy for the morning session.

"And so the watch began.

" I soon came to know individually the dozen or more turtles that kept to my side of the pond. Shortly after the cold mist would lift and melt away they would stick up their heads through the quiet water; and as the sun slanted down over the ragged rim of tree tops the slow things would float into the warm, lighted spots, or crawl out and doze comfortably on the hummocks and snags.

" What fragrant mornings those were! How fresh and new and unbreathed! The pond odors, the woods odors, the odors of the ploughed fields—of water lily, and wild grape, and the dew-laid soil! I can taste them yet, and hear them yet—the still, large sounds of the waking day—

the pickerel breaking the quiet with his swirl; the king-
fisher dropping anchor; the stir of feet and wings among
the trees.   And then the thought of the great book being
held up for me!   Those were rare mornings!

" But there began to be a good many of them, for the
turtles showed no desire to lay.   They sprawled in the
sun, and never one came out upon the sand as if she
intended to help on the great professor's book.   The
embryology of her eggs was of small concern to her; her
contribution to the Natural History of the United States
could wait.

"And it did wait.   I began my watch on the fourteenth
of May; June first found me still among the cedars, still
waiting, as I had waited every morning, Sundays and
rainy days alike.   June first saw a perfect morning, but
every turtle slid out upon her log, as if egg laying might
be a matter strictly of next year.

" I began to grow uneasy—not impatient yet, for a
naturalist learns his lesson of patience early, and for all
his years; but I began to fear lest, by some subtile sense,
my presence might somehow be known to the creatures;
that they might have gone to some other place to lay,
while I was away at the schoolroom.

" I watched on to the end of the first week, on to
the end of the second week in June, seeing the mists rise
and vanish every morning, and along with them vanish,
more and more, the poetry of my early morning vigil.
Poetry and rheumatism cannot long dwell together in the
same clump of cedars, and I had begun to feel the
rheumatism.   A month of morning mists wrapping me
around had at last soaked through to my bones.   But
Agassiz was waiting, and the world was waiting, for those
turtle eggs; and I would wait.   It was all I could do, for

335

there is no use bringing a china nest egg to a turtle; she is not open to any such delicate suggestion.

" Then came a mid-June Sunday morning, with dawn breaking a little after three: a warm, wide-awake dawn, with the level mist lifted from the level surface of the pond a full hour higher than I had seen it any morning before.

" This was the day: I knew it. I have heard persons say that they can hear the grass grow; that they know by some extra sense when danger is nigh. That we have these extra senses I fully believe, and I believe they can be sharpened by cultivation. For a month I had been watching, brooding over this pond, and now I knew. I felt a stirring of the pulse of things that the cold-hearted turtles could no more escape than could the clods and I.

" Leaving my horse unhitched, as if he too understood, I slipped eagerly into my covert for a look at the pond. As I did so, a large pickerel ploughed a furrow out through the spatter-docks, and in his wake rose the head of an enormous turtle. Swinging slowly around, the creature headed straight for the shore, and without a pause scrambled out on the sand.

" She was about the size of a big scoop shovel; but that was not what excited me, so much as her manner, and the gait at which she moved; for there was method in it, and fixed purpose. On she came, shuffling over the sand toward the higher open fields, with a hurried, determined seesaw that was taking her somewhere in particular, and that was bound to get her there on time.

" I held my breath. Had she been a dinosaurian making Mesozoic footprints, I could not have been more fearful. For footprints in the Mesozoic mud, or in the sands of time, were as nothing to me when compared with fresh turtle eggs in the sands of this pond.

336

"But over the strip of sand, without a stop, she paddled, and up a narrow cow path into the high grass along a fence. Then up the narrow cow path, on all fours, just like another turtle, I paddled, and into the high wet grass along the fence.

"I kept well within sound of her, for she moved recklessly, leaving a trail of flattened grass a foot and a half wide. I wanted to stand up, and I don't believe I could have turned her back with a rail, but I was afraid if she saw me that she might return indefinitely to the pond; so on I went, flat to the ground, squeezing through the lower rails of the fence, as if the field beyond were a melon patch. It was nothing of the kind, only a wild, uncomfortable pasture, full of dewberry vines, and very discouraging. They were excessively wet vines and briery. I pulled my coat sleeves as far over my fists as I could get them, and, with the tin pail of sand swinging from between my teeth to avoid noise, I stumped fiercely, but silently, on after the turtle.

"She was laying her course, I thought, straight down the length of this dreadful pasture, when, not far from the fence, she suddenly hove to, warped herself short about, and came back, barely clearing me, at a clip that was thrilling. I warped about, too, and in her wake bore down across the corner of the pasture, across the powdery public road, and on to a fence along a field of young corn.

"I was somewhat wet by this time, but not so wet as I had been before, wallowing through the deep, dry dust of the road. Hurrying up behind a large tree by the fence, I peered down the corn rows and saw the turtle stop, and begin to paw about in the loose soft soil. She was going to lay!

"I held on to the tree and watched, as she tried this place, and that place, and the other place—the eternally feminine! But the place, evidently, was hard to find.

337

What could a female turtle do with a whole field of possible nests to choose from? Then at last she found it, and, whirling about, she backed quickly at it, and, tail first, began to bury herself before my staring eyes.

" Those were not the supreme moments of my life; perhaps those moments came later that day; but those certainly were among the slowest, most dreadfully mixed of moments that I ever experienced. They were hours long. There she was, her shell just showing, like some old hulk in the sand along shore. And how long would she stay there? And how should I know if she had laid an egg?

" I could still wait. And so I waited, when, over the freshly awakened fields, floated four mellow strokes from the distant town clock.

" Four o'clock! Why, there was no train until seven! No train for three hours! The eggs would spoil! Then with a rush it came over me that this was Sunday morning, and there was no regular seven o'clock train—none till after nine.

" I think I should have fainted had not the turtle just then begun crawling off. I was weak and dizzy; but there, there in the sand, were the eggs! And Agassiz! And the great book! And I cleared the fence, and the forty miles that lay between me and Cambridge, at a single jump. He should have them, trains or no. Those eggs should go to Agassiz by seven o'clock, if I had to gallop every mile of the way. Forty miles! Any horse could cover it in three hours, if he had to; and, upsetting the astonished turtle, I scooped out her round white eggs.

" On a bed of sand in the bottom of the pail I laid them, with what care my trembling fingers allowed; filled in between them with more sand; so with another layer to the rim; and, covering all smoothly with more sand, I ran back for my horse.

" That horse knew, as well as I, that the turtle had laid, and that he was to get those eggs to Agassiz. He turned out of that field into the road on two wheels, a thing he had not done for twenty years, doubling me up before the dashboard, the pail of eggs miraculously lodged between my knees.

" I let him out. If only he could keep this pace all the way to Cambridge! Or even halfway there; and I should have time to finish the trip on foot. I shouted him on, holding to the dasher with one hand, the pail of eggs with the other, not daring to get off my knees, though the bang on them, as we pounded down the wood road, was terrific. But nothing must happen to the eggs; they must not be jarred, or even turned over in the sand before they came to Agassiz.

" In order to get out on the pike it was necessary to drive back away from Boston toward the town. We had nearly covered the distance, and were rounding a turn from the woods into the open fields, when, ahead of me, at the station it seemed, I heard the quick sharp whistle of a locomotive.

" What did it mean? Then followed the puff, puff, puff of a starting train. But what train? Which way going? And, jumping to my feet for a longer view, I pulled into a side road that paralleled the track, and headed hard for the station.

" We reeled along. The station was still out of sight, but from behind the bushes that shut it from view rose the smoke of a moving engine. It was perhaps a mile away, but we were approaching, head-on, and, topping a little hill, I swept down upon a freight train, the black smoke pouring from the stack, as the mighty creature pulled itself together for its swift run down the rails.

" My horse was on the gallop, going with the track, and straight toward the coming train. The sight of it almost maddened me—the bare thought of it, on the road to Boston! On I went; on it came, a half-a quarter of a mile between us, when suddenly my road shot out along an unfenced field with only a level stretch of sod between me and the engine.

" With a pull that lifted the horse from his feet, I swung him into the field and sent him straight as an arrow for the track. That train should carry me and my eggs to Boston!

" The engineer pulled the rope. He saw me standing up in the rig, saw my hat blow off, saw me wave my arms, saw the tin pail swing in my teeth, and he jerked out a succession of sharp halts! But it was he who should halt, not I; and on we went, the horse with a flounder landing the carriage on top of the track.

" The train was already grinding to a stop; but before it was near a stand-still I had backed off the track, jumped out, and, running down the rails with the astonished engineers gaping at me, had swung aboard the cab.

" They offered no resistance; they hadn't had time. Nor did they have the disposition, for I looked strange, not to say dangerous. Hatless, dew-soaked, smeared with yellow mud, and holding, as if it were a baby or a bomb, a little tin pail of sand.

" Crazy," the fireman muttered, looking to the engineer for his cue.

" I had been crazy, perhaps, but I was not crazy now. ' Throw her wide open,' I commanded. ' Wide open! These are fresh turtle eggs for Professor Agassiz of Cambridge. He must have them before breakfast.'

" Then they knew I was crazy, and, evidently thinking it best to humor me, threw the throttle wide open, and away we went.

" I kissed my hand to the horse, grazing unconcernedly in the open field, and gave a smile to my crew. That was all I could give them, and hold myself and the eggs together. But the smile was enough. And they smiled through their smut at me, though one of them held fast to his shovel, while the other kept his hand upon a big ugly wrench. Neither of them spoke to me, but above the roar of the swaying engine I caught enough of their broken talk to understand that they were driving under a full head of steam, with the intention of handing me over to the Boston police, as perhaps the easiest way of disposing of me.

" I was only afraid that they would try it at the next station. But that station whizzed past without a bit of slack, and the next, and the next; when it came over me that this was the through freight, which should have passed in the night, and was making up lost time.

" Only the fear of the shovel and the wrench kept me from shaking hands with both men at this discovery. But I beamed at them; and they at me. I was enjoying it. The unwonted jar beneath my feet was wrinkling my diaphragm with spasms of delight. And the fireman beamed at the engineer, with a look that said, " See the lunatic grin; he likes it! "

" He did like it. How the iron wheels sang to me as they took the rails! How the rushing wind in my ears sang to me! From my stand on the fireman's side of the cab I could catch a glimpse of the track just ahead of the engine, where the ties seemed to leap into the throat of the mile-devouring monster. The joy of it! Of seeing space swallowed by the mile!

" I shifted the eggs from hand to hand and thought of my horse, of Agassiz, of the great book, of my great luck, luck, luck, until the multitudinous tongues of the thundering train were all chiming " luck! luck! luck! " They knew! They understood! This beast of fire and

tireless wheels was doing its very best to get the eggs to
Agassiz!

"We swung out past the Blue Hills, and yonder
flashed the morning sun from the towering dome of the
State House. I might have leaped from the cab and run
the rest of the way on foot, had I not caught the eye
of the engineer watching me narrowly. I was not in
Boston yet, nor in Cambridge either. I was an escaped
lunatic, who had held up a train, and forced it to carry
me to Boston.

"Perhaps I had overdone my lunacy business. Suppose
these two men should take it into their heads to turn me
over to the police, whether I would or no? I could never
explain the case in time to get the eggs to Agassiz. I
looked at my watch. There were still a few minutes left,
in which I might explain to these men, who, all at once,
had become my captors. But it was too late. Nothing
could avail against my actions, my appearance, and my
little pail of sand.

"I had not thought of my appearance before. Here
I was, face and clothes caked with yellow mud, my hair
wild and matted, my hat gone, and in my full-grown
hands a tiny tin pail of sand, as if I had been digging
all night with a tiny tin shovel on the shore! And thus
to appear in the decent streets of Boston of a Sunday
morning!

"I began to feel like a hunted criminal. The situation
was serious, or might be, and rather desperately funny
at its best. I must in some way have shown my new
fears, for both men watched me more sharply.

"Suddenly, as we were nearing the outer freight yard,
the train slowed down and came to a stop. I was ready
to jump, but I had no chance. They had nothing to do,
apparently, but to guard me. I looked at my watch again.

342

What time we had made! It was only six o'clock, with a whole hour to get to Cambridge.

" But I didn't like this delay. Five minutes—ten— went by.

" Gentlemen," I began, but was cut short by an express train coming past. We were moving again, on into a siding; on to the main track; and on with a bump and a crash and a succession of crashes, running the length of the train; on at a turtle's pace, but on, when the fireman, quickly jumping for the bell rope, left the way to the step free, and the chance had come!

" I never touched the step, but landed in the soft sand at the side of the track, and made a line for the yard fence.

" There was no hue or cry. I glanced over my shoulder to see if they were after me. Evidently their hands were full, and they didn't know I had gone.

" But I had gone; and was ready to drop over the high board fence, when it occurred to me that I might drop into a policeman's arms. Hanging my pail in a splint on top of a post, I peered cautiously over—a very wise thing to do before you jump a high board fence. There, crossing the open square toward the station, was a big, burly fellow with a club looking for me.

" I flattened for a moment, when someone in the yard yelled at me. I preferred the policeman, and, grabbing my pail, I slid over to the street. The policeman moved on past the corner of the station out of sight. The square was free, and yonder stood a cab!

" Time was flying now. Here was the last lap. The cabman saw me coming, and squared away. I waved a paper dollar at him, but he only stared the more. A dollar can cover a good deal, but I was too much for one dollar. I pulled out another, thrust them both at him, and dodged into the cab, calling, " Cambridge!"

" He would have taken me straight to the police station had I not said, " Harvard College. Professor Agassiz's house! I've got eggs for Agassiz "; and pushed another dollar up at him through the hole.

" It was nearly half past six.

" ' Let him go!' I ordered. " Here's another dollar if you make Agassiz's house in twenty minutes. Let him out; never mind the police!"

" He evidently knew the police, or there were none around at that time on a Sunday morning. We went down the sleeping streets as I had gone down the wood roads from the pond two hours before, but with the rattle and crash now of a fire brigade. Whirling a corner into Cambridge Street, we took the bridge at a gallop, the driver shouting, shouting out something in Irish to a pair of waving arms and a belt and brass buttons.

"Across the bridge with a rattle and jolt that put the eggs in jeopardy, and on over the cobblestones, we went. Half standing, to lessen the jar, I held the pail in one hand and held myself by the other, not daring to let go even to look at my watch.

" But I was afraid to look at the watch. I was afraid to see how near to seven o'clock it might be. The sweat was dropping from my nose, so close was I running to the limit of my time.

" Suddenly there was a lurch, and I dived forward, ramming my head into the front of the cab, coming up with a rebound that landed me across the small of my back on the seat, and sent half of my pail of eggs helter-skelter over the floor.

" We had stopped. Here was Agassiz's house; and without taking time to pick up the scattered eggs I tumbled out, and pounded at the door.

344

"No one was astir in the house. But I would stir them. And I did. Right in the midst of the racket the door opened. It was the maid.

"'Agassiz,' I gasped, 'I want Professor Agassiz, quick!' And I pushed by her into the hall.

"'Go 'way, sir. I'll call the police. Professor Agassiz is in bed. Go 'way, sir.'

"'Call him—Agassiz—instantly, or I'll call him myself.'

"But I didn't; for just then a door overhead was flung open, a great white-robed figure appeared on the dim landing above, and a quick loud voice called excitedly:—

"'Let him in! Let him in! I know him. He has my turtle eggs!'

"And the apparition, slipperless, and clad in anything but an academic gown, came sailing down the stairs.

"The maid fled. The great man, his arms extended, laid hold of me with both hands, and, dragging me and my precious pail into his study, with a swift, clean stroke laid open one of the eggs, as the watch in my trembling hands ticked its way to seven as if nothing unusual were happening to the history of the world."

"You were in time, then?" I said.

"To the tick. There stands my copy of the great book. I am proud of the humble part I had in it."

"ON BEING THE RIGHT SIZE"

From Possible Worlds by J. B. S. HALDANE

The most obvious differences between different animals are differences of size, but for some reason the zoologists have paid singularly little attention to them. In a large textbook of zoology before me I find no indication that the eagle is larger than the sparrow, or the hippopotamus

345

bigger than the hare, though some grudging admissions are made in the case of the mouse and the whale. But yet it is easy to show that a hare could not be as large as a hippopotamus, or a whale as small as a herring. For every type of animal there is a most convenient size, and a large change in size inevitably carries with it a change of form.

Let us take the most obvious of possible cases, and consider a giant man sixty feet high—about the height of Giant Pope and Giant Pagan in the illustrated Pilgrim's Progress of my childhood. These monsters were not only ten times as high as Christian, but ten times as wide and ten times as thick, so that their total weight was a thousand times his, or about eighty to ninety tons. Unfortunately the cross sections of their bones were only a hundred times those of Christian, so that every square inch of giant bone had to support ten times the weight borne by a square inch of human bone. As the human thigh-bone breaks under about ten times the human weight, Pope and Pagan would have broken their thighs every time they took a step. This was doubtless why they were sitting down in the picture I remember. But it lessens one's respect for Christian and Jack the Giant Killer.

To turn to zoology, suppose that a gazelle, a graceful little creature with long thin legs, is to become large, it will break its bones unless it does one of two things. It may make its legs short and thick, like the rhinoceros, so that every pound of weight has still about the same area of bone to support it. Or it can compress its body and stretch out his legs obliquely to gain stability, like the giraffe. I mention these two beasts because they happen to belong to the same order as the gazelle, and both are quite successful mechanically, being remarkably fast runners.

346

Gravity, a mere nuisance to Christian, was a terror to Pope, Pagan, and Despair. To the mouse and any smaller animal it presents practically no dangers. You can drop a mouse down a thousand-yard mine shaft; and, on arriving at the bottom, it gets a slight shock and walks away, provided that the ground is fairly soft. A rat is killed, a man is broken, a horse splashes. For the resistance presented to movement by the air is proportional to the surface of the moving object. Divide an animal's length, breadth, and height each by ten; its weight is reduced to a thousandth, but its surface only to a hundredth. So the resistance to falling in the case of the small animal is relatively ten times greater than the driving force.

An insect, therefore, is not afraid of gravity; it can fall without danger, and can cling to the ceiling with remarkably little trouble. It can go in for elegant and fantastic forms of support like that of the daddy-longlegs. But there is a force which is as formidable to an insect as gravitation to a mammal. This is surface tension. A man out of a bath carries with him a film of water of about one-fiftieth of an inch in thickness. This weighs roughly a pound. A wet mouse has to carry about its own weight of water. A wet fly has to lift many times its own weight and, as everyone knows, a fly once wetted by water or any other liquid is in a very serious position indeed. An insect going for a drink is in as great danger as a man leaning out over a precipice in search of food. If it once falls into the grip of the surface tension of the water—that is to say, gets wet—it is likely to remain so until it drowns. A few insects, such as water-beetles, contrive to be unwettable; the majority keep well away from their drink by means of a long proboscis.

Of course tall land animals have other difficulties. They have to pump their blood to greater heights than a man, and therefore, require a larger blood pressure and tougher blood-vessels. A great many men die from burst arteries, especially in the brain, and this danger is presumably still greater for an elephant or a giraffe. But animals of all kinds find difficulties in size for the following reason. A typical small animal, say a microscopic worm or rotifer, has a smooth skin through which all the oxygen it requires can soak in, a straight gut with sufficient surface to absorb its food, and a single kidney. Increase its dimensions tenfold in every direction, and its weight is increased a thousand times, so that if it is to use its muscles as efficiently as its miniature counterpart, it will need a thousand times as much food and oxygen per day and will excrete a thousand times as much of waste products.

Now if its shape is unaltered its surface will be increased only a hundredfold, and ten times as much oxygen must enter per minute through each square millimetre of skin, ten times as much food through each square millimetre of intestine. When a limit is reached to their absorptive powers their surface has to be increased by some special device. For example, a part of the skin may be drawn out into tufts to make gills or pushed in to make lungs, thus increasing the oxygen-absorbing surface in proportion to the animal's bulk. A man, for example, has a hundred square yards of lung. Similarly, the gut, instead of being smooth and straight, becomes coiled and develops a velvety surface, and other organs increase in complication. The higher animals are not larger than the lower because they are more complicated. They are more complicated because they are larger. Just the same is true of plants. The simplest plants, such as the green algae growing in stagnant water or on the bark of trees, are mere round cells. The higher plants increase their surface by putting out leaves and roots. Comparative anatomy is largely the story of the struggle to increase surface in proportion to volume.

Some of the methods of increasing the surface are useful up to a point, but not capable of a very wide adaptation. For example, while vertebrates carry the oxygen from the gills or lungs all over the body in the blood, insects take air directly to every part of their body by tiny blind tubes called tracheae which open to the surface at many different points. Now, although by their breathing movements they can renew the air in the outer part of the tracheal system, the oxygen has to penetrate the finer branches by means of diffusion. Gases can diffuse easily through very small distances, not many times larger than the average length travelled by a gas molecule between collisions with other molecules. But when such vast journeys—from the point of view of a molecule—as a quarter of an inch have to be made, the process becomes slow. So the portions of an insect's body more than a quarter of an inch from the air would always be short of oxygen. In consequence hardly any insects are much more than half an inch thick. Land crabs are built on the same general plan as insects, but are much clumsier. Yet like ourselves they carry oxygen around in their blood, and are therefore able to grow far larger than any insects. If the insects had hit on a plan for driving air through their tissues instead of letting it soak in, they might well have become as large as lobsters, though other considerations would have prevented them from becoming as large as man.

Exactly the same difficulties attach to flying. It is an elementary principle of aeronautics that the minimum speed needed to keep an aeroplane of a given shape in the air varies as the square root of its length. If its linear dimensions are increased four times, it must fly twice as fast. Now the power needed for the minimum speed increases more rapidly than the weight of the machine. So the larger aeroplane, which weighs sixty-four times as much as the smaller, needs one hundred and twenty-eight times its horsepower to keep up. Applying the same principles to the birds, we find that the limit to their size is soon reached. An angel whose muscles developed no more power weight for weight than those of an eagle or a pigeon would require a breast projecting for about four feet to house the muscles engaged in working its wings, while to economize in weight, its legs would have to be reduced to mere stilts. Actually a large bird such as an eagle or kite does not keep in the air mainly by moving its wings. It is generally to be seen soaring, that is to say balanced on a rising column of air. And even soaring becomes more and more difficult with increasing size. Were this not the case eagles might be as large as tigers and as formidable to man as hostile aeroplanes.

But it is time that we pass to some of the advantages of size. One of the most obvious is that it enables one to keep warm. All warm-blooded animals at rest lose the same amount of heat from a unit area of skin, for which purpose they need a food-supply proportional to their surface and not to their weight. Five thousand mice weigh as much as a man. Their combined surface and food or oxygen consumption are about seventeen times a man's. In fact a mouse eats about one quarter its own weight of food every day, which is mainly used in keeping it warm. For the same reason small animals cannot live in cold countries. In the arctic regions there are no reptiles or amphibians, and no small mammals. The smallest mammal in Spitzbergen is the fox. The small birds fly away in winter, while the insects die, though their eggs can survive six months or more of frost. The most successful mammals are bears, seals, and walruses.

350

Similarly, the eye is a rather inefficient organ until it reaches a large size. The back of the human eye on which an image of the outside world is thrown, and which corresponds to the film of a camera, is composed of a mosaic of " rods and cones " whose diameter is little more than a length of an average light wave. Each eye has about a half a million, and for two objects to be distinguishable their images must fall on separate rods or cones. It is obvious that with fewer but larger rods and cones we should see less distinctly. If they were twice as broad two points would have to be twice as far apart before we could distinguish them at a given distance. But if their size were diminished and their number increased we should see no better. For it is impossible to form a definite image smaller than a wave-length of light. Hence a mouse's eye is not a small-scale model of a human eye. Its rods and cones are not much smaller than ours, and therefore there are far fewer of them. A mouse could not distinguish one human face from another six feet away. In order that they should be any use at all the eyes of small animals have to be much larger in proportion to their bodies than our own. Large animals on the other hand only require relatively small eyes, and those of the whale and elephant are little larger than our own.

For rather more recondite reasons the same general principle holds true of the brain. If we compare the brain-weights of a set of very similar animals such as the cat, cheetah, leopard, and tiger, we find that as we quadruple the body-weight the brain-weight is only doubled. The larger animal with proportionately larger bones can economize on brain, eyes, and certain other organs.

Such are a very few of the considerations which show that for every type of animal there is an optimum size. Yet although Galileo demonstrated the contrary more than three hundred years ago, people still believe that if a flea were as large as a man it could jump a thousand feet into the air. As a matter of fact the height to which an animal can jump is more nearly independent of its size than proportional to it. A flea can jump about two feet, a man about five. To jump a given height, if we neglect the resistance of the air, requires an expenditure of energy proportional to the jumper's weight. But if the jumping muscles form a constant fraction of the animal's body, the energy developed per ounce of muscle is independent of the size, provided it can be developed quickly enough in the small animal. As a matter of fact an insect's muscles, although they can contract more quickly than our own, appear to be less efficient; as otherwise a flea or grasshopper could rise six feet into the air.

" BIOLOGY AND MEDICINE "

by ALAN GREGG

The philosopher Santayana has remarked that he who feels prepared to ignore history is doomed to repeat it. In the history of scientific discovery there are lessons that the Atomic Energy Commission is heeding, deliberately and energetically, lest the frustrations and futilities that attend other discoveries repeat themselves in the study and development of atomic energy.

Sulphuric ether was discovered by Valerius Cordus in 1540. For over three hundred years it remained a chemical commonplace, dangerously inflammable, almost unused, though employed playfully by students as a brisk and potent intoxicant. Then Crawford Long and W. T. G. Morton in 1842-44 found and showed its wonderful value as an anesthetic. It may take long years to make a substance that is known to science useful to man. Think of the sum total of unnecessary pain during three hundred years of the failure to explore the effect of ether on man. Once a new substance is made, or a new process invented, years—even centuries—may elapse before all its properties or uses have been discovered and put in practice.

Roentgen discovered X-rays in 1895. The immediately obvious application in the detection and correction of fractured bones was made rather promptly. In 1902 Cannon, by using X-ray photographs of barium swallowed by experimental animals, defined one of the effects of strong emotions on the stomach and intestines. He thus laid one of the foundations for psychosomatic medicine— a far cry from classical physics. Still later in the use of hard X-rays upon tumors and soft X-rays upon the skin and hair, physicists and physicians found uses of X-rays not dreamed of by Roentgen or his contemporaries. The uses a new substance may possess are as unpredictable and as yet certain as the future shape of a tree lying invisible in its seed.

Gasoline—at first a worthless and dangerous byproduct of distilling kerosene from crude petroleum—was thrown away by the millions of barrels, until its value was shown when used in engines designed to turn its explosive energy into mechanical work. As both result and cause of developments of the internal combustion engine, came the automobile, the tractor, and the airplane—long after gasoline was first produced and thrown away.

However, with energetic and alert study the gap between a discovery and its major application may not last long. Only fourteen years elapsed between Fleming's discovery of the antibiotic effects of a common mold and the production of penicillin in significant quantities for use in human therapy.

But we cannot safely overlook the possibility of danger lurking in any activity that leads to discovery. Research experiments may create substances or unleash forces so

353

powerful in their effects on living tissues that investigation of their properties is no idle curiosity or speculative diversion. It is an impelling necessity. We cannot afford to be casual or careless. The appalling burns from the ignorant and casual use in the early days of X-rays and radium stand on the record as a somber warning.

If scientific research offers unimaginable opportunities for good, it imposes unexampled obligations to protect ourselves against equally unforeseeable dangers. Thanks to examples (from other fields) of wasteful waiting and reckless inadvertence, the Atomic Energy Commission is devoting extensive and unflagging attention to the biological and medical effects of radiant energy—both those that may prove to be beneficent and those that may maim or kill. When man first discovered fire he began a long apprenticeship to caution in dealing with what is both useful and dangerous—and the end is not yet.

The story of the Garden of Eden and the myth of the Promethean fire find uncanny parallels in the huge responsibilities of the Atomic Energy Commission to control the unprecedented forces of atomic energy for the welfare of man. To control the use of this power, to explore its nature, its implications and potential applications, and at the same time to protect us all against its dangers—these responsibilities set a series of tasks that also are without precedent and all but immeasurable. . . .

Perhaps the kernel of the situation lies in the fact that the greater man's knowledge of the laws of nature the more substances he can create that have never actually been found in nature. We can thus not only make completely unfamiliar substances but also release forces that in quality or intensity are not to be found in the natural world. Virtually a second world for study and exploration comes thus into being as a result of profoundly understanding the laws that govern the phenomena of the world about us—the first world we studied and explored. Nor is this the end of the possibilities before us. There is almost an infinity of possible applications of new substances and new forces. Indeed the case for finding the uses of new substances for human needs, the harnessing of new forms of energy to serve human purposes, rests in the phrase of Protagoras the Sophist: *homo mensura*— " man is the measure of all things." And what is to measure the needs and purposes of man?

" BEQUEST TO THE ACADEMIC YOUTH OF MY COUNTRY "

by IVAN PAVLOV (1936)

What shall I wish for the young students of my country? First of all, sequence, consequence and again consequence. In gaining knowledge you must accustom yourself to the strictest sequence. You must be familiar with the very groundwork of science before you try to climb the heights. Never start on the " next " before you have mastered the " previous." Do not try to conceal the shortcomings of your knowledge by guesses and hypotheses. Accustom yourself to the roughest and simplest scientific tools. Perfect as the wing of a bird may be, it will never enable the bird to fly if unsupported by the air. Facts are the air of science. Without them the man of science can never rise. Without them your theories are vain surmises. But while you are studying, observing, experimenting, do not remain content with the surface of things. Do not become a mere recorder of facts, but try to penetrate the mystery of their origin. Seek obstinately for the laws that govern them. And then—modesty. Never think you know all. Though others may flatter you, retain the courage to say, " I am ignorant." Never be proud. And lastly, science must be your passion. Remember that science claims a man's whole life. Had he two lives they would not suffice. Science demands an undivided allegiance from its followers. In your work and in your research there must always be passion.

PART THREE: HISTORY AND THE SOCIAL SCIENCES

PARAGRAPHS FROM *HISTORY*

by RALPH WALDO EMERSON, 1850.

> There is no great and no small
> To the Soul that maketh all
> And where it cometh, all things are:
> And it cometh everywhere.
>
> I am owner of the sphere,
> Of the seven stars and the solar year,
> Of Caesar's hand, and Plato's brain,
> Of Lord Christ's heart, and Shakespeare's strain.

There is one mind common to all individual men. Every man is an inlet to the same and to all of the same. He that is once admitted to the right of reason is made a freeman of the whole estate. What Plato has thought he may think; what a saint has felt he may feel; what at any time has fallen any man he can understand. Who hath access to this universal mind is a party to all that is or can be done, for this is the only and sovereign agent.

Of the works of this mind history is the record. Its genius is illustrated by the entire series of days. Man is explicable by nothing less than all his history. Without hurry, without rest, the human spirit goes forth from the beginning to embody every faculty, every thought, every emotion, which belongs to it in appropriate events. But the thought is always prior to the fact; all the facts of history pre-exist in the mind as laws. Each law in turn is made by circumstances predominant, and the limits of nature give power to but one at a time. A man is the whole encyclopaedia of facts. The creation of a thousand forests is in one acorn; and Egypt, Greece, Rome, Gaul,

Britain, America, lie enfolded already in the first man. Epoch after epoch, camp, kingdom, empire, republic, democracy, are merely the application of his manifold spirit to the manifold world.

This human mind wrote history, and this must read it. The Sphinx must solve her own riddle. If the whole of history is in one man, it is all to be explained from individual experience. There is a relation between the hours of our life and the centuries of time. As the air I breathe is drawn from the great repositories of nature, as the light on my book is yielded by a star a hundred millions of miles distant, as the poise of my body depends on the equilibrium of centrifugal and centripetal forces, so the hours should be instructed by the ages, and the ages explained by the hours. Of the universal mind each individual man is one more incarnation. All its properties consist in him. Each new fact in his private experience flashes a light on what great bodies of men have done, and the crises of his life refer to national crises. Every revolution was first a thought in one man's mind, and when the same thought occurs to another man it is the key to that era. Every reform was once a private opinion, and when it shall be a private opinion, again it will solve the problem of the age. The fact narrated must correspond to something in me to be credible or intelligible. We as we read must become Greeks, Romans, Turks, priest and king, martyr and executioner, must fasten these images to some reality in our secret experience, or we shall learn nothing rightly. What befell Asdrubal or Caesar Borgia is as much an illustration of the mind's powers and depravations as what has befallen us. Each new law and political movement has meaning for you. Stand before each of its tablets and say, "Under this mask did my Proteus nature hide itself." This remedies the defect of our too great nearness to ourselves. This throws our actions into perspective; and as crabs, goats, scorpions, the balance, and the waterpot lose their meanness when hung as signs in the zodiac, so I can see my own vices without heat in the distant person of Solomon, Alcibiades, and Catiline.

It is the universal nature which gives worth to particular men and things. Human life as containing this is mysterious and inviolable, and we hedge it round with penalties and laws. All laws derive hence their ultimate reason; all express more or less distinctly some command of this supreme, illimitable essence. Property also holds of the soul, covers great spiritual facts, and instinctively we at first hold to it with swords and laws, and wide and complex combinations. The obscure consciousness of this fact is the light of all our day, the claim of claims; the plea for education, for justice, for charity, the foundation of friendship and love, and of the heroism and grandeur which belong to acts of self-reliance. It is remarkable that involuntarily we always read as superior beings. Universal history, the poets, the romancers, do not in their stateliest pictures—in the sacerdotal, the imperial palaces, in the triumphs of will or of genius—anywhere lose our ear, anywhere make us feel that we intrude, that this is for better men; but rather is it true, that in their grandest strokes we feel most at home. All that Shakespeare says of the king; yonder slip of a boy that reads in the corner feels to be true of himself. We sympathize in the great moments of history, in the great discoveries, the great resistances, the great prosperities of men;— because there law was enacted, the sea was searched, the land was found, or the blow was struck for us, as we ourselves in that place would have done or applauded.

We have the same interest in condition and character. We honour the rich, because they have externally the freedom, power, and grace which we feel to be proper to man, proper to us. So all that is said of the wise man by Stoic, or oriental, or modern essayist, describes by each reader his own idea, describes his unattained but attainable self. All literature writes the character of the wise man. Books, monuments, pictures, conversation, are portraits in which he finds the lineaments he is forming. The silent and the eloquent praise him and accost him, and he is stimulated wherever he moves as by personal allusions. A true aspirant, therefore, never needs look for allusions personal and laudatory in discourse. He hears the commendation, not of himself, but more sweet, of that character he seeks, in every word that is said concerning character, yea, further, in every fact and circumstance— in the running river and the rustling corn. Praise is looked, homage tendered, love flows from mute nature, from the mountains and the lights of the firmament.

These hints, dropped as it were from sleep and night, let us use in broad day. The student is to read history actively and not passively; to esteem his own life the text, and books the commentary. Thus compelled, the Muse of history will utter oracles, as never to those who do not respect themselves. I have no expectation that any man will read history aright, who thinks that what was done in a remote age, by men whose names have resounded far, has any deeper sense than what he is doing to-day.

The world exists for the education of each man. There is no age, or state of society, or mode of action in history, to which there is not somewhat corresponding in his life. Everything tends in a wonderful manner to abbreviate itself and yield its own virtue to him. He should see that he can live all history in his own person. He must sit solidly at home, and not suffer himself to be bullied by kings or enemies, but know that he is greater than all the geography and all the government of the world; he must transfer the point of view from which history is commonly read, from Rome, and Athens, and London, to himself, and not deny his conviction that he is in the court, and if England or Egypt have anything to say to him, he will try the case; if not, let them for ever be silent. He must attain and maintain that lofty sight where facts yield their secret sense, and poetry and annals are alike. The instinct of the mind, the purpose of nature, betrays itself in the use we make of the signal narrations of history. Time dissipates to shining ether the solid angularity of facts. No anchor, no cable, no fences, avail to keep a fact a fact. Babylon, Troy, Tyre, Palestine, and even early Rome, are passing already into fiction. The Garden of Eden, the sun standing still in Gibeon, is poetry thence-forward to all nations. Who cares what the fact was, when we have made a constellation of it to hang in heaven an immortal sign? London and Paris and New York must go the same way. "What is History," said Napoleon, "but a fable agreed upon?" This life of ours is stuck round with Egypt, Greece, Gaul, England, War, Colonization, Church, Court, and Commerce, as with so many flowers and wild ornaments grave and gay. I will not make more account of them. I believe in Eternity. I can find Greece, Asia, Italy, Spain, and the Islands— the genius and creative principle of each and of all eras in my own mind.

We are always coming up with the emphatic facts of history in our private experience, and verifying them here. All history becomes subjective; in other words, there is properly no history; only biography. Every mind must know the whole lesson for itself—must go over the whole ground. What it does not see, what it does not live, it will not know.

All inquiry into antiquity—all curiosity respecting the Pyramids, the excavated cities, Stonehenge, the Ohio Circles, Mexico, Memphis—is the desire to do away with this wild, savage, and preposterous There or Then, and introduce in its place the Here and the Now.

All public facts are to be individualized, all private facts are to be generalized. Then at once History becomes fluid and true, and Biography deep and sublime.

What is the foundation of that interest all men feel in Greek history, letters, art, and poetry, in all its periods, from the Heroic or Homeric age down to the domestic life of the Athenians and Spartans, four or five centuries later? What but this, that every man passes personally through a Grecian period. The Grecian state is the era of the bodily nature, the perfection of the senses—of the spiritual nature unfolded in strict unity with the body. In it existed those human forms which supplied the sculptor with his models of Hercules, Phoebus, and Jove; not like the forms abounding in the streets of modern cities, wherein the face is a confused blur of features, but composed of incorrupt, sharply defined, and symmetrical features, whose eye-sockets are so formed that it would be impossible for such eyes to squint, and take furtive glances on this side and on that, but they must turn the whole head.

The costly charm of the ancient tragedy, and indeed of all the old literature, is, that the persons speak simply— speak as persons who have great good sense without knowing it, before yet the reflective habit has become the predominant habit of the mind. Our admiration of the antique is not admiration of the old, but of the natural. The Greeks are not reflective, but perfect in their senses and in their health, with the finest physical organization in the world. Adults acted with the simplicity and grace of children. They made vases, tragedies, and statues, such as healthy senses should—that is, in good taste.

As near and proper to us is also that old fable of the Sphinx, who was said to sit in the roadside and put riddles to every passenger. If the man could not answer she swallowed him alive. If he could solve the riddle the Sphinx was slain. What is our life but an endless flight of winged facts or events! In splendid variety these changes come, all putting questions to the human spirit. Those men who cannot answer by a superior wisdom these facts or questions of time, serve them. Facts encumber them, tyrannize over them, and make the men of routine the men of sense, in whom a literal obedience to facts has extinguished every spark of that light by which man is truly man. But if the man is true to his better instincts or sentiments, and refuses the dominion of facts, as one that comes of a higher race, remains fast by the soul and sees the principle, then the facts fall aptly and supple into their places; they know their master, and the meanest of them glorifies him.

But along with the civil and metaphysical history of man, another history goes daily forward—that of the external world—in which he is not less strictly implicated. He is the compend of time; he is also the correlative of nature. His power consists in the multitude of his affinities, in the fact that his life is intertwined with the whole chain of organic and inorganic being. In old Rome the public roads beginning at the Forum proceeded north, south, east, west, to the centre of every province of the empire, making each market-town of Persia, Spain, and Britain pervious to the soldiers of the capital: so out of the human heart go, as it were, highways to the heart of every object in nature, to reduce it under the dominion of man. A man is a bundle of relations, a knot of roots, whose flower and fruitage is the world. His faculties refer to natures out of him, and predict the world he is to inhabit, as the fins of the fish foreshow that water exists, or the wings of an eagle in the egg presuppose air. He cannot live without a world.

You shall not tell me by languages and titles a catalogue of the volumes you have read. You shall make me feel what periods you have lived. A man shall be the Temple of Fame. He shall walk, as the poets have described that goddess, in a robe painted all over with wonderful events and experiences;—his own from the features, by their exalted intelligence, shall be that variegated vest. I shall find in him the Foreworld; in his childhood the Age of Gold; the Apples of Knowledge; the Argonautic Expedition; the calling of Abraham; the building of the Temple; the Advent of Christ; the Dark Ages; the Revival of Letters; the Reformation; the discovery of new lands; the opening of new sciences, and new regions in man. He shall be the priest of Pan, and bring with him into humble cottages the blessing of the morning stars and all the recorded benefits of heaven and earth.

Is there somewhat overweening in this claim? Then I reject all I have written, for what is the use of pretending to know what we know not? But it is the fault of our rhetoric that we cannot strongly state one fact without seeming to belie some other. I hold your actual knowledge very cheap. Hear the rats in the wall, see the lizard on the fence, the fungus under foot, the lichen on the log. What do I know sympathetically, morally, of either of these worlds of life? As old as the Caucasian man—perhaps older—these creatures have kept their counsel beside him, and there is no record of any word or sign that has passed from one to the other. What connection do the books show between the fifty and sixty chemical elements, and the historical eras? Nay, what does history yet record of the metaphysical annals of man? What light does it shed on those mysteries which we hide under the names Death and Immortality? Yet every history should be written in a wisdom which divined the range of our affinities and looked at facts as symbols. I am ashamed to see what a shallow village tale our so-called History is. How many times we must say Rome, and Paris, and Constantinople! What does Rome know of rat and lizard? What are Olympiads and Consulates to these neighbouring systems of being? Nay, what food or experience or succour have they for the Esquimaux seal-hunter, for the Kanaka in his canoe, for the fisherman, the stevedore, the porter?

Broader and deeper we must write our annals—from an ethical reformation, from an influx of the ever new, ever sanative conscience,—if we would trulier express our central and wide-related nature, instead of his old chronology of selfishness and pride to which we have too long lent our eyes.

COURSE OF POSITIVE PHILOSOPHY

" Concerning the Hierarchy of the Positive Sciences "

by AUGUSTE COMTE (1798-1857)

All human activities are either of speculation or of action. Thus the most general division of our knowledge is into theoretical and practical. Starting with this division, it is evident that only theoretical knowledge should be our concern here. For our task is not that of observing the entire system of human ideas; on the contrary we are interested only in those fundamental concepts under the diverse orders of phenomena which furnish a solid basis for all other combinations and which are not themselves based on any previous intellectual system. Hence we should consider speculation, not application, except where we can clarify the former in terms of the latter. This is probably what Bacon intended, though imperfectly, by that *first philosophy* which he considered to be an extract from the totality of the sciences, and which has been so variously and so strangely conceived by the metaphysicians who have undertaken to comment on his work.

Without doubt when one envisages the complete ensemble of the works of the human mind he is obliged to look upon the study of nature as furnishing the truly rational basis for action. If we know the laws of phenomena we can predict them, and, in an active life, control them to our advantage. Our natural and direct means of acting on bodies which surround us are extremely weak and quite disproportionate to our needs. Every time we succeed in acting on nature it is only because our knowledge of natural laws permits us to introduce, among the determining circumstances under the influence of which the diverse phenomena are brought about, certain modifying elements. These factors, however weak they may be, suffice in certain cases to modify for our benefit the operation of the external causes. In short, *from science comes prevision; from prevision comes action.* Such is the simple formula which expresses exactly the general relation of science to art, taking these two terms in their broadest meanings.

In view of the present development of our intelligence we are not yet ready to apply the sciences directly to the arts, at least in the most perfect cases. However there exists between these two classes an intermediate group which, although somewhat indefinite from the philosophical point of view, is more clearly recognizable when we consider the social group which is concerned with its special problems. Between the pure scientists and the group which busies itself with practical works there is beginning to be formed an intermediate class called *engineers,* whose special job it is to organize the relations between theory and practice. Without concerning themselves at all with the progress of scientific knowledge they accept the sciences in their existing state in order to deduce from them the industrial applications of which they are susceptible. Such at any rate is the tendency; there is still much confusion. The body of doctrine which is distinctive of this class, and which ought to constitute the theories of the various arts, could unquestionably provoke philosophical considerations of great interest and genuine importance.

It is essential to distinguish in relation to all orders of phenomena two kinds of natural sciences. The abstract or general sciences have as their object the discovery of the laws which govern the different classes of phenomena in all conceivable cases; the concrete, particular, or descriptive sciences (natural sciences, properly so-called) have as their task the application of these laws to the actual history of the different kinds of existent beings. The former are fundamental, and we shall be concerned exclusively with them in what follows; the latter, however important, are really purely secondary and ought not to constitute a part of a work which is by nature so extensive that some limitation is required. This distinction should be clear to those who have special acquaintance with the different positive sciences, stated in scientific treatises in the comparison of dogmatic physics with what is properly called natural history. This distinction, whose importance has not been sufficiently recognized, will now be clarified by examples.

Compare general physiology, on the one hand, with zoology and botany, on the other. The study of the laws of life in general is quite a different matter from the determination of the mode of existence of each living being in particular. The latter study, furthermore, is necessarily founded on the former. Or consider chemistry in relation to mineralogy; again the former is evidently the rational foundation of the latter. In chemistry one considers all possible combinations of molecules in all imaginable circumstances; in mineralogy one concerns himself only with certain of these combinations which are realized in the constitution of the earth and which are under the influence of the circumstances peculiar to this location. Although the two sciences are concerned with the same objects, each has its own point of view. Most of the facts considered by the former have only an artificial existence. A substance such as chlorine or potassium will have an extreme importance in chemistry by virtue of the extent and energy of its affinities, while it will have almost no importance in mineralogy; on the other hand a compound such as granite or quartz, although a very significant substance for mineralogy, is in relation to chemistry of only minor interest.

The logical necessity for this fundamental distinction between the two great sections of natural philosophy is seen even more clearly in the fact that each section of concrete physics not only presupposes the cultivation of the corresponding section of abstract physics but also demands knowledge of the general laws relative to all orders of phenomena. For example, the special study of the earth considered in its widest extent demands not only a preliminary acquaintance with physics and chemistry but also knowledge of astronomy and even, from another side, physiology; thus it comprehends the entire system of the fundamental sciences. This is precisely the reason why *concrete physics* has made so little progress up to now; it could only begin to be studied in a truly rational manner after *abstract physics* in all of its principal branches had taken on a definite character—something which has occurred only recently.

Thus far we have seen the following: *1*. That science consists of two parts, one devoted to speculation, the other to application; we shall be concerned only with the former. *2*. That theoretical science, or science properly understood, consists of two kinds, general and particular; we shall be concerned here only with the former and limit ourselves to abstract physics, however interesting concrete physics may be. Now that we have precisely delimited the subject of the book we may proceed to a rational classification of the basic sciences which is really satisfactory. This is the encyclopedic question which is the special subject of this chapter.

Every science can be viewed according to two modes of development—the *historical* and the *dogmatic*. All other viewpoints are only a combination of these two. According to the first, one considers the science successively, following the order by which the human mind has really acquired the knowledge, and adopting as far as possible the existing concepts. According to the second, one presents the system of ideas as they would be conceived today by a mind which, placed at the proper point of view and provided with sufficient knowledge, is concerned with remaking the science into a totality.

The general problem of education consists in enabling a single intelligence, frequently a mediocre one, to arrive in a few years at the same point of development as that which has been attained by a large number of superior minds, working throughout their lives, and applying themselves successively over a series of centuries to the study of a single subject. It is clear from this that although learning is infinitely easier and quicker than invention, the end of education could not possibly be achieved if we compelled each individual to pass successively through the same intermediary stages as those followed by the collective mind. Consequently the dogmatic order is indispensable. This is especially apparent in the case of the more advanced sciences, the exposition of which contains almost no trace of the historical connections of their details.

As a result of this discussion positive philosophy is naturally divided into five basic sciences, whose succession is determined by a necessary and invariable subordination, founded, independently of all hypothetical consideration, on a simple but profound comparison of the corresponding phenomena. These are astronomy, physics, chemistry, physiology and finally social physics. The first considers phenomena which are the most general, the most simple, the most abstract, and the most removed from humanity; these phenomena influence all others without being influenced by them. Phenomena considered by the last science are, on the contrary, the most particular, the most complex, the most concrete, and the most directly of interest to man.

Selected Paragraphs from

" SCIENCE AS A VOCATION " *by* MAX WEBER

You wish me to speak about " Science as a Vocation." Now, we political economists have a pedantic custom, which I should like to follow, of always beginning with the external conditions. In this case, we begin with the question: What are the conditions of science as a vocation in the material sense of the term? Today this question means, practically and essentially: What are the prospects of a graduate student who is resolved to dedicate himself professionally to science in university life? In order to understand the peculiarity of German conditions it is expedient to proceed by comparison and to realize the conditions abroad. In this respect, the United States stands in the sharpest contrast with Germany, so we shall focus upon that country.

Ladies and gentlemen. In the field of science only he who is devoted solely to the work at hand has " personality." And this holds not only for the field of science; we know of no great artist who has ever done anything but serve his work and only his work. As far as his art is concerned, even with a personality of Goethe's rank, it has been detrimental to take the liberty of trying to make his " life " into a work of art. . . . In the field of science, however, the man who makes himself the impresario of the subject to which he should be devoted, and steps upon the stage and seeks to legitimate himself through " experience," asking: How can I prove that I am something other than a mere "specialist" and how can I manage to say something in form or in content that nobody else has ever said? — such a man is no "personality." Today such conduct is a crowd phenomenon, and it always makes a petty impression and debases the one who is thus concerned. Instead of this, an inner devotion to the task, and that alone, should lift the scientist to the height and dignity of the subject he pretends to serve. And in this it is not different with the artist. . . . In contrast with these preconditions which scientific work shares with art, science has a fate that profoundly distinguishes it from artistic work. Scientific work is chained to the course of progress; whereas in the realm of art there is no progress in the same sense. It is not true that the work of art of a period that has worked out new technical means, or, for instance, the laws of perspective, stands therefore artistically higher than a work of art devoid of all knowledge of those means and laws—if its form does justice to the material, that is, if its object has been chosen and formed so that it could be artistically mastered without applying those conditions and means. A work of art which is genuine " fulfilment " is never surpassed; it will never be antiquated. Individuals may differ in appreciating the personal significance of works of art, but no one will ever be able to say of such a work that it is outstripped by another work which is also " fulfilment."

In science, each of us knows that what he has accomplished will be antiquated in ten, twenty, fifty years. That is the fate to which science is subjected; it is the very meaning of scientific work, to which it is devoted in a quite specific sense, as compared with other spheres of culture for which in general the same holds. Every scientific " fulfilment " raises new " questions "; it asks to be " surpassed " and outdated. Whoever wishes to serve science has to resign himself to this fact. Scientific works certainly can last as " gratifications " because of their artistic quality, or they may remain important as a means of training. Yet they will be surpassed scientifically —let that be repeated—for it is our common fate and, more, our common goal. We cannot work without hoping that others will advance further than we have. In principle, this progress goes on *ad infinitum*. And with this we come to inquire into the meaning of science. For after all, it is not self-evident that something subordinate to such a law is sensible and meaningful in itself. Why does one engage in doing something that in reality never comes, and never can come, to an end? One does it, first, for purely practical, in the broader sense of the word, for technical, purposes: in order to be able to orient our practical activities to the expectations that scientific experience places at our disposal. Good. Yet this has meaning only to practitioners. What is the attitude of the academic man towards his vocation—that is, if he is at all in quest of such a personal attitude? He maintains that he engages in " science for science's sake " and not merely because others, by exploiting science, bring about commercial or technical success and can better feed, dress, illuminate, and govern. But what does he who allows himself to be integrated into this specialized organization, running on *ad infinitum,* hope to accomplish that is significant in these productions that are always destined to be outdated? This question requires a few general considerations.

Scientific progress is a fraction, the most important fraction, of the process of intellectualization which we have been undergoing for thousands of years and which nowadays is usually judged in such an extremely negative way. Let us first clarify what this intellectualist rationalization, created by science and by scientifically oriented technology, means practically. . . . The increasing intellectualization and rationalization do not . . . indicate an increased and general knowledge of the conditions under which one lives. . . . They mean that principally there are no mysterious incalculable forces that come into play, but rather that one can, in principle, master all things by calculation. This means that *the world is disenchanted.* One need no longer have recourse to magical means in order to master or implore the spirits, as did the savage, for whom such mysterious powers existed. Technical means and calculations perform the service. This above all is what intellectualization means.

Now, this process of disenchantment, which has continued to exist in Occidental culture for millennia, and, in general, this " progress," to which science belongs as a link and motive force, do they have any meanings that go beyond the purely practical and technical? You will find this question raised in the most principled form in the works of Leo Tolstoi. He came to raise the question in a peculiar way. All his broodings increasingly revolved around the problem of whether or not death is a meaningful phenomenon. And his answer was: for civilized man death has no meaning. It has none because the individual life of civilized man, placed into an infinite " progress," according to its own imminent meaning should never come to an end; for there is always a further step ahead of one who stands in the march of progress. And no man who comes to die stands upon the peak which lies in infinity. Abraham, or some peasant of the past, died " old and satiated with life " because he stood in the organic cycle of life; because his life, in terms of its meaning and on the eve of his days, had given to him what life had to offer; because for him there remained no puzzles he might wish to solve; and therefore he could have had " enough " of life. Whereas civilized man, placed in the midst of the continuous enrichment of culture by ideas, knowledge, and problems, may become " tired of life " but not " satiated with life." He catches only the most minute part of what the life of the spirit brings forth ever anew, and what he seizes is always something provisional and not definitive, and therefore death for him is a meaningless occurrence; by its very " progressiveness " it gives death the imprint of meaninglessness. Throughout his late novels one meets with this thought as the keynote of the Tolstoyan art.

What stand should one take? Has " progress " as such a recognizable meaning that goes beyond the technical, so that to serve it is a meaningful vocation? The question must be raised. But this is no longer merely the question of man's calling for science, hence, the problem of what science as a vocation means to its devoted disciples. . . . Here the contrast between the past and the present is tremendous. You will recall the wonderful image at the beginning of the seventh book of Plato's Republic: those enchained cavemen whose faces are turned toward the stone wall before them. Behind them lies the source of the light which they cannot see. They are concerned only with the shadowy images that this light throws upon the wall, and they seek to fathom their interrelations. Finally one of them succeeds in shattering his fetters, turns around, and sees the sun. Blinded, he gropes about and stammers of what he saw. The others say he is raving. But gradually he learns to behold the light, and then his task is to descend to the cavemen and to lead them to the light. He is the philosopher; the sun, however, is the truth of science which alone seizes not upon illusions and shadows but upon the true being.

The second great tool of scientific work, the rational experiment, made its appearance at the side of this discovery of the Hellenic spirit during the Renaissance period. The experiment is a means of reliably controlling experience. Without it, present-day empirical science would be impossible. There were experiments earlier; for instance, in India physiological experiments were made in the service of ascetic yoga technique; in Hellenic antiquity, mathematical experiments were made for purposes of war technology; and in the Middle Ages, for purposes of mining. But to raise the experiment to a principle of research was the achievement of the Renaissance. They were the great innovators in art, who were the pioneers of experiment. Leonardo and his like and, above all, the sixteenth-century experimenters in music with their experimental pianos were characteristic. From these circles the experiment entered science, especially through Galileo, and it entered theory through Bacon; and then it was taken over by the various exact disciplines of the continental universities, first of all those of Italy and then those of the Netherlands.

What did science mean to these men who stood at the threshold of modern times? To artistic experimenters of the type of Leonardo and the musical innovators, science meant the path to true art, and that meant for them the path to true nature. Art was to be raised to the rank of a science, and this meant at the same time and above all to raise the artist to the rank of the doctor, socially and with reference to the meaning of his life. This is the ambition on which, for instance, Leonardo's sketch book was based.

But during the period of the rise of the exact sciences one expected a great deal more. If you recall Swammerdam's statement, " Here I bring you the proof of God's providence in the anatomy of a louse," you will see what the scientific worker, influenced (indirectly) by Protestantism and Puritanism, conceived to be his task: to show the path to God. People no longer found this path among the philosophers, with their concepts and deductions. All pietist theology of the time, above all Spener, knew that God was not to be found along the road by which the Middle Ages had sought him. God is hidden, His ways are not our ways, His thoughts are not our thoughts. In the exact sciences, however, where one could physically grasp His works, one hoped to come upon the traces of what He planned for the world. And today? Who—aside from certain big children who are indeed found in the natural sciences—still believes that the findings of astronomy, biology, physics, or chemistry could teach us anything about the meaning of the world? If there is any such " meaning," along what road could one come upon its tracks? If these natural sciences lead to anything in this way, they are apt to make the belief that there is such a thing as the " meaning " of the universe die out at its very roots.

And finally, science as a way " to God " ? Science, this specifically irreligious power? That science today is irreligious no one will doubt in his innermost being, even if he will not admit it to himself. Redemption from the rationalism and intellectualism of science is the fundamental presupposition of living in union with the divine. This, or something similar in meaning, is one of the fundamental watchwords one hears among German youth, whose feelings are attuned to religion or who crave religious experiences. They crave not only religious experience but experience as such. The only thing that is strange is the method that is now followed : the spheres of the irrational, the only spheres that intellectualism has not yet touched, are now raised into consciousness and put under its lens. For in practice this is where the modern intellectualist form of romantic irrationalism leads. This method of emancipation from intellectualism may well bring about the very opposite of what those who take to it conceive as its goal.

Science today is a " vocation " organized in special disciplines in the service of self-clarification and knowledge of interrelated facts. It is not the gift of grace of seers and prophets dispensing sacred values and revelations, nor does it partake of the contemplation of sages and philosophers about the meaning of the universe. This, to be sure, is the inescapable condition of our historical situation. We cannot evade it so long as we remain true to ourselves. And if Tolstoi's question recurs to you : as science does not, who is to answer the question : " What shall we do, and, how shall we arrange our lives? " or, in the words used here tonight: " Which of the warring gods should we serve? Or should we serve perhaps an entirely different god, and who is he? " then one can say that only a prophet or a savior can give the answers. If there is no such man, or if his message is no longer believed in, then you will certainly not compel him to appear on this earth by having thousands of professors, as privileged hirelings of the state, attempt as petty prophets in their lecture-rooms to take over his role. All they will accomplish is to show that they are unaware of the decisive state of affairs: the prophet for whom so many of our younger generation yearn simply does not exist. But this knowledge in its forceful significance has never become vital for them. The inward interest of a truly religiously " musical " man can never be served by veiling to him and to others the fundamental fact that he is destined to live in a godless and prophetless time by giving him the *ersatz* of armchair prophecy. The integrity of his religious organ, it seems to me, must rebel against this.

The fate of our times is characterized by rationalization and intellectualization and, above all, by the " disenchantment of the world." Precisely the ultimate and most sublime values have retreated from public life either into the transcendental realm of mystic life or into the brotherliness of direct and personal human relations. It is not accidental that our greatest art is intimate and not monumental, nor is it accidental that today only within the smallest and intimate circles, in personal human situations, in pianissimo, that something is pulsating that corresponds to the prophetic pneuma, which in former times swept through the great communities like a firebrand, welding them together. If we attempt to force and to " invent " a monumental style in art, such miserable monstrosities are produced as the many monuments of the last twenty years. If one tries intellectually to construe new religions without a new and genuine prophecy, then, in an inner sense, something similar will result, but with still worse effects. And academic prophecy, finally, will create only fanatical sects but never a genuine community.

378

To the person who cannot bear the fate of the times like a man, one must say: may he rather return silently, without the usual publicity build-up of renegades, but simply and plainly. The arms of the old churches are opened widely and compassionately for him. After all, they do not make it hard for him. One way or another he has to bring his "intellectual sacrifice"—that is inevitable. If he can really do it, we shall not rebuke him. For such an intellectual sacrifice in favor of an unconditional religious devotion is ethically quite a different matter than the evasion of the plain duty of intellectual integrity, which sets in if one lacks the courage to clarify one's own ultimate standpoint and rather facilitates this duty by feeble relative judgments. In my eyes, such religious return stands higher than the academic prophecy, which does not clearly realize that in the lecture-rooms of the university no other virtue holds but plain intellectual integrity. Integrity, however, compels us to state that for the many who today tarry for new prophets and saviors, the situation is the same as resounds in the beautiful Edomite watchman's song of the period of exile that has been included among Isaiah's oracles: He calleth to me out of Seir, Watchman, what of the night? The watchman said, The morning cometh, and also the night: if ye will enquire, enquire ye: return, come. The people to whom this was said has enquired and tarried for more than two millennia, and we are shaken when we realize its fate. From this we want to draw the lesson that nothing is gained by yearning and tarrying alone, and we shall act differently. We shall set to work and meet the "demands of the day," in human relations as well as in our vocation. This, however, is plain and simple, if each finds and obeys the demon who holds the fibers of his very life.

PART FOUR: PHILOSOPHY

" WHY PHILOSOPHY? "

by SUSANNE K. LANGER, 1961.

A hundred years ago our highly respectable ancestors were shaking their heads over the unrespectable modern ways of the younger generation. A thousand years ago their ancestors undoubtedly did the same thing and wondered what the world was coming to. Of course, it is possible for a society to come to a disastrous end. The Neanderthal race probably came to as bad an end as their eldest moralists could have predicted—if they had speech, which is uncertain—for they seem to have been exterminated and frequently eaten by their taller and technologically more advanced competitors, the Cro-Magnon people. The Tasmanians met their end when civilized Christian men from Europe discovered them. They were not eaten, but it might have seemed more orderly and respectable to them if they had been.

Social life is always modern and would always come to bad ends if it came to ends at all. But it rarely does, because we usually don't let it. Before evils reach their final, fatal stage, we do something about them. But it is remarkable how close to the brink of destruction we often let evils take us, and how much suffering society will tolerate before it moves to free itself from an incubus —pest, famine, anarchy, superstition, degeneracy, mass warfare.

In every age some social advances are materializing; and as its old people look with misgiving on the bold innovations, its young people look with pity and a little scorn on the stuffy past. The young are making the new world and, in the excitement of making it, they overlook what their elders are seeing—that with every change, even the most desired, some new problems are created.

380

To weary or unimaginative minds the best way to deal with any new potential evil is to nip it in the bud by forgoing the social change which might create it—stick to hand industry, for example, because the factory system threatens to weld men into ignorant masses and to dehumanize them; keep women subjugated, lest they lose their charm and domestic virtues by foolishly aping men.

History does not stand still and cannot be held back by bogging down in old activities. In the world that shaped them, those successful activities already bore the seeds of the future. That future is now upon us, and all its potential evils have become imminent and must be dealt with. A potential evil is not a finished fact; it is a problem. A great mind is one that sees the problematical content of radical changes and dares to tackle it, to face the problems and solve them as part and parcel of the advance into a new order, whether in science, government, economics, ethics or whatever field.

In our present age of rapid changes, anybody can see that problems crop up at the same accelerating rate at which political and technological developments are going. What is not plain for everyone to see is that as the changes in the human scene increase, the problems they engender run into one another and ultimately run deeper, to the common roots of all our special activities, the basic attitudes and ideas embodied in European culture. That culture has recently changed so profoundly that even its conceptual framework shows the strain; and doubts arise in thoughtful minds whether our most time-honored words, such as " matter," " infinity," " individual," " community," " mind," " truth," still mean what they used to mean a hundred years ago. If not, then what do they mean? If we don't know exactly, then how do we know what we are saying when we use them?

The answer is, of course, that we do not know exactly what we are saying, nor even precisely what we want to say. So long as we doubt what our general terms really mean, we cannot even think clear thoughts, for all thinking on a theoretical level is implemented wholly by words, and if the implements are faulty, thinking peters out in confusion. These problems of meaning are essentially philosophical problems which have to be resolved somehow before we can deal with facts.

For some inscrutable reason, the word "philosophical" makes most people decide on the spot that the problem is not for them. Usually they say with great conviction and a touch of self-approval, " I haven't got that kind of mind." But if you ask what kind of mind one needs for philosophical reflection, they do not claim to know. They have healthy, normal minds; philosophy is for some extraordinary sort of brain.

Perhaps there is a bit of truth in that opinion. As one of the great philosophers of our century, Alfred North Whitehead, said, " It requires a very unusual mind to undertake the analysis of the obvious." To undertake it, yes; words we use all the time without stopping to ask or to specify what they mean must have obvious meanings, and to question these takes an unusual sort of mind. But to follow the analysis, once somebody has undertaken it, requires no more than a clear head. It is not lack of some special talent, but of philosophical training that makes the average person afraid of dealing with concepts. The chances are that he does not even know what philosophy is, and therefore looks with undue awe at philosophers, much as persons who know nothing about medicine look at doctors as though they were magicians. It is a serious charge against our educational system that most high-school graduates should not know what philosophy is and shy away from it as something esoteric and beyond them.

The most immediate remedy for this state of affairs is, of course, to make up the deficit ourselves, inquire what philosophy is, whether it really bears on matters that are vital to us, and if so, how we should revise our approach to such matters. So let us consider, in the first place, what is a philosophical issue, as distinct not only from a practical one but also from scientific work; secondly, how genuinely philosophical problems arise in scientific work so that such work must stop until they are resolved, and how they arise in ordinary practical and moral life, to bedevil our emotional stability; and finally, how we can tackle these deepest questions, and what we are likely to have to deal with before we are through.

What, then, is a philosophical problem and how does it differ from scientific and practical ones? The latter kinds are more familiar to us and they have something in common, which is that a correct answer to them is a statement of fact. Such questions and statements are called "empirical," which means "known by sense-experience." Many scientific statements do not seem to be empirical, being the results of mathematical calculations; but, what finally validates them is always experiment, actual observation, and if this does not corroborate them, the whole assertion is false and has to be reconsidered.

A philosophical problem, on the other hand, is a problem of meaning. Its answer is not a statement of fact, but an interpretation of words or statements, especially a pursuit of their implications—of which people are usually quite unaware. Philosophical statements are not empirical, but conceptual. If, for instance, you ask, " What causes a geyser to erupt periodically? " that is an empirical question, a scientific one. But: " What do you mean by 'causing'? " is a philosophical problem—one of the most far-reaching, in fact, in the philosophy of science.

Some people might be tempted to reply that it is also one of the most far-fetched. Everybody thinks he knows what " causing " means, so why bother with a precise definition?

The answer is, because we know the meaning of this and many other words only so long as our discourse is on a familiar, everyday level. Any child can understand what you mean when you say that accumulating steam *causes* geysers to spout. This, however, is not the level on which the mind of a pioneering scientist moves. He needs high-precision concepts as much as he needs high-precision instruments. The way to attain such concepts is to subject the rough-and-ready notions of ordinary discourse to more and more rigorous definition until we know exactly what our words mean and all the necessary concepts have become clear.

Philosophy, then, is the clarification and articulation of concepts. This definition may not fit some people's ideas of the deepest thoughts men have had; "philosophy" is commonly taken to mean general reflection on life, moral adages, logical justification of religious beliefs or speculations on the nature of the universe which go beyond what is scientifically known. All these notions do fit some aspects or some consequences of philosophical thought, but they constitute neither its substance nor its discipline. A philosophical statement always involves us in some trafficking with the meaning of a term or an assertion, pushed to its furthest consequences. It makes explicit what is implicit in our beliefs or denials—that is, what we are assuming, usually without realizing it, when we make what seems like a plausible assertion. In fact, one does not even have to assert anything; just to ask a question is to use a whole lot of ideas hidden in the structure of language, in figures of speech that have become our figures of thought, in prepositions and verb forms and other items of discourse hard to define, but even harder to dispense with. If you ask what was the place, date and hour of an accident, you assume our whole conventional system of dividing time into years, months, days and hours, and the equally conventional spatial frame of four compass points, wherein every place on the earth can be uniquely determined. All these implicit concepts belong to the intellectual machinery of our daily living and of theoretical thought well beyond the practical moment; they make up our common sense.

No one would deny that a scientist has to have common sense. But it is surprising that almost every epoch-making advance in scientific thought begins with an idea that sounds absurd and perverse and affronts people's common sense. When physical theories contradict one another or don't fit the demonstrable facts, the trouble usually lies in our way of seeing and describing the facts open to our observation. Let us take an example from the history of civilization that we all heard about in our school days— the old conception of the earth and its location in space, which ruled both geography and astronomy until about 500 years ago.

The earth was generally taken to be a disk floating in space, and the heavenly bodies were thought to rise beyond its eastern edge, sail through an airy dome that arched over its expanse and sink behind the western edge. As long as this view prevailed, the geographical directions of the earth—north and south, east and west, upward and downward—could be simply extended into space as absolute, cosmic directions. All terrestrial life was, of course, supposed to be on top of the disk. Even the belief that the earth was round, which was fairly prevalent by the sixteenth century, did not materially disturb the picture of its celestial setting; so the proposal of some

intrepid adventurers to sail westward in search of India—
a known country and therefore on top of the earth—
naturally met with the objection that on the nether surface
the adventurers would be upside down. There could be
no water or life, but only solid matter on the underside
of the hypothetical globe, for anything else would fall off.
I do not know how people like Columbus thought of the
passage through the antipodes; they did not expect to be
upside down, but their spatial concepts probably defied
geometrical thinking. They were in open conflict with
common sense.

Since Columbus did not reach India, the facts were
not actually given for some thirty years. But when
Magellan's men, who had sailed westward around Cape
Horn, came back to Europe from the east without having
fallen into space or ever having found themselves walking
the deck like flies on a ceiling, it became clear to all
candid minds that common sense can play us false. This
must have caused some consternation. An undeniable
physical fact contradicted an equally undeniable truth
implied by everybody's most elementary knowledge of
space. How could an object standing upright on a globe
be moved through an arc of 180 degrees, always keeping
the same end in contact with the globe, and not be upside
down when it reached the underside?

The solution was a philosophical insight into the
meaning of " up " and " down "—the realization that these
terms can have meaning only in relation to the earth;
namely, " away from the center of the globe " and " toward
the center of the globe," respectively. A startling consequence of this new meaning was that the earth has no
underside. All its places are equally " on top."

To think of the universe as a space to which " up "
and " down " could not be applied was a monkey puzzle.
How else could one think of space? Astronomers working

with purely mathematical constructions could dispense with spatial imagery; they gradually realized the limited and relative meaning of those words, but other people could not reinterpret them in any illuminating way. This was probably the first time the philosophical concepts of science really parted company with common sense, so that intelligent persons even, without special logical training, could neither agree nor disagree with what the " natural philosophers "—whom today we would call " scientists "—said about cosmic space.

Perhaps no one except a few discerning churchmen realized from the beginning how revolutionary the new astronomy without absolute directions was, how it deprived the universe of all fixed places, realms of glory, of trial and of punishment, and confounded the religious world-image based on the spiritual meanings and physical symbols of up and down, high and low. To them it did presage much more than the defeat of all their Aristotelian physics; it threatened to shatter the stage on which the drama of creation and salvation was taking place and to jeopardize its clear rational structure. When Galileo invited three eminent divines to look through his telescope, they could not bring themselves to view what one of them called " the disgusting spectacle of nature contradicting reason." The scientists themselves, having made the philosophical shift from orientation on the earth to a different sort of orientation without any fixed basic directions, only gradually realized the full implications of their working notions—that objects had no weight in space, but what functioned on earth as weight had to be redefined as " mass " in the new astronomical heavens—and other equally radical new conceptions which were perfectly natural in their frame of thought but sounded bizarre to the uninitiated.

Many facts, of course, were far from clear, but one of the special assets of a logically trained mind is the power to suspend an unsolved problem, knowing all the time what and where it is, until some new idea or finding moves it forward for solution. For instance, the reason why earthly objects fall to the ground—that is, toward the earth—was not understood until Newton expressed the concept of gravity in such a way that it applied to all objects without exception, planets in galaxies and apples on twigs.

Today's common sense has caught up with the pioneer thought of men like Galileo and incorporated Newtonian physics as part of its own warp and woof. But it has no sooner done so than its smooth fabric is ruptured again by the unimaginable scheme of a new geometry dealing in more than three dimensions and the mysteries of relativity physics. Evidently we are not through yet with the " Copernican revolution "—the philosophical reinterpretation of experience which gave rise to our physical sciences and is still egged on by their growing demands. Our epoch-making scientists like Einstein and Planck are known as physicists, but they are, above all, philosophers of modern science; it is due to their abstract logical thought that we have our highly tangible products of technology.

This technology, however, has stirred up hornets' nests in all human affairs by utterly transforming the conditions of life in every quarter—domestic, economic, political, social. Industry has changed beyond recognition, commerce spreads over countries that were scarcely known to exist a generation ago, new nations emerge, governments rise and fall, wars become monstrous. Every change carries its own problems with it. The marriage pattern of lifelong partnership is breaking up, divorce being quite generally countenanced. What becomes of our time-honored social unit, the family? If that disintegrates, what can we put in its stead? Probably nothing; you can substitute one element for another only where the same place is to be filled, but with a radical change in the social structure of all mankind, the place for a fundamental social unit is not likely to be the same.

Again, what substitute could we find in the future for international wars, now that destructive powers are so great that to settle disputes by bombs is like roasting a pig by burning down the house? In a political setup that follows the lines of a world economy, as some future setup probably will, there may well be no place to fill with a " substitute for war." Substitutes for spontaneous fighting, yes; but international wars are not spontaneous. They are prepared moves that belong to the old system of tribal organization, which is being strained to its uttermost limits today when the tribes have expanded into giant nations.

Faced with such staggering and sudden changes in the conditions of life—all sparked by the meteoric new physical science—we realize with dismay that we have no science but physics (chemistry has lately come into the same camp, and biology, as it becomes scientific, is merging into chemistry) and that we can plan and control nothing but machines. Where are those social sciences that we have been hearing about since the early nineteenth century? We hear about them still, and thousands of able people are ranked in their service, but we certainly do not feel we can bank on them to do wonders in a time of crisis, as we trust nuclear physicists to meet any demand.

How deep does the difference between the physical and the social sciences go? I think it goes to the philosophical roots of knowledge, the conceptual substructure. In the study of society—psychology, anthropology, jurisprudence, pedagogy and other departments—there has never been a radical break through the framework of common sense by entirely abstract concepts. No Copernicus, Galileo or Newton has defied imagination with completely unfamiliar elements of reality and silly-sounding propositions which prove to be true. The technical terms of social science are familiar words, such as " need," " motivation," " interest," " dominance," which are commonly defined in terms of other equally familiar words, with the result that their ordinary meanings are somewhat narrowed or widened, but not radically transcended. They cannot be manipulated, combined and operated on like true abstract elements, but only used to express facts first established in common-sense terms. The philosophical groundwork of our moral and social thinking has not been done, and until it is, the social sciences will not become intrinsically scientific.

Yet it may be that the great break-through of abstract thought is just in the offing, because something is happening in society similar to what happened in the physical realm 500 years ago, precipitating the " new natural philosophy." The words we have always used to describe and discuss social situations seem to lose their precise meanings, because we have to fit them to circumstances that did not exist before. There was a time when we were quite sure what the word " community " meant—a group of persons living in a certain locality and sharing all public interests, and some private ones, with other persons in the same locality. It made sense to ask whether an individual belonged to one specific community or another, whether Mr. James Henry Abbington was a Bostonian or a Philadelphian. But now we talk about the " world community " and think we are merely stretching the term. Can we still ask whether Mr. James Henry Abbington is a member of that community or another?

Does our mere extension of a term really make him and comrade Ivan Ostov and chief warrior Mpungu members of the same community in a precise sense—dwellers in a certain locality who hold their public interests in common? Surely the sense of the word has slipped, but no one knows in what direction or how far.

This is but one example of how philosophical issues slowly take shape in political and moral life. There are dozens of terms in our general discourse which have taken on new meanings, usually without quite losing the old, so their import is blurred like a double-exposed picture. When ideas are in such a state of disintegration, the time is ripe for entirely new forms of conception, a radical reinterpretation of the major facts—in short, for a philosophical advance in the field of baffled research.

Why is that great reconstruction not under way? Because we are not training enough philosophers to cope with so tough a problem. Our leading philosophers talk about man, society and God, about anxiety, commitment, identification and other currently interesting problems of life. They do so in response to the widespread cry for religious rescue which arises especially from Europe after a half century of disaster—loss of faith, loss of physical and mental security, broken fortunes and broken morale. But movements like existentialism or our own personalism and new humanism are not intellectual revolutions. They develop attitudes, not instruments of thought.

The physicists who laid the conceptual foundations of their science were men of philosophical genius, trained for the task of abstract reasoning because reason was valued and cultivated in their day. Such genius has two essential factors—imagination and logic. Logic is analytic and critical, but not by itself constructive; that is, it provides no formula for producing new ideas. It can only permit them or expose them as inconsistent and unusable.

Only imagination can furnish new ways of seeing and putting things. But imagination has its own dangers—it is essentially unrealistic and tends to run riot. We all know from our dreams how far it can range. If imagination were the whole stuff of genius, what geniuses most of us would be between midnight and morning! Perhaps we would wear electrodes on our heads with gadgets to record our achievements.

In dreams or in waking life, imagination is spontaneous; and its special forms—pictorial, poetic or conceptual— are native to the individuals who possess them. But the instrumental factor in genius can be acquired. Logic is the tool of scientific imagination. In a mind which uses that tool with ease, logic has a feed-back function—it guides the creative imagination in progress from moment to moment. This saves the trained thinker from constantly scrapping big, developed ideas because they are illogical and having to start anew. He rarely gets as far as that, though it may happen that a thrilling inspiration is finally found to contain some hopeless fallacy. Most of the time a purely habitual, logical control monitors his mental processes.

But all these reflections do not answer the question why the social sciences cannot get off the ground. If they require basic research—conceptual analysis, new interpretations—why do we not train people for the task?

The answer points to a grave condition in our whole educational pattern, visible on every level, from symposia and commencement speeches to the courses listed in school catalogs—we do not cultivate philosophical thought at all. We do not value abstract conception and pure logic, nor train our youth in system construction or formalization of any sort. We do not even teach algebra as a generalization of arithmetic, nor point out that the negative numbers exemplify the same abstract structure as the positive, so their orders are mirror images of each other. We teach algebra as a set of instructions for solving problems in a conceptual frame vaguely taken for granted. Problem solving is our obsession. Even rats and monkeys in our laboratories spend their " behaving " hours in the problem box, and their food-getting and shock-evading are supposed to furnish the blue-print for our own intelligence.

From such an educational background no band of brilliant philosophical minds can arise to create a new frame of thought and set the social sciences on their way. Genius naturally arises from a high level of ordinary professional work, and this in turn requires a general popular interest. We have few first-rate poets today, because the lay public does not read, write and recite poetry as it did a hundred years ago. We do have great painters, because painting commands both popular and expert interest, galleries and museums are active, and amateurs numerous.

Many people are aware that humanity is on the edge of destruction for lack of social concepts to match its physical powers, and a growing number of us even realize that intensive philosophical work is the need of the hour. But there will be no philosophical pioneering until we reform our whole educational scheme and aim it squarely at the cultivation of reason, not viewed as a device for getting food and evading foes, but as a precision instrument for a high imagination to work with. Only then will great thinkers arise—this time, probably, in the sciences of life—as they arose in the Renaissance to give astronomy and physics the impetus that still carries them. But without public sympathy, without a high level of competence in the relevant studies of psychology, ethnology and others—and a general stirring of intellectual life in lay circles—the most daring new ideas may be lost for lack of enthusiasts to follow them up. The outriders cannot proceed alone; they have to keep contact with the homesteaders in their wake, who come to take possession.

Education is one of our urgent concerns today, because history has shown us dramatically the truth of Lord Bacon's dictum, " Knowledge is power." If the public mind ever fully realized that the spearhead of scientific progress is philosophical imagination and pure rationality, no practical difficulty could deter us from a revolution in the teaching of philosophy and in the demands made on philosophers to set the pace for the next advance of knowledge—the science of society.

INDEX OF SUBJECTS

INDEX OF NAMES

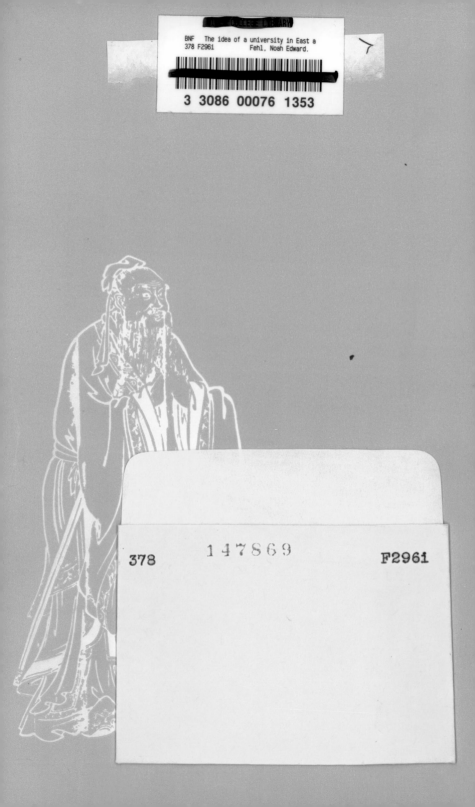